THE GUIDE TO THE FEDERAL BUDGET

THE GUIDE TO THE
FEDERAL BUDGET

FISCAL 1996

STANLEY E. COLLENDER

Director, Federal Budget Policy
Price Waterhouse LLP

THE URBAN INSTITUTE PRESS
Washington, D.C.

THE URBAN INSTITUTE PRESS
2100 M Street, N.W.
Washington, D.C. 20037

Library of Congress Cataloging in Publication Data

LC 82-643840

ISSN 0730-9511

ISBN 0-87766-632-6 (alk. paper)
ISBN 0-87766-631-8 (alk. paper; casebound)

Urban Institute books are printed on acid-free paper whenever possible.

Printed in the United States of America.

Distributed by:
      University Press of America
4720 Boston Way   3 Henrietta Street
Lanham, MD 20706   London   WC2E 8LU   ENGLAND

THE URBAN INSTITUTE is a nonprofit policy research and educational organization established in Washington, D.C., in 1968. Its staff investigates the social and economic problems confronting the nation and public and private means to alleviate them. The Institute disseminates significant findings of its research through the publications program of its Press. The goals of the Institute are to sharpen thinking about societal problems and efforts to solve them, improve government decisions and performance, and increase citizen awareness of important policy choices.

Through work that ranges from broad conceptual studies to administrative and technical assistance, Institute researchers contribute to the stock of knowledge available to guide decision making in the public interest.

Conclusions or opinions expressed in Institute publications are those of the authors and do not necessarily reflect the views of staff members, officers or trustees of the Institute, advisory groups, or any organizations that provide financial support to the Institute.

CONTENTS

Tables

Figures

Imagine that you are playing golf, you're on the ninth hole, and you get the ball in the cup in three strokes instead of the par four listed on your scorecard. In golf terms, you have just gotten a birdie and finished the hole in one less stroke than you were expected to need.

But while you have one stroke less for the last hole, you also have three strokes more than you had after the first eight.

As implausible as it may seem, what I have just described is an almost perfect analogy for the debate that took place in 1994 on the fiscal 1995 federal budget.

The Clinton Administration started the year by projecting a big drop in the deficit, from $235 billion in fiscal 1994 to $165 billion in fiscal 1995.[1] The White House called this projected $70 billion reduction a major achievement and said that, because of this decline, nothing further needed to be done on the deficit as part of the fiscal 1995 budget process. The administration saw this as the budget equivalent of a birdie—one less stroke than had been expected.

Critics charged, however, that $165 billion was nothing to be proud of, that this was big compared with a balanced budget, and that the deficit needed to be reduced further. They saw the projected red ink as the budget equivalent of three strokes more.

So which was it—one less or three more?

The answer, of course, is both; it just depends on what question you're answering.

In golf, if the question is how did you do compared to par (that is, what you were expected to do), then three strokes instead of four means that the answer is clearly "one less." If the question is what is your total score, then the answer just as unambiguously is "three more." In other words, the same result produces two different answers even though there is no dispute about what actually happened.

The same is true as far as the federal budget is concerned. There was no doubt that a $165 billion deficit was far less than the previous year's deficit. But there was also no doubt that that same deficit was substantially more than no deficit at all.

So although both sides in the fiscal 1995 budget debate agreed on the mathematics, they did not agree on what question should have been asked. Some wanted to use the previous year as the standard by which the need for further action should have been determined. Others wanted to use a balanced budget.

Ultimately, those who felt that nothing further needed to be done on the deficit this past year prevailed and so the debate on the budget was almost a nonevent compared to what occurred the previous year.

This is not to say, however, that the budget process was unimportant in 1994. Quite to the contrary, budget process rules and procedures were key elements in many of the most important issues that were debated.

For example, much of the debate over health care reform was centered on the budget impact of the various plans as estimated by the Congressional Budget Office. The legislation implementing the General Agreement on Tariffs and Trade (GATT) had to conform to the pay-as-you-go rules that require revenue losses to be offset by cuts in mandatory programs or increases in other receipts and the Senate requirement that the bill not increase the deficit in either the first year, over the first five years, and over the second five years.

In addition, the crime bill had to get at least 60 votes in the Senate because of a rule (section 306 of the Congressional Budget Act) that subjects any bill that proposes to change the budget process to a point of order unless that change is first reported by the Senate Budget Committee. When the crime bill triggered this provision because of the reduction in the discretionary spending cap it included (see chapter 2), crime bill opponents were given a way to stop the bill from being adopted and backers had to scramble for several days to get the necessary support.

The situation for the debate over the fiscal 1996 budget, which will take place in calendar 1995, is likely to be far different because the deficit will almost certainly reemerge as a major issue. There are three main reasons.

First, the fiscal 1996 projected deficit will be higher than the one forecast for fiscal 1995. In its August 1994 report on the budget outlook,[2] the Congressional Budget Office projected that the fiscal 1996 deficit would be $176 billion, $14 billion more than the $162 billion deficit it forecast for 1995. This will be the first time since Bill Clinton took office that the deficit will be projected to rise from one year to the next,[3] and this will put additional pressure on the White House and Congress to propose further reductions.

Second, Congress will be more budget aware in 1995 than it was in 1993 and 1994. The results of the 1994 elections show clearly not only that both houses of Congress are now under Republican control, but that the new first-term representatives and senators are more fiscally conservative than the people they replaced. And when you consider the fact that the 103rd Congress of 1993–1994 generally was more fiscally conservative than the 102nd Congress it replaced, it becomes evident that the House and Senate are not only likely to be receptive to deficit reduction proposals, they are likely to demand them.

Third, it now appears that legislation will have to be adopted during 1995 that will increase the limit on the federal debt. This bill has often been the legislative vehicle for deficit reductions and budget process changes. For example, in 1985 the Balanced Budget and Emergency Deficit Control Act (Gramm-Rudman-Hollings) was adopted as an amendment to a debt limit increase. In 1987, the revised version of Gramm-Rudman-Hollings—the Balanced Budget and Emergency Deficit Control Reaffirmation Act—was also adopted as an amendment to a debt limit bill. And in 1990, the Budget Enforcement Act was also an amendment to a debt limit increase.

If a deficit reduction package has not been adopted by the time the existing ceiling on federal borrowing is reached, there is a strong possibility that the debt limit again will be used to force action on either spending cuts and revenue increases or on budget process changes.

Budget process changes are also likely to be considered in 1995 both because they were a major part of the "Contract with America" that House Republican incumbents and challengers used so successfully during the campaign and because a consensus started to develop in 1994 about what they might be. Seven revisions now seem to be the most likely.

1. Appropriations Caps. An extension of the annual cap on discretionary spending is likely. The existing caps, which were created in 1990 by the Budget Enforcement Act and then extended by the 1993 budget agreement between Congress and the Clinton Administration, will expire at the end of fiscal 1998. This means that, without an extension, discretionary spending will no longer be constrained as of fiscal 1999.

The most likely extension will be for two more years, or through fiscal 2000. This will provide Congress and the White House with spending limits over the full five-year period (fiscal 1996–2000) over which budget projections will be made while the fiscal 1996 budget is debated. But it is also possible that the caps will be extended through fiscal 2002, so that the fiscal 1998 budget, the one the Clinton Administration submits after the 1996 election, is covered by a five-year forecast.

The key question, however, will be the level at which the caps are extended. If the changes are part of a deficit reduction effort, the caps could be lowered from their current levels to force additional cuts in discretionary spending. However, if, as many expect, the fiscal 1996 deficit reduction effort focuses on entitlement programs, the caps could assume increases for inflation or that spending stay at the fiscal 1998 level.

2. Balanced Budget Amendment. There appears to be substantial support for an amendment to the U.S. Constitution that would require the federal budget to be balanced each year. Indeed, this was a major provision of the Republican "Contract with America." (See chapter 1.)

3. Baseline Budgeting. There appears to be substantial support in Congress for eliminating the use of the current services baseline (the budget equivalent of the par on a golf course), which compares proposed increases or decreases in appropriations with a baseline level that assumes programs will grow by the rate of inflation. In 1994 the House voted to do away with the baseline and instead to measure all proposals against the actual level of spending in the current year. The Senate did not act on the bill, however, so the baseline will continue at least for the time being to be the standard against which all appropriations changes are judged.

4. Entitlement Caps. It is not yet clear how they will work or how they will get past the extraordinary political problems involved, but some type of limit on entitlement spending is likely to be considered during 1995.

Under the current pay-as-you-go rules of the Budget Enforcement Act, spending on existing entitlements is unconstrained. As long as the higher-than-projected spending occurs as a result of existing law (i.e., more people are eligible for the same programs, cost-of-living adjustments are higher than expected because of higher inflation, current beneficiaries are using more services, etc.), it does not have to be offset with cuts in other entitlement programs or revenue increases.[4]

An entitlement cap would change this by limiting the overall amount of spending on these programs regardless of the reason it occurred. If spending exceeded the cap, then some mechanism would force offsets to be adopted. This could be an automatic across-the-board cut in all entitlement programs such as now occurs in sequestration (see chapters 2 and 6), a requirement that the president propose and Congress pass separate legislation to bring spending down to the cap, or an automatic reduction of some type in the offending program.

It is important to note that all of the major health care reform proposals that were considered in 1994—Democratic and Republican alike—included some type of limit on health care entitlement spending. They also included limits on the amount of revenue that could be lost through the new tax expenditures that would have been created.

Whether tax expenditures are covered under entitlement caps is likely to be one of the more contentious issues in this debate. Many budget observers believe that these reductions in tax liabilities are the revenue equivalent of entitlements and, therefore, should be limited in the same way as spending.

5. Deficit Maximums. An extension of the current deficit maximums (see chapter 2), which expire at the end of fiscal 1995, is also likely to be considered. Some budget observers believe that the maximums are too ineffective to be of much use and so should be eliminated. Others want to strengthen their enforcement and extend the maximums through the same year as the appropriations caps.

The major problems in dealing with the deficit maximums may well be political rather than substantive. Will it be possible for a member of either house to vote against extending the maximums, regardless of how ineffective they may be, when that vote could be characterized as being in favor of a higher deficit? Will it be possible for members to vote against a possible return to a Gramm-Rudman-Hollings procedure that would fix the deficit maximums at specified levels and then impose an across-the-board cut if they are not achieved? (See chapter 2.)

6. Emergency Spending Limits. The House voted in 1994 to put limits on the way it provides funds for emergencies while the Senate did not consider the proposal. But the overwhelming vote in the House means that this change is likely to find its way into any budget process bill next year.

7. Expedited Rescission/Line-Item Veto. The House this year also passed an expedited rescission proposal that would have forced Congress to consider presidential proposals not to spend funds more quickly than it is currently required to do (see chapter 7). Like the other House-passed changes, the Senate also did not consider this proposal and so the existing procedure remains in place, although it will probably be part of any budget process debate in 1995.

However, even the expedited rescission plan that passed the House did not satisfy a number of members, especially Republicans, who felt that it was a poor substitute for what they really wanted to give the president—a line-item veto.

Politically, a line-item veto would be a win-win-win situation for Republicans. First, its enactment in 1995 would mean that Bill Clinton could be blamed for not proposing additional spending cuts. Second, Republicans would be able to claim that they had acted in a bipartisan way by giving an extraordinary budget power to a Democrat. Third, if, as many Republicans hope, a Republican is elected to the White House in 1996, it would mean that Republicans had succeeded in giving a president of their own party this same extraordinary power.

As a result, don't be surprised if Democrats try to include some type of sunset provision in any line-item veto proposal that is considered. This provision would require that a line-item veto be reenacted at some point (say, after the next election) for it to continue. This would eliminate the possibility that it would automatically be available to a Republican president in 1997.

* * * * *

Anyone who has worked in Washington knows that, for a big city, this is a very small town. There are always stories about things said at a restaurant table one afternoon that show up on the front pages of a newspaper the next morning, and of supposedly confidential memos that turn up on Capitol Hill or in lobbyists' offices before they get to the person for which they were intended.

This is why through all the years in which this book has been published I have not mentioned my many sources of budget information by name. All of those who belong in this category should know how appreciative I am. So many people are finding ever more and more complex ways of taking advantage of the already arcane budget rules that no one person can possibly know everything there is to know about how particular procedures apply to new situations. I truly am grateful for everyone's help and support, especially for their willingness to discuss and debate the increasingly finer points of federal budgeting when they have other pressing matters.

I owe Felicity Skidmore and her able crew at the Urban Institute Press many thanks for their usual great job in pushing and prodding me to get my work done, and for getting their work done with so little pushing and prodding from me.

My colleagues in Price Waterhouse LLP's federal budget policy group—Beverly Campbell, Sarah Ducich, and Terry Nyhous—continued throughout this year to be a constant source of wonder. Sometimes it was wondered at how we managed not to kill ourselves while getting all of the work done for clients. Other times we wondered about how we ever came to devote our professional lives to this stuff. But I never wondered about Bev's, Sarah's, or Terry's capabilities, professionalism, or friendship, and I truly appreciate it all.

Anyone who has read any of the prefaces from the previous thirteen editions of *The Guide* knows that the most important person in my life is Maura McGinn, my wife of now almost ten years. Like all of the others, this edition is dedicated to Maura as a way of saying thanks for everything she does and says.

Maura's influence on the previous editions was mostly indirect. However, in addition to all of the general emotional, psychic, and inspirational support she again provided, her impact on the fiscal 1996 edition was for the first time also very specific and particularly important. Had it not been for Maura's insistence, I would have never tried so hard to reinvigorate my golf game over the past year and so probably would not have thought of the analogy I used to start this preface. This has always been the toughest part of the book for me to write and so for that inspiration alone I am overwhelmingly grateful.

Stanley E. Collender
Washington, D.C.
November 1994

Notes

1. U.S. Office of Management and Budget, *Budget of the United States Government, Fiscal Year 1995* (U.S. Government Printing Office, Washington, D.C.: February 1994).

2. Congressional Budget Office, *The Economic and Budget Outlook, An Update* (U.S. Government Printing Office, Washington, D.C.: August 1994).

3. The fiscal 1992 deficit was $290 billion, the fiscal 1993 deficit was $255 billion, and the fiscal 1994 deficit was $203 billion.

4. This is different from the situation for spending resulting from newly enacted programs or program increases which, according to the pay-as-you-go rules, must be completely offset (see chapter 6).

ABOUT THE AUTHOR

Stanley E. Collender is director of federal budget policy for Price Waterhouse LLP. He is also editor-in-chief of *Federal Budget Report*, Price Waterhouse LLP's biweekly newsletter on the federal budget and congressional budget process, which he founded in 1981. Before joining Price Waterhouse LLP, Mr. Collender was president of the Budget Research Group, Inc., a private, Washington-based consulting organization that specialized in the federal budget.

Mr. Collender has been involved with the congressional budget process since 1975. He is one of only a handful of people who have worked for both the House and Senate Budget Committees. As a member of the House Budget Committee staff, he served as administrator of the Task Force on State and Local Government. For the Senate Budget Committee, he was responsible for analyzing military spending. Mr. Collender also served as the administrator of the Task Force on the Budget of the Northeast-Midwest Congressional Coalition, a bipartisan group of representatives from the states in those regions.

Mr. Collender's experience also includes service on the staffs of Representatives Thomas Downey, Fortney Stark, Jr., and Elizabeth Holtzman. He also served as the administrative assistant to the deputy assistant secretary for health planning in the Department of Health, Education, and Welfare.

Mr. Collender frequently appears as an expert on the federal budget on a number of television and radio programs. During the past few years these have included "Good Morning America," National Public Radio's "Morning Edition," CNBC, C-SPAN, and CNN. He is often quoted in major newspapers and magazines, including *The New York Times, The Washington Post, Wall Street Journal, Business Week, National Journal, Congressional Quarterly, U.S. News and World Report, The Christian Science Monitor,* and *Bond Week* as well as all of the major wire services. He regularly speaks on the budget to audiences across the country and consults with numerous corporations, banks, investment banks, and associations.

Mr. Collender holds a master's degree in public policy from the University of California, Berkeley, and a bachelor's degree from New York University. He lives in the Washington, D.C., area with his wife, Maura McGinn.

Chapter One

THE FEDERAL BUDGET
AS A SECOND LANGUAGE

Before anyone attempts to understand the budget process or to analyze individual budget documents, it is important to master the following key terms and concepts. (For further information on the language of the budget, refer to the updated glossary at the end of the book.)

AUTHORIZATION VERSUS APPROPRIATION

Two steps must usually occur before the federal government can spend money on an activity. First, an authorization must be passed allowing a program to exist. The authorization is the substantive legislation that establishes the purpose and guidelines for a given activity and usually sets the limit on the amount that can be spent. The authorization does not, however, provide the actual dollars for a program or enable an agency or department to spend funds in the future.

Second, an appropriation must be passed. The appropriation enables an agency or department to (1) make spending commitments and (2) spend money.

Except in the case of entitlements, an appropriation is the key determinant of how much will be spent on a program. In almost all cases, however, an appropriation for a given activity is not supposed to be made until the authorization is enacted. No money can be spent on a program unless it first has been allowed (authorized) to exist. Conversely, if a program is authorized but no money is provided (appropriated) for its implementation, that activity cannot be carried out. Therefore, both an authorization and an appropriation are necessary for an activity to be included in the budget.[1]

A particularly confusing aspect of these two legislative requirements is that both authorizations and appropriations often describe an activity in dollar terms. For example, the fiscal 1982 authorization for the administrative expenses of the United States Railway Association stated: "There are authorized to be appropriated to the Association for purposes of carrying out its administrative expenses under this Act not to exceed $13,000,000 . . . ,"[2] whereas the fiscal 1982 appropriation for the same organization stated: "For necessary administrative expenses to enable the United States Railway Association to carry out its functions . . . $13,000,000."[3]

Despite the fact that both seem to be providing $13 million, only the appropriation was actually doing so. The dollar figures in the authorization served only as an upper limit on what could be appropriated. An appropriation is not supposed to exceed the authorization.

An entitlement is a particular type of authorization that requires the federal government to pay benefits to any person or unit of government that meets the eligibility requirements it establishes. An entitlement differs from other authorizations because it constitutes a legally binding commitment on the federal government. Although, like all other programs, an entitlement requires an appropriation, that appropriation is often permanent and indefinite so that the amount spent each year is not determined through the annual appropriations process. The amount needed to pay all the eligible beneficiaries is provided automatically.

In fact, eligible potential recipients may sue the federal government if entitlement benefits are denied to them because funds are not appropriated. The authorization, therefore, is the key legislation in deciding how much will be spent on an entitlement and relegates the appropriation to little more than a formality. Examples of entitlement programs are Medicare, Medicaid, and Social Security.

BUDGET AUTHORITY VERSUS OUTLAYS

The dollar amounts listed in both authorization and appropriation bills are stated in terms of "budget authority." Budget Authority (BA) is the permission granted to an agency or department to make commitments to spend money—such as hiring workers and signing contracts to purchase some item. In most cases, budget authority is not the amount of spending that will occur but the level of new spending commitments that will be made. Although budget authority will lead to the spending of money, it is not the actual exchange of cash.

Outlays (O) are the actual dollars that either have been or will be spent on a particular activity. Outlays are the direct result of budget authority, that is, the commitment to spend money made either this year or in previous years. The overall level of outlays compared with the overall level of revenues determines whether the budget is in surplus or deficit.

Figures for both budget authority and outlays are needed because many federal activities are not completed within a single fiscal year and it is important to know both what the total cost will be (budget authority) and what will have to be spent this year (outlays). By looking beyond this year's spending requirements to the overall cost of the activity, the president and Congress can know the future spending commitments they are making as well as the cash required immediately.

Knowing future spending commitments is particularly important for activities that take several years to complete—for example, the procurement of an aircraft carrier. In this case, outlays in the first year will be relatively small because it takes a long time to start construction. The budget authority in the first year, however, will be large because it will reflect the full cost of the ship. In the second year there will be no new budget authority because the full cost was provided in the previous year's budget. Outlays for this ship, however, will begin to increase in the second year as construction continues and accelerates. This pattern of outlays but no new budget authority will continue each year until the procurement is completed.

A good analogy is the purchase of an automobile with a three-year loan. When the purchase of the car (at a total cost of $20,000, for example) is arranged, the buyer and seller sign a contract for the full amount and the "budget authority" is $20,000. But the actual amount spent ("outlays") in the first year is only equal to the down payment ($5,000, in this example) plus the monthly payments (another $5,000). In the second year no new budget authority is needed because the loan already has been arranged and the commitment made, but the outlays are equal to the monthly payments ($5,000 in this case). In the third and final year again there would be no new budget authority, but the outlays again would equal $5,000, at which point the loan would be repaid. Table 1 shows how the federal budget typically depicts this situation.

It should be clear from table 1 that neither budget authority nor outlays alone are sufficient to tell the full budgetary consequences of purchasing this car. By looking only at budget authority in fiscal 1995, the program might seem too expensive to undertake because the full

Table 1 PURCHASE OF AUTOMOBILE (in thousands of dollars)

	Fiscal Year		
	1995	1996	1997
Budget Authority (BA)	20.0	0.0	0.0
Outlays (O)	10.0	5.0	5.0

cost of the car appears to be needed in that year. Yet by looking only at the budget authority in fiscal years 1996 and 1997, the car looks too good to pass up because it appears to cost nothing even though substantial spending is, in fact, required. But if you look only at the outlays in a particular year you would not know the full cost of the car because only the yearly spending requirements are obvious.

Some federal activities, notably the payment of salaries and entitlements, usually "spend out" within the fiscal year in which the budget authority is provided. In these cases, budget authority and outlays are approximately equal. In some cases, however, the level of outlays appears to be greater than the level of budget authority. This situation generally is the result of budget authority that was provided in previous years but is only now being spent. The level of outlays for a particular year is, therefore, a combination of budget authority provided that year and in previous years.

It is difficult, however, to determine simply by looking at the tables in the budget whether outlays are the result of budget authority provided this year or in previous years; usually some knowledge of the program is necessary. Take the previous example of an automobile purchased with a three-year loan. Table 2 shows how the federal budget typically would depict the situation if a second car is purchased in a similar manner and at the same cost in fiscal 1996.

It would be wrong to assume that the $15,000 in outlays in fiscal 1996 is the result of the $20,000 in budget authority provided in fiscal 1996. In fact, only $10,000 comes from this new budget authority. The remaining $5,000 comes from budget authority provided in fiscal 1995 that is now coming due (the monthly payments from the automobile purchased in that year). Even if the decision was made not to buy the

Table 2 PURCHASE OF TWO AUTOMOBILES (in thousands of dollars)

	Fiscal Year		
	1995	1996	1997
Budget Authority (BA)	20.0	20.0	0.0
Outlays (O)	10.0	15.0	10.0

second car in 1996 and the entire $20,000 in budget authority were cut from the 1996 budget, $5,000 still would be spent in fiscal 1996 as the result of the previous spending decision. Fiscal 1997 spending, however, would drop to $5,000.

Figure 1 depicts the relationship between budget authority and outlays in the Clinton fiscal 1995 budget as a whole. The president proposed a budget with outlays of $1,518.9 billion (upper right-hand corner). Only 78.0 percent of that amount, or $1,184.0 billion, was projected to result from the requested fiscal 1995 budget authority of $1,537.0 billion (upper left-hand corner), however. The remaining 22.0 percent, or $334.9 billion, was the result of unspent budget authority granted in previous years (lower left-hand corner). The $353.0 billion in budget authority requested for fiscal 1995 that was not expected to result in fiscal 1995 outlays was to be added to the $621.4 billion in budget authority provided in previous years that was expected to continue to remain unspent. This $974.5 billion was the total amount

Figure 1 RELATION OF BUDGET AUTHORITY TO OUTLAYS

RELATIONSHIP OF BUDGET AUTHORITY TO OUTLAYS FOR FY 1995
(in billions of dollars)

New Authority Recommended for 1995 **1,537.0**

To be spent in 1995 **1,184.0**

Outlays in 1995 **1,518.9**

To be spent in Future Years

To be spent in 1995 334.9

To be spent in 1995

353.0

Authority written off, expired, and adjusted (net)

Unspent Authority Enacted in Prior Years **972.2**

15.9

To be spent in Future Years **621.4**

Unspent Authority for Outlays in Future Years **974.5**

Source: Office of Management and Budget (OMB), *Budget of the United States Government, Fiscal Year 1995, Analytical Perspectives* (Washington, D.C.: U.S. Government Printing Office, 1994), p. 268.

of unspent budget authority that was projected to result in outlays in fiscal 1996 and beyond (bottom right-hand corner).[4]

CONTROLLABLE VERSUS UNCONTROLLABLE SPENDING AND DISCRETIONARY VERSUS MANDATORY SPENDING

The $974.5 billion in unspent budget authority is a significant part of what is classified as "relatively uncontrollable" spending. Such spending is not out of control in the literal sense. It consists of outlays that result from prior-year commitments of the federal government, including previously granted budget authority, entitlements, open-ended programs, and permanent appropriations (interest on the national debt, for example) that require no further action by Congress and the president. For example, of the $1,151.8 billion in outlays in the Reagan fiscal 1990 budget, $902.9 billion—78.4 percent—was classified by the administration as relatively uncontrollable.

"Controllable" spending is spending that will occur only if Congress passes and the president signs an appropriation for it.

"Uncontrollable" is something of a misnomer; if Congress and the president choose to act, in many cases they can change laws to alter the amount expected to be spent or to stop such spending entirely. In other words, controllable spending will occur only if Congress and the president take some action (such as an appropriation) to cause it. Uncontrollable spending will occur unless Congress and the president take some action to stop it.

The difference between controllable and uncontrollable spending took on new importance because of passage of the Budget Enforcement Act (BEA) of 1990.[5] The act drew a sharp distinction between "discretionary appropriations," which are virtually the same as controllable spending, and "mandatory spending," which is virtually the same as uncontrollable spending, and created different limitation mechanisms for each (see chapter 2).

BEA states that discretionary appropriations are "budgetary resources provided in appropriations acts." This means that Congress must pass and the president must sign legislation each year providing for these funds to be spent. BEA defines mandatory spending as budget authority provided by laws other than appropriations (primarily authorizations), entitlement authority, and the food stamp program. This means that, for the most part, the funds will be spent even

if Congress does not pass and the president does not sign new legislation this year.

ECONOMIC ASSUMPTIONS

The federal budget is very sensitive to changes in the economy. The
levels of many spending programs change as interest rates, inflation,
and unemployment increase or decrease. Similarly, the amount of
revenues collected by the government changes as the economy, usually
measured by the gross domestic product (GDP),[6] declines or grows
because businesses and individuals pay taxes according to their earnings. Whenever the president and Congress formulate the budget,
therefore, they must make certain assumptions about how well or how
poorly the economy is likely to do.

Economic assumptions frequently have been a source of constant
confusion and controversy. Because the president, the House and Senate Budget Committees, and the Congressional Budget Office (CBO)
often use different economic projections, the budgets are not always
comparable. In addition, the same budgets with different economic
assumptions produce different results. For example, the Bush fiscal
1990 budget projected a deficit of $92.5 billion using economic as-
sumptions that many believed were optimistic. Using its own forecast
that differed substantially from the president's, CBO re-estimated the
Bush deficit to be $120 billion, $27.5 billion higher. Both of these
estimates were for the same budget and included the same spending
and tax proposals.

Table 3 shows the differences that existed between the Clinton
Administration and CBO economic assumptions for 1994 and 1995.

Appendix C provides current estimates for the impact of several
changes in the economy on revenues, outlays, and the deficit.

BUDGET FUNCTION

The president's budget and the congressional budget resolution are
supposed to present each program according to the principal national
need it is intended to serve.[7] These needs constitute general areas of
federal activity (agriculture, health, general government, and so on)
and are referred to as "functions." Every program, regardless of the

Table 3 CLINTON VERSUS CBO 1995 ECONOMIC ASSUMPTIONS

	Actual 1992	Estimated 1993	Forecast	
			1994	1995
Fourth Quarter to Fourth Quarter (Percentage change)				
Nominal GDP				
CBO	6.7	4.9	5.7	5.4
Administration	6.7	5.0	5.8	5.6
Real GDP				
CBO	3.9	2.3	2.8	2.7
Administration	3.9	2.3	3.0	2.7
Consumer Price Index				
CBO	3.1	2.7	2.9	3.0
Administration	3.1	2.8	3.0	3.2
Calendar Year Averages (Percent)				
Civilian Unemployment Rate				
CBO	7.4	6.8	6.8	6.5
Administration	7.4	6.8	6.9	6.5
Three-Month Treasury Bill Rate				
CBO	3.4	3.0	3.5	4.3
Administration	3.5	3.0	3.4	3.8
Ten-Year Treasury Note Rate				
CBO	7.0	5.9	5.8	6.0
Administration	7.0	5.9	5.8	5.8

Source: U.S. Congress, Congressional Budget Office, *An Analysis of the President's Budgetary Proposals for Fiscal 1995* (Washington, D.C.: U.S. Government Printing Office, 1994), p. 20.

agency or department that administers it, is placed in the one function of the budget that best describes its most important purpose.

A function is not the same as the budget of a particular department. The National Defense function, for example, is different from the Department of Defense budget because the function also includes several nuclear weapons programs administered by the Department of Energy. In addition, a department's budget often is part of several functions. The Treasury Department, for instance, administers programs in a number of functions, including Commerce and Housing Credit, General Government, and International Affairs. A function also does not correspond precisely to an authorization or appropriation bill, which usually deals with parts of several functions at the same time. Finally, a function is not the same as the three categories of discretionary spending—defense, international, and domestic—that were established by the Budget Enforcement Act for fiscal years 1991–1993.

Table 4   FUNCTIONS OF THE FISCAL 1995 BUDGET

Number	Title
050	National Defense
150	International Affairs
250	General Science, Space, and Technology
270	Energy
300	Natural Resources and Environment
350	Agriculture
370	Commerce and Housing Credit
400	Transportation
450	Community and Regional Development
500	Education, Training, Employment, and Social Services
550	Health
570	Medicare
600	Income Security
650	Social Security[8]
700	Veterans Benefits and Services
750	Administration of Justice
800	General Government
900	Net Interest
920	Allowances
950	Undistributed Offsetting Receipts

Each function is separated into subfunctions, which divide the programs according to the "major mission" they fulfill. The first two digits of a subfunction are the same as the digits for the main function; only the last digit is different. For example, function 400, Transportation, contains the following four subfunctions—401, Ground Transportation; 402, Air Transportation; 403, Water Transportation; and 407, Other Transportation.

Table 4 provides a list of the 20 functions. Appendix D of this book describes each function and includes a list of the major agencies, departments, and programs each contains.

SEQUESTERS VERSUS IMPOUNDMENTS[9]

The Balanced Budget and Emergency Deficit Control Act of 1985[10] (commonly known as Gramm–Rudman–Hollings, or "GRH") created a new budget procedure—sequestration.

The Budget Enforcement Act substantially revised sequestration. Under BEA, federal spending was divided into four categories for fiscal 1991–1993—domestic discretionary, defense discretionary, international discretionary, and all mandatory programs. For fiscal 1994 through 1998, BEA combined the three discretionary categories into one (see chapters 2 and 7).[11]

For discretionary programs, the president must issue an order to cut spending if the director of the Office of Management and Budget determines that the limit or "cap" has been exceeded or "breached."

For mandatory spending and revenues, over the entire 1991–1998 period the president must issue a sequester order if a law has been enacted that will increase the deficit and that deficit increase is not offset with either an equal mandatory spending cut or a revenue increase or a combination of both.

This is very different from another budgeting tool that can be used to reduce spending—impoundments. An impoundment is when the president proposes not to spend all or part of an enacted appropriation. The president has the total authority to determine whether and when an impoundment will be proposed and which programs will be affected to what extent. However, under the provisions of the Congressional Budget and Impoundment Control Act of 1974,[12] Congress has the responsibility to review and pass judgment on all proposed impoundments. Without congressional approval, an impoundment cannot become effective and, therefore, spending cannot be cut.

BASELINES

A baseline is a projection of what will happen to spending and revenues based on certain assumptions.[13] For example, suppose the federal government spent $100 on a certain program in fiscal 1995, and the baseline assumption is that it will grow every year by 5 percent. This assumption could be based on anything—an automatic cost of living adjustment that is included in the law that created the program; an assumption that enough funds will be provided to keep the program even with inflation; an expected increase in the number of people eligible for the program; and so on. Regardless of the reason, as table 5 shows, a 5 percent annual increase means that the baseline for this

Table 5 BASELINE CHANGES BASED ON 5 PERCENT PER YEAR GROWTH

1995	1996	1997	1998	1999
100.0	105.0	110.3	115.8	121.6

program would grow from $100 in 1995 to almost $122 four years later if the specified assumptions were realized.

A baseline is important because it provides a way to determine the impact of a proposal on what is expected to happen under certain assumptions. In the example shown in table 5, suppose that in 1996 the president proposes to increase spending in this program to $106. This is an increase over the amount spent in 1995 of $6. However, it is an increase of only $1 over the baseline—the amount that is assumed would be spent anyway.

Baselines are not unique to federal budgeting; they are actually part of everyday life. For example, workers who complain that they did not get enough of a raise in their salaries to stay even with inflation are actually using a baseline that is based on an assumption that their earnings would or should grow by that amount each year.[14]

Federal budget baselines were intended to be used to show how a proposal compared to the amount needed to keep a program at a constant level of services. The problem is that over the years the original purpose for baselines has often been forgotten or ignored and the comparisons of a proposed level of spending with the baseline often have been misused. For example, a member of Congress who wanted to defeat a proposed funding level for the coming year that was at the baseline might refer to it as a budget "freeze" when in fact it represents an increase over the amount expected to be spent in the current year. Or a member who wants to cut a program below the amount expected to be spent this year might find that opponents make the proposed reduction look larger by comparing it to the baseline rather than the prior year.

In 1989, baselines became increasingly controversial because of OMB Director Richard Darman's attempt to avoid using the current services baseline and instead to compare everything to what was actually spent the previous year. Current services not only assumes an increase for inflation in most programs, for entitlements it also assumes additional increases to cover such changes as increased numbers of people who are expected to be legally eligible to participate in the program. In these programs, the baseline amount can, therefore, be significantly above the amount that was spent the previous year, even though there is no change in policy.

Darman was upset because the Bush Administration's proposals to spend more than the previous year looked like cuts in comparison to the baseline. When compared with the previous year's actual amount, however, the proposals appeared to be rather generous.

What Darman really wanted to do was play the same game that he was accusing others of playing by using a different baseline, one that would show the president's proposals in the best possible light. Those that preferred the current services baseline wanted to be able to claim that the administration was cutting spending even though the amount that would be spent was more than was spent the previous year. Darman wanted to claim that the president was increasing spending even though the amount to be spent under the administration's proposal was less than was needed to maintain the same level of services.

The baseline controversy erupted again in 1994. The House—led by Reps. Charles Stenhom (D-TX), John Kasich (R-OH), and Tim Penny (D-MN)—voted to eliminate the use of the baseline and to instead use the prior year's level as a base to judge all proposals. The Senate did not act on the change, however, so the existing baseline continues to be the standard.

What is most interesting is that, using different baselines, both sides in a dispute will agree completely on what was spent last year and what is being proposed. The baselines they use will allow the two sides to reach very different conclusions about exactly the same budget figures.

It is important to remember that baselines are not forecasts of what is going to happen. All they do is show how spending or revenues will change if the assumptions hold true.

The Budget Enforcement Act uses baselines extensively. The most important use is for the "pay-as-you-go" sequester system for mandatory spending and revenues. If spending on mandatory programs rises above its baseline or revenues fall below its baseline because of new legislation enacted by Congress and the White House and that change is not offset by either an equal mandatory spending cut or revenue increase or both, then a sequester is triggered.

ON-BUDGET VERSUS OFF-BUDGET

Not everything the federal government spends money on is reflected in the budget totals. Certain federal entities, programs, and some parts of programs have been specifically excluded from the budget. The Budget Enforcement Act, for example, excluded the receipts and disbursements of Social Security[15] (the Old-Age and Survivors Insurance Fund and the Disability Insurance Fund) from the president's budget and the congressional budget resolution. Programs that have been excluded like this are called "off-budget." Because the spending on these programs is not included in the budget totals, the deficit is not affected by it.

There is no standard list of reasons as to why some program is not included in the budget totals; the decision is almost always political and can be changed depending on the year and situation. For example, until 1981 the purchase of oil for the strategic petroleum reserve was "on-budget," that is, any spending was included in the budget and the deficit was affected accordingly. In 1981, the Reagan Administration proposed and Congress agreed to take this spending off-budget. There was no specific reason for this other than the fact that the price of oil had increased and the White House did not want the deficit growing by as much as would have occurred. Rather than propose to increase revenues or cut other programs to control the deficit, Reagan proposed to take the spending off-budget. In 1985 this program was put back on the budget again when Gramm–Rudman–Hollings was enacted.

The issue of on-budget versus off-budget spending became a somewhat more popular issue in 1989 because of the savings and loan bailout legislation. The Bush Administration wanted the expected $50 billion in spending between fiscal 1989 and 1991 to be off-budget, while Congress wanted it to be on-budget but to exempt it from the GRH deficit calculations. The compromise was that the first $20 billion would be on-budget and the next $30 billion would be off-budget.

DEFICIT VERSUS DEBT

The federal "deficit" and the national "debt" are often incorrectly used interchangeably.

The deficit is the annual difference between the outlays and revenues that occurs in any fiscal year. The deficit for fiscal 1994 was $203 billion.

The government can incur a deficit, that is, spend more than its revenues, by borrowing the difference.[16] The total amount the government has borrowed, that is, all of the deficits from the previous years that have not been paid off, plus the interest that has accrued on the amount borrowed, equals the national debt. As a result, the debt is significantly larger than the deficit. At the end of fiscal 1994, the national debt equalled about $4.6 *trillion*.

Any time the budget is in deficit, the debt will increase because the government must borrow more. Therefore, although deficit reduction efforts such as the ones enacted in 1990 and 1993[17] reduce the deficit, the debt continues to increase because the deficit was not eliminated and the government continues to borrow.

The only way to prevent the deficit from increasing is for the budget to be balanced, that is, for there to be no deficit. The only way to reduce the debt is for the government to run a surplus and for that surplus to be used to buy back previously issued federal securities.

Interest on the national debt is an on-budget expenditure and is displayed in the Net Interest function of the budget. Therefore, a reduction in the amount of interest paid by the government is listed as a reduction in spending.

BALANCED BUDGET VERSUS BALANCED BUDGET AMENDMENT

Technically, a balanced federal budget is one where spending exactly equals receipts, that is, where "outlays" equal "revenues." These days, however, the budget is frequently said to be "in balance" if revenues equal or *exceed* outlays. In other words, a balanced federal budget is often considered to be a budget that is not in deficit.

A balanced budget is different from the proposed balanced budget amendment to the U.S. Constitution. The amendment would establish a constitutional requirement that the federal budget be balanced each year. It would not, however, actually balance the budget; that would still have to be done by Congress adopting and the president signing legislation that would result in the necessary spending cuts and revenue increases.

Therefore, having a balanced budget requirement (be it constitutional or statutory) is not the same as having a balanced budget. The first might lead to the second, but there is no guarantee.

The concept of a constitutional requirement for a balanced budget became newly popular during the debate on the fiscal 1993 budget when both houses of Congress seriously considered but failed to adopt any of the plans that were proposed by various representatives and senators. At least one of the proposed amendments received a majority of votes in both the House and Senate. They did not, however, receive the two-thirds majority required of all proposed constitutional amendments. A balanced budget amendment was considered again in 1994. It failed to get a two-thirds majority in the Senate or even a simple majority in the House. A balanced budget amendment was also a principal element in the "Contract with America" signed by House Republican incumbents and challengers just before the 1994 elections.

Notes

1. The reasons for this dual requirement are mostly political. For a good discussion of how this process came to be, see Allen Schick, *Congress and Money: Budgeting, Spending, and Taxing* (Washington, D.C.: Urban Institute Press, 1980).

2. Public Law 97-35.

3. Public Law 97-102.

4. Theoretically, if the federal government stopped all new spending, budget authority and outlays could eventually be reconciled so that they would equal each other. However, budget authority that was unused for some reason (unspent appropriations, rescissions, and so on) would also have to be taken into account.

5. Public Law 101-508.

6. The Commerce Department announced in 1990 that it would substitute "gross domestic product" or "GDP" for gross national product starting in 1992.

7. The budgets produced by the Bush and Clinton Administrations have not followed this requirement as strictly as previous administrations. Although the budgets have included tables that have displayed the budget by function, the narrative discussion has generally ignored the functional scheme entirely. This has made it far more difficult to understand and analyze the proposals.

8. Social Security was removed from the budget by the Omnibus Budget Reconciliation Act of 1990 (Public Law 101-508). The Social Security function may not, therefore, show up in every functional table.

9. See chapter 6 for a further discussion of sequesters and chapter 7 for further explanation of impoundments.

10. Public Law 99-177.

11. Under the Budget Enforcement Act of 1990, the caps on discretionary spending were established through fiscal 1995. The Omnibus Budget Reconciliation Act of 1993 (P.L. 103-66) extended the caps through fiscal 1998.

12. Public Law 93-344.

13. Section 13101 of the Budget Enforcement Act of 1990 modified section 257 of the Balanced Budget and Emergency Deficit Reduction Act of 1985, which provides a full description of how the baseline is to be calculated.

14. It is important to note that this assumption need not be written in a contract for it to be assumed and the baseline to be used. Similarly, there is no requirement that a baseline be specified in law for it to be used in the federal budget debate.

15. The administrative expenses of Social Security continue to be "on-budget" because of a ruling by the Office of Management and Budget which, according to the Budget Enforcement Act, makes the final decision about such questions.

16. The federal government borrows principally by selling short-term (bills), medium-term (notes), and long-term (bonds) securities.

17. Omnibus Budget Reconciliation Act of 1990 (P.L. 101-508) and Omnibus Budget Reconciliation Act of 1993 (P.L. 103-66).

Part One

THE CONGRESSIONAL BUDGET PROCESS

Chapter Two

OVERVIEW: THE BUDGET ENFORCEMENT ACT BUDGET PROCESS

With little or no debate and absolutely no congressional hearings, the potentially most significant change in the federal budget process—the Budget Enforcement Act of 1990 (BEA)[1]—was passed by the House and Senate on October 27, 1990, and signed by President Bush on November 5, 1990.[2] The most important provisions of BEA were extended through the end of fiscal 1998 when the Omnibus Budget Reconciliation Act of 1993 was signed by President Clinton on August 10, 1993.[3]

BEA significantly revised the budget process that was first created by the Balanced Budget and Emergency Deficit Control Act of 1985,[4] which is better known by the names of its three original sponsors—Senators Phil Gramm (R-TX), Warren Rudman (R-NH), and Ernest Hollings (D-SC). This first version of Gramm–Rudman–Hollings (GRH I) was then revised by the Balanced Budget and Emergency Deficit Control Reaffirmation Act of 1987[5] (GRH II).

The extraordinarily limited public discussion that took place before GRH I and II and BEA were enacted is in sharp contrast to the length of time it took for Congress to pass the legislation that created what is now considered by many to be the original budget process, the Congressional Budget and Impoundment Control Act of 1974.[6] That legislation was adopted almost 21 months after a special joint study commission had been formed, after five different committees in the House and Senate had an opportunity to consider the various problems that had been plaguing consideration of the budget by Congress, and after lengthy debate on the floors of the full House and Senate.[7]

The different paths that the original, GRH, and BEA budget processes took to enactment says much about why each was adopted and what each was and is expected to achieve. The 1974 process was not intended to guarantee any particular outcome, but simply to create a framework for congressional budget decisions. Although many of those who voted for the legislation thought that the process would reduce the deficit or change federal spending priorities, the only true purposes of the law were to revise congressional procedures so that the budget debate would occur more systematically and to enhance accountability in Congress for budget decisions.

The 1974 process was debated at a time when there was little public clamor for action on the deficit. To be sure, some observers considered the deficit to be troublesome. However, it was relatively small,[8] and few people, including those in the media and the general public, seemed to care about it. As a result, the 1974 budget process paid no attention to the deficit. This is not to say that the process could not have been used to reduce the deficit, only that it did not require any such action.

In contrast, both versions of GRH were enacted with reducing the deficit as their almost only purpose. The reason? The federal deficit grew dramatically while the 1974 budget process was in effect. Although the budget process was not the reason the deficit grew, it was a highly visible target for much of the blame.

In addition, unlike the political environment that existed when the 1974 act was debated, Congress considered GRH I at a time when the federal budget and its $200 billion deficit were big news. Starting with Ronald Reagan's 1980 campaign for the White House (when the deficit was one of the leading issues), and continuing through the first Reagan Administration (when Office of Management and Budget [OMB] Director David Stockman became one of the most powerful and visible members of the president's cabinet), Americans had become increasingly concerned about the budget and its ever-growing deficit.

As a result, in late 1985, Congress felt pressure to develop what appeared to be a solution to the deficit problem and to do so quickly, no matter how radical a change from existing practices and procedures the solution might be. Therefore, once GRH I was passed by the Senate as an amendment to another largely unrelated piece of legislation, it rapidly gained supporters and flew through both houses even though there had been no hearings on it and few people were sure exactly how (or even whether) it would work.

The two most significant changes created by GRH were (1) the setting of specific deficit targets—"maximum deficit amounts"—that the president and Congress had to follow, and (2) a new enforcement mechanism—"sequestration"—that was used to cut all eligible federal spending by whatever was needed to reach the maximum deficit amount if the president and Congress were unable or unwilling to do so.

BEA retains both these GRH features but relies on them for quite different purposes. On the one hand, a maximum deficit amount still exists through fiscal 1995, but for a variety of reasons and in a number of ways it is far less important than the maximum deficit amounts were under GRH. On the other hand, the purposes and uses of sequestration have been expanded significantly.

BEA not only changed the basic procedures and timetable by which the federal budget is decided, it also changed the major purpose of the debate. **Under the BEA procedures, reducing the deficit is no longer the major goal; limiting spending and guaranteeing that the baseline level of revenues is collected are now the budget process's primary aims.**

This is not to say that deficit reduction was not expected to occur once BEA went into effect. In fact, the Office of Management and Budget initially forecasted a greatly reduced deficit. But that was mostly as a result of projections that the economy would grow significantly and interest rates and inflation would fall[9] and that several so-called "one-time" factors such as the savings and loan bailout and Operation Desert Storm would stop requiring federal spending.

BEA does not force Congress and the president to do anything about the deficit. This is in sharp contrast to what occurred under GRH, where an across-the-board cut in spending would have been threatened and Congress and the White House most likely would have compromised on a deficit reduction plan if a deficit in excess of the maximum had been projected.

There were a number of reasons for this 180-degree change in goals from GRH to BEA. Some budget watchers believe that it was mostly a White House ploy. After all, BEA's assumed policies of freezing spending and then allowing economic growth to reduce the deficit were remarkably similar to the "flexible freeze" that candidate George Bush talked about during the 1988 presidential campaign.

Others believe that it was an alliance of administration officials—led by OMB Director Richard Darman—and congressional appropriators—led by Senate Appropriations Committee Chairman Robert Byrd (D-WV)—who joined forces to carve out new powers for themselves at the expense of deficit reduction.

Others point out that the overall impact of the changes was to make it easier for all federal officials—White House and Congress, Republicans and Democrats, Senate and House—to avoid making any additional tough choices on spending and taxes until at least after the 1992 presidential and congressional elections were over. This meant that immediately prior to the voting there would be none of the political problems that had plagued the previous budget debates—no more year-long stalemates, no more apparent congressional or presidential ineptitude on the budget, and no more hard votes. According to this line of thinking, the BEA changes would have nothing but a positive impact on everyone's reelection chances.[10]

Undoubtedly all of these reasons were true to some extent. But before any final conclusion is drawn as to why the BEA revisions were adopted it should be remembered that they were:

1. *Made by a very small number of people.* Probably no more than half a dozen members of Congress, congressional staff, and Bush Administration officials really knew and understood the implications of what was discussed;
2. *Made in relative secrecy.* There was little debate on the floor of either the House or Senate, the staff discussions and drafting sessions were conducted behind closed doors, and there were only very limited copies of the legislation available to representatives and senators when the final vote was taken; and,
3. *Completed at the very last minute.* Negotiations on BEA were conducted and drafting continued until only hours before the final vote was taken in the House at about 7:00 a.m. on October 27, 1990. The Senate approved the legislation less than 12 hours later.

This makes it hard to say that BEA was well-conceived or carefully planned, or that anyone really could see the "big picture" as to what was being contemplated. Therefore, as was the case when GRH I and GRH II were implemented for the first time, when Congress and the White House developed the first (fiscal 1992) budget according to the BEA rules they were using an untested and largely unknown procedure to determine that year's spending and taxing policies. In light of the secrecy with which it was enacted, it is hardly surprising that the intricacies of the BEA process were still poorly understood by many until well into the following year's budget debate.

BASIC PROVISIONS OF THE BUDGET ENFORCEMENT ACT

The GRH process was based solely on the deficit. If, on October 15, OMB projected that the deficit would exceed the maximum allowed for the year, sequestration would occur and all eligible programs would be cut across-the-board by whatever amount was needed to reduce the deficit to the target. The spending cuts would be divided evenly between eligible domestic and military programs.

The sequester would occur regardless of the reason the deficit exceeded the maximum. The across-the-board cuts would have gone into place whether or not the economy was performing as well as expected; revenues were below projections; or additional spending was enacted for emergency reasons such as a flood, hurricane, or military operation. Military, international affairs, and domestic appropriations would have been cut whenever sequestration took place. Some entitlements would also have been cut, although the vast majority of these programs were either partially or completely exempt.

An additional feature of GRH was that, regardless of how the economy performed, the maximum deficit did not change. If, as often happened, the economy turned out to be less robust than had been forecast, revenues would be lower and spending higher than expected so the projected deficit would be larger. This typically forced Congress and the White House to enact a larger deficit reduction plan to reach the maximum which, to say the least, was politically difficult.

All these features were changed by BEA.

Maximum Deficits. The BEA process significantly revised the deficit maximums. As table 6 shows, the BEA maximums were substantially above both the GRH I and GRH II targets for fiscal 1991 and 1992, the years the two laws overlapped. They are even higher than what might otherwise seem appropriate because the Social Security trust fund and U.S. Postal Service were not included in BEA deficit calculations.[11]

Table 6 GRH AND BEA DEFICIT MAXIMUMS (billions of dollars)

	1986	1987	1988	1989	1990	1991	1992	1993	1994	1995
GRH I	172	144	108	72	36	0				
GRH II			144	136	100	64	28			
BEA						327[a]	360[b]	428[b]	324[c]	244[d]

[a]Section 601(a)(1) of Public Law 93-344 (as amended).
[b]Office of Management and Budget. "OMB Final Sequestration Report to the President and Congress for Fiscal Year 1993," October 23, 1992, p. 15.
[c]Office of Management and Budget. "OMB Sequestration Update Report to the President and Congress," August 20, 1993, p. 13.
[d]Office of Management and Budget. "OMB Sequestration Update Report to the President and Congress," August 19, 1994, p. 15.

Unlike what happened under GRH when deficit maximums were fixed, the BEA deficit maximums are revised one or more times each year.

The first type of revision, which occurred when the president submitted the budget to Congress,[12] adjusted the maximums to reflect the administration's economic forecast and any technical changes and changes in "concepts and definitions." The president's economic forecast was then "locked in" for the entire debate on that year's budget. Even if the real projected deficit rose because of a worsening economic picture, that was irrelevant as far the budget process is concerned. Congress and the White House continued to deliberate as if the president's forecast and the deficits it produced are what was actually occurring.

The second type of revision was that the deficit maximum was adjusted throughout the year to take into account any of the allowed changes in the discretionary spending cap (discussed below).

The practical effect of these revisions was to increase[13] the deficit maximum at the beginning of each year if, as has happened frequently in the past, the economy did not perform as well as was projected and to then increase it further if certain other allowable developments occur during the year. This effectively prevented the problem that was typical of the GRH I and II years—a growing baseline deficit, a fixed deficit maximum and, therefore, as the year's debate continued, the need for an increasingly larger deficit reduction to avoid sequestration. Under BEA, the increased deficit either was not taken into account or the deficit maximum increased along with the changes.

A good example of the overwhelming difference these new rules made was what happened in 1990. As table 7 shows, in January the budget submitted by President Bush to Congress projected a fiscal 1991 deficit of $101 billion. This meant that $37 billion in spending cuts and tax increases were needed to meet the GRH maximum of $64 billion. By October the projected deficit had risen to $295 billion,

Table 7 FISCAL 1991 BASELINE DEFICIT FORECASTS (billions of dollars)

Month	Projected Deficit	GRH Maximum	Difference
January, 1990	101	64	37
May	138	64	74
June	159	64	95
July	169	64	105
August	170	64	106
October	295	64	231

largely because of economic and technical revisions. This meant that $231 billion was needed to meet the GRH maximum.

Under the GRH rules, as the projected deficit increased, the budget process increased the pressure on Congress and the White House to reduce it because the size of the impending sequester got larger. Had the BEA rules been in effect when the 1991 budget was debated, however, the increasing deficit that was caused by the weakening economy and technical revisions would have created no additional pressure because the deficit reduction needed to satisfy the budget process's requirements would not have changed.

The GRH type of sequester (referred to as an "excess deficit" sequester by BEA) technically can still occur if the deficit maximum for the year is exceeded for reasons other than economic or technical revisions. However, the other changes made by BEA make it highly unlikely that this will happen.

The rules regarding the BEA deficit maximums could have changed dramatically after fiscal 1993, but did not. On January 21,[14] 1993, President Clinton had to decide whether to continue to allow the maximum deficit amounts to "float" for fiscal 1994 with changes in the economy. The president decided to let them float, so the deficit maximum rules that were in effect for fiscal 1991–1993 continued and there was no chance of an excess deficit sequester occurring. Had the president decided not to let them float, the BEA process would have looked like the Gramm–Rudman–Hollings process and an excess deficit sequester would have again been possible.

On January 21, 1994, the president made this same decision for fiscal 1995.

GRH provided a $10 billion margin for error, that is, the deficit had to be reduced to within $10 billion of the maximum to avoid sequestration. BEA changed the margin for an excess deficit sequester. It was $0 in fiscal 1992 and 1993 and $15 billion in fiscal 1994 and 1995.

There are no deficit maximums for any years after fiscal 1995.[15]

Discretionary Spending (Appropriations) Limits. One of the two key enforcement mechanisms created by BEA was the establishment of appropriations limits ("caps") and the creation of a sequestration process to make sure that they are not exceeded ("breached").

As table 8 shows, for fiscal 1991–1993, all discretionary spending was divided into three categories (defense, international, and domestic), and it was each of these individual caps that was enforced. As shown in table 9, for 1994 through 1998, the three categories were combined into a single category and it is this total that will be en-

Table 8 BEA DISCRETIONARY SPENDING CAPS 1991–1995
         (billions of dollars)

	1991	1992	1993	1994	1995
Defense					
Budget Authority	332.9	305.3	289.7		
Outlays	330.8	310.3	298.9		
International					
Budget Authority	21.3	22.2	35.1		
Outlays	20.3	19.8	20.6		
Domestic					
Budget Authority	182.9	209.2	210.5		
Outlays	200.5	215.6	230.7		
Total Discretionary					
Budget Authority				524.1	515.9
Outlays				547.2	544.8

Source: Office of Management and Budget, "OMB Sequestration Update Report to the President and Congress," August 19, 1994, p. 6.

forced. Both the budget authority and outlay caps are binding. Legislation that breaches either can trigger a sequester.

The discretionary caps were changed in 1994 by the Violent Crime Control and Law Enforcement Act (P.L. 103-322). That act lowered the caps each year through fiscal 1998 by differing amounts and transferred the spending to a new "Violent Crime Reduction Trust Fund." Like all trust funds, this one can only be used for the purposes specified in the act.

In effect, the Violent Crime Control and Law Enforcement Act recreated the situation that existed prior to fiscal 1994 when there were three separate categories of discretionary spending. Now there are two—crime control and everything else.

Table 9 BEA DISCRETIONARY SPENDING CAPS 1994–1998[16]
         (billions of dollars)

	1994	1995	1996	1997	1998
Total Discretionary					
Budget Authority	524.1	515.9	514.3	522.6	524.6
Outlays	547.2	544.8	547.1	544.1	542.3

Source: Office of Management and Budget, "OMB Sequestration Update Report to the President and Congress," August 19, 1994, p. 6, and Violent Crime Control and Law Enforcement Act of 1994 (P.L. 103-322).

NOTE: The numbers for fiscal 1996–1998 will be revised in the 1996 budget submitted by the president to Congress.

Like the annual maximum deficits, these caps are adjusted each year by the president when the budget is submitted to Congress to account for a revised inflation forecast, updated technical assumptions, and any changes in concepts and definitions. Unlike the deficit maximums, however, through fiscal 1995 the caps are revised to take other factors into account as the debate continues through the year. These include additional funding provided for increased enforcement of Internal Revenue Service regulations (up to a specified limit);[17] increases in the U.S. contributions to the International Monetary Fund; and any emergency appropriations requested by the president and approved by Congress.[18]

There are actually three different possible discretionary spending sequesters. The "end-of-session" sequester occurs **15 days after Congress adjourns** each year if the budget authority or outlay cap is breached because of enacted legislation. Unlike the GRH sequester, which divided the sequester cuts between eligible military and domestic programs, this sequester will cut all discretionary spending to make up for any breach.

The second or "within session" sequester occurs **between the time that Congress reconvenes each year and June 30** if a supplemental appropriation or other legislation is enacted that breaches a cap for the fiscal year currently underway. This sequester occurs 15 days after the legislation is signed by the president.

Finally, if a supplemental appropriation or other legislation is enacted **after June 30** that breaches a cap for the fiscal year currently underway, a "look-back" sequester occurs immediately that reduces the next year's cap by the same amount.

Three additional features of the appropriations caps are crucial to understanding both how they work and their ultimate purpose.

First, spending cannot be increased above the cap even if it is offset with increased revenues or lower entitlement spending. The reason is that the cap would still be breached and it is the spending limit that is the key to this process, not the impact on the deficit of any proposal.

Second, discretionary spending cannot be reduced to pay for increases in entitlements or reductions in revenues. Although Congress and the president can decide to spend less on appropriations, they can only do so to reduce the deficit, not to offset other budget changes.

Third, BEA provides a "special allowance" for budget authority and outlays to create a cushion for estimating differences between CBO and OMB. For fiscal 1994 through 1998, the budget authority allowance is equal to 0.1 percent of the adjusted limit on total discretionary budget authority for the year. Total appropriations that CBO considers to be within the budget authority cap but OMB scores as over will not trigger a sequester as long as the difference is within the allowance.

The outlay allowance is also intended to deal with any OMB and CBO estimating differences. For both fiscal 1994 and 1995, the allowance is $6.5 billion for all discretionary spending. For fiscal 1996 through 1998, the allowance is 0.5 percent of the adjusted discretionary outlay limit. The outlay allowance for any year is reduced by the outlays associated with the budget authority allowances.

Pay-As-You-Go (PAYGO). The most controversial changes adopted in the BEA budget process deal with revenues and mandatory spending programs.

Revenues and mandatory programs are now assumed to grow only at the baseline levels each year. The baseline is the amount of spending that will occur and revenues that will be collected based on the assumption that current law will continue and that the economic forecast included in the president's budget will occur. All existing mandatory programs (except those with outlays of less than $50 million) and revenue provisions are assumed to continue indefinitely.

Under the rules, OMB maintains a PAYGO "scorecard," a running total of any enacted legislation dealing with revenues and mandatory spending. BEA requires that the net effect of all such legislation must be not to increase the deficit. A net tax loss must be offset by either an increase in other revenues or a decrease in mandatory spending. Similarly, a net increase in mandatory spending must be offset by either a decrease in other mandatory spending or an increase in revenues.

This is unlike the situation with the discretionary spending caps. As far as PAYGO is concerned, the offset can be in either spending cuts or tax increases. In other words, a revenue decrease can be matched with either an equal cut in other mandatory programs or an increase in revenues.

If revenue or mandatory program legislation is not completely offset by the end of that session of Congress, then a potentially very controversial sequester occurs that cuts mandatory programs to make up the difference. The sequester occurs 15 days after Congress adjourns for the year.

BEA retained all the entitlement exemptions that existed under GRH II. As a result, the cuts that can be made in mandatory programs when a sequester occurs are quite limited—only about $25 billion to $30 billion in total.

One change from the GRH rules is in Medicare. Under GRH Medicare could be cut only by a maximum of 2 percent; it can now be cut by 4 percent if a pay-as-you-go sequester occurs.

An additional direct spending enforcement procedure was added to the budget process through an executive order signed by President Clinton on August 4, 1993.[19] According to that order, this new procedure was established "to create a mechanism to monitor total costs of direct spending programs, and, in the event that actual or projected costs exceed targeted levels, to require that the budget address adjustments in direct spending." The key word is monitor. This new procedure is supposed to draw attention to any unforeseen increases in direct spending but, unlike the BEA pay-as-you-go rules, it does not mandate that anything be done about them.

Furthermore, the president can decide that only part of the increase should be offset or that the increase is completely warranted and, therefore, that no offsets are needed at all.

The new direct spending monitoring process is similar to the deficit monitoring procedure that was created by the Congressional Budget Act of 1974. The budget act required that Congress adopt a budget resolution each year that, for the first time, stated the size of the deficit and forced Congress to vote on it. Action to reduce the deficit was not required, however. Therefore, the budget resolution drew attention to the deficit and created political pressure on representatives and senators to do something about it, but it did not mandate that anything actually be done.

In accordance with the executive order's requirements, Office of Management and Budget Director Leon Panetta submitted a report to Congress 30 days after the Omnibus Budget Reconciliation Act of 1993[20] was enacted that created targets for direct spending for fiscal 1994 through 1997. These targets included all legislation enacted up to five days before the report was submitted and were based on the same economic and technical assumptions that were used in the fiscal 1994 congressional budget resolution.[21] Table 10 shows these targets.

The targets will be adjusted in future years when the president submits the budget to Congress to account for any projected increases in the number of beneficiaries of direct spending programs, any increases or decreases in revenues resulting from legislation enacted since the Omnibus Budget Reconciliation Act of 1993 went into effect, any legislation enacted to deal with prior-year breaches of the targets, and the costs of any direct spending legislation designated as an emergency under the Budget Enforcement Act.

Table 10 DIRECT SPENDING TARGETS 1994–1997
         (in billions of dollars)

1994	1995	1996	1997
752.0	792.7	833.7	901.7

Source: Office of Management and Budget, *Budget of the United States, Fiscal Year 1995, Analytical Perspectives* (Washington, D.C.: U.S. Government Printing Office, 1994), p. 203.

The order requires that the president's budget include an annual review of the targets along with a review of how revenues compare to the levels projected in the Omnibus Budget Reconciliation Act of 1993. If the review indicates that direct spending outlays in the prior year actually exceeded the target, or that direct spending outlays in the current or budget year are projected to exceed those targets, then the president's budget must include an explanation for these increases—a "special direct spending message"—and a recommendation as to whether and how they should be offset.

The president has several choices. First, he or she can propose to eliminate the full excess. Even though the overage is in direct spending, the president can propose any combination of discretionary or direct spending cuts or revenue increases.

Second, the president can propose to eliminate part of the excess. Again, any combination of spending cuts is acceptable.

Third, the president can propose that the excess not be offset at all. This must be accompanied by a statement that, because of economic conditions or "for other specified reasons," no cuts are warranted.

If the president recommends spending reductions, the special direct spending message must include the text of a "special direct spending resolution" with proposed reconciliation directives (see chapter 4) to the House and Senate committees with jurisdiction over the programs to be cut.

However, Congress is not legally required to vote on the special direct spending message. An executive order only creates a requirement for the executive branch; it cannot force Congress to do anything.

To deal with this, the House changed its own rules in 1993 to require that it take a vote on any special direct spending message it receives in accordance with this executive order.[22]

According to the House rules, within 10 days after the special direct spending message is sent to Congress by the president it must be introduced by the chair of the budget committee as a concurrent resolution. The chair is not allowed to make any "substantive revisions" from what the president proposed. This concurrent resolution is then required to be included as a separate title by the budget committee in the budget resolution it approves for the upcoming fiscal year (see chapter 4). This title contains reconciliation instructions to the appropriate House and Senate committees that they propose changes in laws within their jurisdiction to reduce outlays or increase revenues by specified amounts which equal or exceed the reductions recommended by the president.

In drafting the title the House Budget Committee is free to vary from what the president proposed. Total spending cuts and revenue increases cannot, however, be greater than the amount by which the direct spending targets are projected to be exceeded. If this title recommends that no changes be made to eliminate the overage, then it must include a statement to that effect.

If the House approves the title of the budget resolution with the direct spending message reconciliation provisions, then the House committees that received the instructions must develop those spending reductions or revenues increases in accordance with the regular reconciliation procedures (see chapter 4). If the title is disapproved, then nothing further happens and direct spending will be above both the targets. Because of several procedural safeguards that were included in the change in House rules that implemented the executive order, it will be very difficult for the House to avoid taking a vote at all.[23]

All of this may be somewhat moot, however, because the Senate did not follow the House's lead and change its rules to require that the executive order be implemented. Although the Senate can decide to consider a special direct spending message or to take up a House-passed reconciliation bill, it does not have to do so. Because the U.S. Constitution requires that spending cuts have to be adopted as statutory changes that are passed by both houses and signed by the president, the practical result of the Senate's decision not to require itself to implement the president's executive order could mean that the order will have no impact on direct spending levels.

But this does not necessarily mean that the executive order is unimportant. To the contrary, if recent budget history is any guide, it may very well be the beginning of more stringent controls on direct spending. The budget resolutions created by the 1974 Congressional Budget Act first forced attention to be paid to the deficit, and that eventually led to the Balanced Budget and Emergency Deficit Control Act (Gramm–Rudman–Hollings), which was specifically designed to reduce it.

This new procedure could have a similar effect as far as direct spending is concerned. If the direct spending message from the president and the House's response to it lead to a demand that more be done, the executive order could be the forerunner of more specific requirements that direct spending be reduced in some way when the targets are exceeded.

THE POLITICS OF THE BUDGET ENFORCEMENT ACT

BEA clearly changed the responsibilities and powers of most of the key players in the federal budget process.

Office of Management and Budget. For a large number of reasons the biggest winner of all was the White House in general and OMB in particular. Although Congress has tried repeatedly to prove otherwise, the president clearly has the upper hand in requesting that something be designated as an "emergency." And for fiscal 1994 and 1995, it was completely up to the president to decide whether the deficit maximums should be allowed to float.

But the real shift in power comes as a result of the tremendous discretion given to OMB all through the BEA process. It is the president's budget, drafted by OMB, that sets the economic forecast for the year and that is used to update the deficit maximums and the discretionary spending caps.

It is also OMB's figures that are used officially to determine whether any of the three different sequesters is needed and, if so, how much spending must be cut. CBO and the congressional Joint Committee on Taxation (which has the responsibility for making all revenue estimates for the House and Senate) may disagree with OMB, and Congress is supposed to use the estimates provided by these two organizations when it debates legislation. But it is still OMB that has the final say about what level of spending and revenues has been enacted and, therefore, whether a sequester is needed.

As was generally the case during the first two years of the Clinton Administration, OMB can stay out of the legislative process until it must provide a cost or revenue estimate 15 days after a bill has been signed into law. When that occurs, OMB's influence is minimal. However, during the fiscal 1992 and 1993 budget processes, the Bush Administration's OMB attempted to become involved in many different legislative issues early in the process by providing informal spending and revenue estimates. For example, it sometimes threatened a sequester early during a tax-writing or appropriations deliberation if a particular provision being considered was not changed in some way more to the White House's choosing even when another provision costing the same amount was ignored.

Appropriations Committees. The House and Senate Appropriations Committees also have been clear winners in the BEA budget process.

First, because of the appropriations caps the committees know how much they will have to spend before the budget process begins each year. Therefore, they no longer have to endure what in the past was often an interminable wait for the budget resolution to be passed before they find out what they can do.

Second, under the BEA rules, if the budget resolution is not adopted by April 15, the appropriations committees receive their allocations based on the caps in the president's budget. These allocations tell appropriations how much they have to spend and so are a critical element in their work. Therefore, this is another reason the committees can move ahead without having to wait for the budget resolution to be passed.

Third, because there is no longer any chance of an excess-deficit sequester because there are no deficit maximums, the only likely way that a sequester can occur in appropriated programs is if the appropriations committees themselves include additional spending that causes the discretionary caps to be breached. Because this is unlikely, there is little chance that any sequester will occur.

The appropriations committees, therefore, have been able to move ahead with their bills without having to worry about any across-the-board cuts reducing the amounts later in the process.

Fourth, while the discretionary caps prevented the shifting of funds among the three categories in fiscal 1991–1993, there is only a single category for fiscal 1994 through 1998. This means that the appropriations committees will again be able to shift funds among the various programs as they see fit.

Budget Committees. It is hard to find any budget process participant whose responsibilities have been further diminished by BEA than the two budget committees. The appropriations committees determine the priorities, annual deficit reductions are not required, and it will be OMB's decisions that hold the most weight as the process is implemented.

Furthermore, although the formal requirement remains, there really is no need for Congress to pass a budget resolution. Virtually all the decisions that used to be made when the budget resolution was adopted have been determined in advance by both the 1990 deficit reduction agreement and BEA. In addition, the appropriations committees no longer have to wait for the budget committees to draft the budget resolution or for it to be adopted before finding out how much they have to spend.

The budget committees' responsibilities could grow if, as was the case in 1993, the budget resolution is used to develop additional deficit reductions or if it is needed to instruct some committees as part of a pay-as-you-go effort. Neither of these is required by BEA, however, and, in the absence of further deficit reduction efforts that are implemented through the regular budget process, the budget committees most likely will play a smaller role than they did under GRH I and II.

Congressional Budget Office and Joint Committee on Taxation. Technically, CBO's role in the budget process has been strictly advisory since GRH II was enacted in 1987. However, the tremendous need for cost estimates has often put CBO's projections into the forefront of many congressional debates.[24] The best example of this occurred in 1994 during the debate on health care reform when Congress relied heavily on CBO to project the cost of the many plans that were being considered. The debate was even delayed until CBO could develop its estimate. A CBO projection that a plan would increase the deficit often resulted in that proposal either being revised or dropped entirely.

The impact on the Joint Committee on Taxation (JCT) is somewhat less clear. GRH I and II both required that Congress use JCT as the sole authority for all revenue estimates, and that was not changed by BEA. As a result, JCT's estimates have been extremely influential in a number of highly charged debates, and that has frequently brought it both increased public attention and influence.

BUDGET ENFORCEMENT ACT TIMETABLE

BEA made a number of important changes in the dates by which certain steps in the budget process have to be completed. It also added several new procedures and requirements. The schedule is as follows.

Stage 1: The President's Budget—January 2 to March 20, 1995

By February 6. Under GRH II, the president had to submit a budget to Congress by the first Monday in January. The BEA rules provide a one-month window from the first Monday in January to the first Monday in February. Although the conference report explaining the BEA changes strongly suggested that the president aim for the earliest possible date, the general assumption is that the later date is much more likely. For the fiscal 1996 budget, this is February 6.

Five days before the president submits the budget to Congress each year, CBO must issue a sequestration "preview" report. This report provides a starting point for the year's debate by providing estimates for each of the three potential sequesters—discretionary, pay-as-you-go, and excess deficit.

For discretionary spending, the preview report provides an updated spending cap based on the adjustments allowed. For pay-as-you-go, the report provides the net increase or decrease in the deficit that will be caused by revenue and mandatory legislation already enacted and an estimate of the potential pay-as-you-go sequester that could be needed if an offset is not adopted. For the excess-deficit sequester, the preview report provides an estimate of how much the projected deficit will exceed the maximum and the size of the across-the-board cuts (if any) that might be needed to eliminate the excess.

On the same date that the president submits the budget, OMB must issue its own sequestration preview report with the same information that is required of CBO. OMB must explain any differences between its estimates and CBO's, but it is not bound by the CBO figures in any way.

March 20. As was the case with GRH, BEA requires all committees to send a report to the budget committee in their own house explaining their spending and revenue plans for the coming year. These "views and estimates" reports are not binding commitments, just the committees' best guess as of this date as to what they are planning to do with the programs within their jurisdiction. Under GRH the reports were due by February 25. Under BEA, the reports must be sent to the budget committee within six weeks after the president submits the budget to Congress. If the fiscal 1996 president's budget is submitted to Congress on February 6, this date will be March 20.

Stage 2: Congressional Budget Resolution and Reconciliation—March 20 to June 15, 1995

April 15. April 15 is still the date by which Congress is supposed to adopt the budget resolution for the coming year. In most years this date, at best, has been little more than a pie-in-the-sky dream. The fiscal 1995 budget resolution, however, was adopted by the House on March 31 and the Senate on April 1.

For fiscal 1991–1993, virtually all the controversial decisions that the budget committees had to make to put a budget resolution together—e.g., the size of the deficit, the split between domestic and military appropriations, the level of revenues—were made before the debate began. The deficit was the BEA maximum as updated by the president's budget; the domestic-military split was determined by the appropriations caps as updated by the president's budget; and the level of revenues was the pay-as-you-go baseline, again as updated by the president's budget.

Because of this, the job of putting a budget resolution together was relatively noncontroversial. The only potential problem was the decision as to how to allocate the domestic caps among the various domestic functions (Energy vs. Community and Regional Development, for example). Most of this will continue through 1998. The one big change will be the allocation between domestic, military, and international appropriations. That will have to be made during the budget process because the three BEA categories were combined into one starting in fiscal 1994.

There are two situations that could make a budget resolution more controversial. The first is if, as happened during the debate on the fiscal 1994 budget, Congress decides to reduce the deficit more than is required under the BEA rules. The budget resolution would be the most likely legislative vehicle for determining how much spending should be cut and revenues increased, and these decisions are always politically difficult.

The second situation is if the budget resolution is used to determine either how to cut taxes or increase mandatory spending without triggering a pay-as-you-go sequester. The budget resolution would be used to determine how to offset the policy change and would then provide reconciliation instructions to one or more committees to develop the actual spending cuts or tax increases. Again, this would be very difficult politically.

If reconciliation does occur, it is supposed to be completed by June 15.

Stage 3: Authorizations and Appropriations—April 15 to September 30, 1995

April 15. BEA makes April 15 important for another reason. If Congress fails to adopt a budget resolution by this date, the appropriations committees are given their allocations based on the amounts included in the president's budget. This means that they will know the amounts they will have to spend and so be able to start drafting their appropriations bills.

May 15. If a budget resolution has not been adopted by this date, the House may start to pass the fiscal 1996 appropriations anyway.

June 30. The House is expected to pass its version of all 13 appropriations for fiscal 1996 by this date.

September 30. BEA did not change the start of the federal fiscal year. Therefore, September 30 is still the date by which all fiscal 1996 appropriations are supposed to be enacted. Although this deadline has generally been difficult for Congress to meet, all fiscal 1995 appropriations were passed by September 30, 1994.

Stage 4: Sequestration—August 10 until 15 Days after Congress Adjourns

August 10. The president must notify Congress by this date if he or she wants to exempt military uniformed personnel from sequestration if it occurs this year. If the president does partially or completely exempt the military personnel acounts, all other discretionary programs will be cut by a higher percentage to make up the difference.

August 15. CBO must submit to OMB a "sequestration update" report that revises the information provided in the preview report released in January.

August 20. OMB must issue its own sequestration update report to Congress five days after it receives CBO's report. As with the preview report in January, OMB must explain any differences between its estimates and CBO's, but it is the OMB figures that will be controlling in all cases.

Ten and Fifteen Days after the End of the Congressional Session. One of the biggest GRH loopholes existed because of the October 15 sequestration date—any spending increase or revenue decrease that occurred after this date did not have any impact on the deficit as far as GRH was concerned. Because all congressional sessions extended past October 15, there was nothing to stop Congress and the White House from taking actions that would thwart the goal of reducing the deficit as long as they did it after the sequestration deadline.

BEA dealt with this problem by changing the sequester date from October 15 to 15 days after the session of Congress ends. This makes it impossible to get around the sequester deadline because, if Congress is not meeting, no legislation can be enacted. Furthermore, if Congress and the administration try to overcome a sequester during the next session by increasing spending or decreasing revenues in the current year, a "within-session" or "look-back" sequester will be triggered.

CBO must send its final sequester report to OMB 10 days after the session of Congress ends. This report provides final estimates for all the information provided in both the preview and update reports completed earlier in the year and, if it is necessary, the amounts by which discretionary spending and mandatory spending have to be cut.

OMB must send its final sequester report to Congress 5 days later, 15 days after the end of the congressional session. As with all its previous reports, OMB must explain any differences between its figures and CBO's, but it is OMB's numbers that are binding.

The same day that OMB issues its report, the president must issue a sequester order to all federal departments and agencies telling them what cuts, if any, must be made. The order is effective immediately.

Table 11 shows the expected timetable for all congressional and presidential actions on the fiscal 1996 budget.

IMPOUNDMENTS

The impoundment procedures created by the 1974 Congressional Budget Act were not changed significantly by either GRH I or GRH II and not at all by BEA. They continue to be implemented only when the president proposes either not to spend or to delay spending funds previously approved by Congress.[25]

A "rescission" is a presidential proposal not to spend congressionally approved appropriations. The reason for such a proposal can be specific (as when the objectives of the program can be achieved without spending the full amount appropriated) or general (such as fiscal policy considerations). Regardless of the reason, the president must submit a message to Congress requesting the rescission and explaining the reasons for it. If both houses of Congress do not pass a bill approving the proposed rescission within 45 legislative days, the president must spend the money as originally intended.

Appendix E is the rescission message submitted to Congress by President Clinton on November 1, 1993.

Table 11 FISCAL 1996 BEA BUDGET PROCESS

	Deadline	Event
1.	By five days before president submits his budget to Congress (by 2/1/95)	The president submits the fiscal 1996 budget to Congress. OMB issues sequestration preview report.
2.	Between the first Monday in January and the first Monday in February (by 2/6/95)	CBO issues sequestration preview report.
3.	Within six weeks after president submits budget to Congress (by 3/20/95)	All committees must submit their "views and estimates" reports to the budget committee in their own house.
4.	By April 15	Congress must adopt concurrent resolution on the budget for fiscal 1996; if budget resolution is not adopted by this date, appropriations committees will receive their allocations based on the amounts requested in the president's budget.
5.	May 15	The House can begin passing fiscal 1996 appropriations even if a budget resolution has not yet been adopted.
6.	By June 30	The House is supposed to adopt its version of all fiscal 1996 appropriations; last date for triggering "within-session" discretionary sequester.
7.	July 1	First date that a "look-back" discretionary sequester can be triggered.
8.	August 10	The president must notify Congress if and how he or she plans to exempt military uniformed personnel from sequestration.
9.	August 15	CBO issues its sequestration update report.
10.	August 20	OMB issues its sequestration update report.
11.	September 30	Last date for triggering "look-back" discretionary sequester.
12.	October 1	Fiscal 1996 begins.
13.	Ten days after the end of the session of Congress	CBO issues its final sequestration report.
14.	Fifteen days after the end of the session of Congress	OMB issues its final sequestration report; if needed, the president issues a sequestration order to all departments and agencies, which is effective immediately.

A "deferral" is a presidential proposal to delay the spending of congressionally approved appropriations. The delay can be for any length of time but cannot last beyond the end of the fiscal year. Regardless of the length of time, the president must submit a deferral message to Congress. Unlike a rescission, which requires specific approval by Congress, a deferral is automatically assumed to be approved unless, at any time after the president's message has been received, either the House or Senate passes legislation specifically disapproving it.

Deferrals were controversial during the Reagan Administration, which tried to use them to thwart congressional policy. As a result, GRH II codified the informally accepted circumstances under which a president could propose a deferral. They are: "(1) to provide for contingencies; (2) to achieve savings made possible by or through changes in requirements or greater efficiency of operations; or (3) as specifically provided by law."

The use of deferrals was, however, severely limited by the federal courts. As a result, at this point, deferrals for policy reasons are no longer permitted.

The budget and appropriations committees in the Senate and the appropriations committee in the House have assumed responsibility for reviewing presidential impoundment messages. But the statutory monitor of this part of the budget process is the comptroller general who, as head of the General Accounting Office,

> must review each message and advise the Congress of the facts surrounding the action and its probable effect. . . . The comptroller general is also required to report to the Congress reserve or deferral action which has not been reported by the president; and to report and reclassify any incorrect transmittals by the president. **Such reports by the comptroller general have the same legal effect as rescission . . . messages from the president.**[26] (Emphasis added)

The comptroller general also has the power to sue the president if he or she refuses to spend an appropriation after Congress has formally disapproved a proposed rescission or deferral.

Notes

1. Public Law 101-508.

2. BEA technically amends the Budget and Accounting Act, the Congressional Budget and Impoundment Control Act, the Balanced Budget and Emergency Deficit Control

Act, and the Balanced Budget and Emergency Deficit Control Reaffirmation Act. Because the process created by the Budget Enforcement Act is so different from what existed before, this book will refer to BEA as a separate process even though all of the previous laws (as amended) continue to remain in effect.

3. Public Law 103-66.

4. Public Law 99-177.

5. Public Law 100-119.

6. Public Law 93-344.

7. For a good discussion of the legislative history of P.L. 93-344, see Allen Schick, *Congress and Money: Budgeting, Spending, and Taxing* (Washington, D.C.: The Urban Institute Press, 1980), pp. 51–81.

8. The federal deficit was $2.8 billion in fiscal 1970, $23.0 billion in fiscal 1971, $23.4 billion in fiscal 1972, $14.9 billion in 1973, and $6.1 billion in fiscal 1974.

9. The economic forecast used by the Bush Administration in August 1991, when BEA was adopted, was:

[percent; calendar years]

	1991	1992	1993	1994	1995	1996
Growth, Real GNP	0.8	3.6	3.4	3.2	3.0	3.0
Unemployment	6.7	6.3	6.2	5.8	5.4	5.2
3-Month Treasury Bill	5.7	5.9	5.8	5.6	5.4	5.3
Inflation, GNP Deflator	4.2	3.8	3.7	3.5	3.4	3.3

10. This did not work out as had been expected largely because of Ross Perot's presidential campaign, which relied on the deficit as one of its major issues. Perot's emergence as a presidential candidate, of course, had not been anticipated when the 1990 budget agreement was put in place.

11. Section 13301 of BEA states:

   ... the receipts and disbursements of the Federal Old-Age and Survivors Insurance Fund and the Federal Disability Insurance Fund shall not be counted as new budget authority, outlays, receipts, or deficit or surplus for purposes of

   (1) the budget of the United States Government as submitted by the president,
   (2) the congressional budget, or
   (3) the Balanced Budget and Emergency Deficit Control Act of 1985.

12. The president had to make these changes in his fiscal 1992 and 1993 budgets. He had the option of making similar revisions in the deficit targets when the fiscal 1994 and 1995 budgets were submitted.

13. The revisions in the maximum deficit amounts could have been in either direction. That is, if the economy performed better than had been anticipated, the deficit target would be reduced.

14. The January 21 date was chosen very carefully. Because it is the day after the president is inaugurated, it required that the president who would preside over the next four years also determine the rules that would be used to consider the budget during this period. The relevant provisions of BEA are sections 254(a), 254(c), and 253(g)(1)(B) of Public Law 99-177 (as amended).

15. The Omnibus Budget Reconciliation Act of 1993 (Public Law 103-66) extended the discretionary spending caps and pay-as-you-go rules for mandatory spending and rev-

enues through fiscal 1998 but did not extend the deficit maximums.

However, the Senate established a new rule regarding the deficit in the conference report on H.Con.Res. 218 (Report 103-490), the fiscal 1995 congressional budget resolution, that prohibits the Senate from enacting legislation that would increase the deficit over a 10-year period. Section 23 of that report states that it is not in order for the Senate to consider any direct-spending or receipts legislation that, compared to the most recently adopted budget resolution, would increase the deficit in the first fiscal year, over the first five years, or in the second five years.

16. The fiscal 1996–1998 caps will be revised again in the president's fiscal 1996 budget.

17. The limits were $191 million in budget authority and $183 million in outlays for fiscal 1991, $172 million in budget authority and $169 million in outlays for fiscal 1992, $183 million in budget authority and $179 million in outlays for fiscal 1993, $187 million in budget authority and $183 million in outlays for fiscal 1994, and $188 million in budget authority and $184 million in outlays in fiscal 1995.

18. BEA does not provide a specific definition of emergency appropriations. It merely states that they are appropriations designated by the president as "emergency requirements" and designated as such by Congress in a statute. The emergency designation was extended through fiscal 1998.

19. The executive order was signed by President Clinton after a legislative attempt to impose the same process failed and conservative Democrats in the House balked at supporting the Clinton fiscal 1994 deficit reduction plan without it. The direct spending targets and enforcement procedure were originally included in H.R. 2264, the House-passed version of reconciliation for fiscal 1994.

20. The report was a letter from Panetta to House Speaker Thomas Foley and Vice President Albert Gore, Jr. (in his capacity as president of the Senate) dated September 3, 1993.

21. House Concurrent Resolution 64.

22. The House changed its rules when it adopted House Resolution 240, which established the procedure under which the conference report on the Omnibus Budget Reconciliation Act of 1993 was debated. Section 2 of H.Res. 240 stated, "House Resolution 235 is hereby adopted" and H.Res. 235 included the actual change in House rules.

23. If the president submits a direct spending message, it is not in order in the House to consider an appropriation for the coming fiscal year until Congress adopts the budget resolution that includes the appropriate separate title. If the separate title proposes to eliminate less than the full amount by which the direct spending targets will be exceeded, then the House Budget Committee must report a resolution directing the House Government Operations Committee to report legislation increasing the targets by the appropriate amount. It is not in order for the House to consider the budget resolution for the year until it first passes the increases in the targets.

24. The Clinton Administration decided to use the CBO's economic forecast when it put together its fiscal 1994 budget. This gave CBO additional prominence early in the debate. However, that August, the White House used its own economic forecast when it compiled its mid-session review of the budget.

25. GRH II did amend the impoundment control provisions of the Congressional Budget and Impoundment Control Act to prevent the president from proposing two rescissions for the same activity in the same fiscal year. See chapter 7 for an explanation.

26. U.S. Congress, House Committee on the Budget. *The Congressional Budget Process: A General Explanation* (Washington, D.C.: U.S. Government Printing Office, 1981), p. 17.

STAGE ONE: THE PRESIDENT'S BUDGET

Deadline	Action
By February 6	The president submits the fiscal 1996 budget to Congress; Office of Management and Budget (OMB) issues its fiscal 1996 sequester preview report.
At least five days before the president submits the fiscal 1996 budget to Congress	Congressional Budget Office (CBO) issues its fiscal 1995 sequester preview report.
By March 20	Congressional committees submit their "views and estimates" to their respective budget committees.

The congressional budget process for fiscal 1996 will begin between January 2 and February 6, 1995, when the president submits the budget to Congress.[1]

Five days before the president submits the budget to Congress, CBO is required to issue its sequester preview report.

The sequester preview report provides estimates of three things that are crucial to successful implementation of the two primary enforcement mechanisms of the BEA process:

1. *Discretionary Spending.* For the current year (fiscal 1995 in this case) and all subsequent years through fiscal 1998, the revised discretionary spending cap based on the anticipated adjustments in the president's budget and any other adjustments that might have been made since the last sequester report was issued 15 days after Congress adjourned.
2. *Pay-As-You-Go.* For the current year and the budget year (fiscal 1995 and 1996, respectively), a list of each mandatory spending or

revenue law enacted since November 9, 1990, and its impact on the deficit. If the deficit is projected to increase, the report must also include the potential percentage cut in mandatory programs that will be needed to eliminate that increase if Congress and the president do not take action to eliminate it.[2]

The purpose of the sequestration preview report is to provide Congress and the White House with the information they need to determine how much can be spent in the year ahead or how much must be offset as the result of prior-year legislation to avoid a sequester.

For example, if legislation enacted in 1994 during the debate on the fiscal 1995 budget will result in a revenue loss or mandatory spending increase in fiscal 1996 and so will increase the deficit, the preview report will indicate that Congress and the president will be starting the year with the requirement that an offset be enacted. There is no special procedure for enacting the revenue increase or spending cut; presumably it will occur as part of the regular legislative process.

The sequestration preview report, therefore, is really a status report provided just as the budget process begins. It is necessary because some legislative actions will have an impact on spending and revenue implications several years into the future and, under the BEA requirements, lawmakers need to know what this is so that action can be taken to compensate for them.

To a certain extent this procedure is a response to a legislative practice that had become fairly common prior to BEA's enactment— passing a law now that had either no or only a limited budget impact immediately but which did have a large impact in the future. This ploy was possible under the GRH rules; it is not possible under BEA.

Not later than five days after CBO issues its report, OMB must issue its own sequester preview report. OMB must explain any differences between its numbers and CBO's. As with all other steps in the BEA budget process, however, it is OMB's figures that are binding on all participants and the ones that are used throughout the year. The OMB preview report is due on the same day that the president must submit the proposed budget to Congress.[3]

GRH I changed the deadline for the president to submit the budget from 15 days after Congress convenes to the first Monday in January. BEA changed that deadline again—it now must be submitted between the first Monday in January and the first Monday in February.

The reason for this change is that the earlier deadline proved to be increasingly difficult for the White House to meet. Part of the reason for the delay was the length of time it took for Congress and the president to work out the final details on the previous year's budget. When that work dragged on past the start of the fiscal year to November and December, it was very hard for all of the decisions on the following year's budget to be completed and the budget to be drafted and printed by the first Monday in January.

Many of the changes included in BEA have made it easier for the budget process to be completed close to the start of the fiscal year in October, and presumably that should make it easier for the president's budget to be submitted to Congress closer to the beginning rather than the end of the one-month period. The fiscal 1992 Bush budget, however, was submitted on February 4, the last possible date. The fiscal 1993 Bush budget was submitted on January 29, five days before the end of the one-month window. The Clinton fiscal 1995 budget was submitted on February 7, the last day of the period.[4]

Under the BEA procedures, the president's budget provides the economic forecast that must be used throughout the rest of the budget process. It also includes an adjusted cap for discretionary spending that must be used to determine how much can be appropriated. If Congress does not pass its budget resolution by April 15, the cap included in the president's budget can be used to provide the appropriations committee with their allocations (see chapter 5) so that the debate on the appropriations bills can start.

The significance of this first step in the congressional budget process, which was relatively high to begin with, increased even further under BEA. Submission of the budget by the president provides the administration with the power to propose a seemingly cohesive proposal embodying an economic program and spending and taxing priorities, and to present it in one or more documents.[5] Now, however, in addition to providing recommendations, the president's budget also includes information that, while it can be questioned, must be used by all participants for the rest of the year. This is likely to increase the attention the budget gets and the influence it exerts.

The executive budget process is considerably less open than the congressional budget process and, consequently, difficult to describe precisely. Other than the deadline for submitting the budget to Congress, there are no specific statutory dates by which certain decisions must be made.

In addition, the relative importance of decisions made in the executive budget process varies greatly from year to year and from department to department, depending on the personalities, political skills, and relative power of the decision makers. One department may have no choice but to accept an OMB decision, whereas another may be able to get a further review or appeal directly to the president.

In early 1981, for example, OMB and its director, David Stockman, were preeminent forces in compiling the fiscal 1982 budget, largely because cabinet secretaries had just been appointed and knew relatively little about the departments they were to administer.[6] Later in 1981, however, when OMB proposed cuts in military spending, the president overruled Stockman in favor of Secretary of Defense Caspar Weinberger. During the final preparations for the fiscal 1983 budget in November and December 1981, Stockman was repeatedly overruled when agency heads, notably Secretary of Housing and Urban Development Samuel Pierce and Environmental Protection Agency Administrator Ann Gorsuch, also appealed OMB-proposed cuts directly to the president.

BEA created several requirements that the president must follow when the budget is compiled. First, through fiscal 1995, the president's budget had to have a deficit no higher than the maximum deficit amount set for the year. Second, through 1998, discretionary spending must be no higher than the adjusted cap.

The budget that the president submits to Congress is only a proposal. It will be debated, amended, and even ignored at times by Congress during its deliberations over the next eight or nine months. But virtually all congressional budget activities that take place over the rest of the process will, either formally or informally, use the president's budget as a starting point for debate. More importantly, many of the minute decisions made in compiling the president's budget will not be reviewed by Congress because of lack of controversy, interest, staff, or time. Therefore, regardless of what Congress may do to alter the budget at the different stages of its own process, to a large extent the president will dominate many, if not most spending decisions.

The president's decisions have become even more dominant as a result of BEA, which, as noted above, increased the overall importance of the president's budget to the rest of the budget process. In addition, because the president's economic assumptions now must be used by everyone else in the budget process, because the discretionary spending cap eliminates much of the pre-BEA controversy with regard to how much should be devoted to appropriations, and because the floating deficit maximums mean that no further deficit reductions will have to be enacted each year, the president's budget should no longer suffer the relative ignominy of being declared "dead on arrival" as soon as it is received on Capitol Hill. The administration's priorities should, therefore, be the focus of most of the attention.

Congressional hearings on the president's budget generally further emphasize the president's budget agenda because the initial witnesses before almost all committees usually are administration officials. The administration often appears to be conducting the political equivalent of a traveling road show, with key officials (the OMB director, the chair of the Council of Economic Advisors, and the secretary of the Treasury, for example) sometimes testifying together or on consecutive days before the same committees. These hearings take place during the first few days or weeks after the president's budget is submitted to Congress.

Congressional hearings on the president's budget go in two different directions. The budget committees hold hearings to consider the whole budget. Besides hearing from administration officials, the committees are likely to receive testimony from outside economists with different views on what the appropriate fiscal policy should be; interest groups concerned with particular aspects of the budget; other members of Congress; and CBO, which is required to analyze the president's budget and report to Congress.

At the same time, the authorization and appropriations committees hold hearings on the specific parts of the budget within their jurisdiction. They are likely to hear from the cabinet officials whose programs they must review, groups that benefit from or are otherwise interested in those programs, and other members of Congress.

Before passage of the Congressional Budget Act in 1974, all this activity took place over many months. The appropriations committees, in particular, spent much time reviewing the budget requests of each department and agency. The benefit of this line-by-line review was that Congress was able to examine the spending plans in detail. But an extraordinary amount of time was necessary to do the work, and appropriations bills usually were not enacted before the fiscal year began or, sometimes, not until it was well underway.

In part to deal with this problem, all standing committees are now required to report to their respective budget committees no later than six weeks after the president's budget has been submitted to Congress[7] their "views and estimates" of the actions they probably will take on the provisions of the president's budget within their jurisdiction.[8] In calendar 1995, therefore, each committee will have to complete in six weeks a large part of the work that previously might have taken six months or more. But because Congress often is in session only on Tuesday, Wednesday, and Thursday at this time of the year, and because there is a recess scheduled to coincide with the Lincoln and Washington birthday holidays, the amount of time available to review the president's budget actually is considerably less than six weeks. Obviously, the time pressure severely limits the level of detail each committee can consider.

The views and estimates are not binding commitments by the committees but merely a forecast of the actions they might take this session, including support for and deviations from presidential recommendations and committee initiatives not included in the president's budget proposal. Appendix B contains sample pages from the fiscal 1995 views and estimates of two committees.

The views and estimates usually are the first official congressional response to the president's proposals and, therefore, the initial move away from that budget. The actual value of the reports varies greatly from committee to committee, however. Some committees will meet to vote on specific matters to be incorporated in their reports and will include detailed backup materials, justifications, and even supplemental and minority views by members of the committee who disagree with or wish to distinguish themselves in some other way from the majority position. Such committees attempt to determine spending priorities and provide real guidance to their budget committee. Other committees make no such attempt in the belief that any decisions would be premature at this point and might limit their options in the future. The type of report that these committees submit is, therefore, of minimal value and sometimes indicates merely that the committee is unhappy with the budget process or the budget committee.

Nevertheless, the views and estimates are an often overlooked and undervalued part of the budget process. They force the authorization and appropriations committees to review and make some quick initial decisions about the president's budget. They provide the budget committees with guidance as to the intentions of the other committees. And, because the committees have such limited time in which to review the president's budget and make their reports to the respective budget committees, the views and estimates often identify the issues within each committee's purview that (because they have been specifically raised) are likely to be controversial or (because they have been ignored or glossed over) are likely not to be considered at all.

Again, it is important to remember that these reports are in no way binding on the committees that make them. Issues that may be unimportant early in the year may well become highly controversial later.

For the same reason that much of the president's budget will not be debated by Congress, a good deal of the detail necessary to compile the views and estimates also will not be reviewed further, either by the individual committees or by the full House and Senate. There simply is not enough time to reconsider questions on which no substantial controversy exists or which are insignificant compared with the larger issues that must be debated.

As a result, the earlier in the process a particular item or program can be included in the budget, the better its chances are of staying there. If, for example, a new jobs training program in the Department of Labor is included in the president's budget proposal and also is specifically included in the views and estimates by the House Education and Labor and Senate Labor and Human Resources Committees and the Appropriations subcommittees dealing with these programs, the likelihood of it ultimately being funded is significantly increased. Conversely, if the same program is not included in the president's budget and is specifically excluded from the views and estimates, it becomes more difficult to add it to the authorization or appropriations bills later in the process. Therefore, although the president's budget submission is only a proposal and the views and estimates are nonbinding, significant (albeit unofficial) budget decisions are made at both these points.

The views and estimates are submitted by the committees to their respective budget committees, which do not hold separate hearings on them. In 1994, the House and Senate Budget Committees compiled the fiscal 1995 reports they received into a single volume and made them available to other members of Congress and the public.[9]

These views and estimates receive only minimal attention from the media, in no way approaching the notice given the president's budget. The reports then become some of several considerations used by the budget committees to compile the congressional budget resolution, as described in the next chapter.

Notes

1. The 1994 election results may change this. Although the budget process usually begins with the submission of the president's budget, there was some indication shortly after the election that the Republican majority wanted to pass the fiscal 1996 budget resolution *before* President Clinton even sent his budget proposal to Capitol Hill.

2. The Omnibus Budget Reconciliation Act of 1993 (P.L. 103-66) "rebased" the pay-as-you-go scorecard so that all mandatory spending reductions and revenue increases enacted in previous years that had not yet been used to offset mandatory spending increases or revenue decreases could not be used in the future. The effect of the rebasing was to reset the scorecard at zero.

3. BEA does not indicate whether the OMB sequester preview report must be a separate document. It was part of the Bush fiscal 1992, 1993, and 1994 budgets. It was also part of the Clinton 1995 budget.

4. The president's fiscal 1994 budget was submitted to Congress in three different documents and on three dates. The Bush Administration sent Congress what it termed a "budgetary statement," *Budget Baselines, Historical Data, and Alternatives for the Future* on January 6, 1993, two weeks before President Clinton was inaugurated. This document included no policy choices but did provide much of the statistical information that is usually included in the president's budget.

The Clinton Administration's *A Vision of Change for America*, which was submitted to Congress on February 17, 1993, included the president's economic stimulus and deficit reduction proposals. It did not, however, include the detailed department-by-department proposals for fiscal 1994. That was provided on April 8, when the White House sent Congress its proposed *Budget of the United States Government* for fiscal 1994.

5. Prior to the fiscal 1991 budget, the president's budget was presented in seven separate documents—the Budget of the United States Government; the Budget of the United States Government in Brief; Historical Tables; Special Analyses; the Budget of the United States Government, Appendix; Management of the United States Government; and Major Policy Initiatives. The fiscal 1991 and 1992 Bush budgets combined all of these documents into a single volume. The fiscal 1993 Bush budget and Clinton fiscal 1994 budget were submitted in two documents. The fiscal 1995 Clinton budget was submitted in four documents. (See chapters 8–10 for more information on the president's budget.)

6. William Greider, "The Education of David Stockman," *Atlantic Monthly,* December 1981, pp. 27–54.

7. This was a change from GRH, which required that the views and estimates be submitted by February 25.

8. The Joint Economic Committee is required to submit a report recommending appropriate fiscal policies to achieve the goals of the Employment Act of 1946.

9. U.S. Congress. House of Representatives, Committee on the Budget, *Views and Estimates of the Committees of the House on the Congressional Budget for Fiscal 1995* (Washington, D.C.: U.S. Government Printing Office, 1994), Committee Print CP-5. See also U.S. Congress. Senate, Committee on the Budget, *FY 1995 Concurrent Resolution on the Budget* (Washington, D.C.: U.S. Government Printing Office, 1994), Senate Report 103–238.

Chapter Four

STAGE TWO: THE CONGRESSIONAL BUDGET RESOLUTION AND RECONCILIATION

Deadline	Action
By April 15, 1995	Congress completes action on the fiscal 1996 congressional budget resolution.
By June 15	Congress completes action on the fiscal 1996 reconciliation bill.

Because of the Budget Enforcement Act, the congressional budget resolution will either be the least or most important stage in the congressional budget process each year.

On the one hand, the budget resolution could be a nonevent if, as happened during consideration of the fiscal 1995 budget, the president and Congress decide to make no further reductions in the deficit than those already in place. This will mean that the discretionary spending cap set in BEA and adjusted in the president's budget will be the one included in the budget resolution, and the baseline levels of revenues and mandatory spending will be the ones that were included in the president's budget.

In this situation the congressional budget resolution will precisely mirror the aggregate amounts included in the president's budget so there will be little of the acrimony that has existed between the White House and Congress on these matters over the past decade. Not only will the deficit essentially be set, but the split between revenues and spending will also be fixed.

On the other hand, the budget resolution could be a highly controversial and politically difficult stage if either:

1. Congress decides that the deficit should be cut below the baseline level or the level proposed in the president's budget;
2. Congress decides to increase mandatory spending or decrease revenues more than would occur under the baseline assumptions and,

therefore, has to use the reconciliation procedures to order committees to develop offsetting spending cuts or tax increases to comply with the BEA pay-as-you-go provisions;
3. Congress has to use reconciliation to develop pay-as-you-go offsets
to pay for a previously enacted mandatory spending increase or
revenue reduction that will increase the deficit in the budget year
(fiscal 1996 in this case); or
4. The president's budget includes a special direct spending message
in accordance with the new executive order dealing with entitlements (see chapter 2) and the budget resolution must be used as a
vehicle for congressional action on it.

If any of these four situations occur, many of the problems that have
plagued Congress's deliberations on the budget resolution over the
past decade will exist again, and the likelihood of the resolution being
adopted by the April 15 deadline will be greatly decreased.

CONGRESSIONAL BUDGET RESOLUTION

The congressional budget resolution is Congress's budget. It sets the
total level of budget authority, outlays, and revenues (and, therefore,
the deficit or surplus) and determines priorities by dividing these
totals among the budget functions. The major purpose of the budget
resolution is to provide a fiscal blueprint for all congressional committees; once it is adopted it will be used through the year to determine whether spending and revenues comply with the limits set.
Legislation that would increase spending above the maximums or
decrease revenues below the minimums established in the budget
resolution is subject to a number of restrictions.

Under the general procedures established by BEA, the budget resolution is expected to be more of a nonevent than anything else. In
general, it is expected to simply ratify the levels that were determined
when BEA was adopted. Indeed, this was one of BEA's major attrac-
tions to many in Congress and the Bush Administration—nothing
further would have to be done on the deficit as long as the discretionary spending caps and mandatory spending and revenue baselines
were maintained. Under this situation, it was assumed that the budget
resolution would be passed quickly and easily.

The pay-as-you-go rules are the big exception. Although BEA does
not specifically require it, the assumption is that any plan to increase

mandatory spending or reduce revenues will be worked out in the budget resolution. Presumably, the proposals would be included in the views and estimates (see chapter 3) received from the various committees and it would be the budget committees that would have to figure out how to satisfy the pay-as-you-go provisions. The budget committees would then draft the budget resolution assuming both the proposed spending increases and/or revenues reductions and the proposed offsets. The offsets would then not just be assumed to occur but would be ordered through reconciliation instructions.

One of the ways to avoid having to determine early in the year how legislation will be offset and, therefore, using reconciliation to accomplish it is the use of "reserve funds" in a budget resolution. To use a reserve fund, the budget resolution includes language that allows the budget committee to change a committee's spending allocation when it passes deficit-neutral legislation on specified subjects later in the year. Without this device, the legislation reported by a committee would almost certainly cause its allocation to be exceeded and so would subject it to a point of order.

There are three keys to reserve funds. First, so far they have applied only to the Senate. Second, reserve funds do not allow a proposal to increase the deficit; the increases in spending or reductions in revenues must still be completely offset so as not to trigger other Budget Enforcement Act prohibitions.

Third, reserve funds can only be used for the specific purposes stated in the budget resolution. For example, the fiscal 1994 congressional budget resolution (see appendix A) had seven different reserve funds for various subjects including improving the health and nutrition of children, preserving and rebuilding the United States Maritime Industry, and "reforming the financing of federal elections."

As the past few years have amply demonstrated, any budget resolution that assumes mandatory spending cuts and revenue increases will be difficult for Congress to pass. This will be especially true if the president has not included such changes in his budget, because that will mean that Congress will have to take all the political heat for these votes. Because Congress tends to prefer to work jointly with the White House in such situations, congressional leaders generally try either to work out the details in advance with the president (possibly before the budget is sent to Capitol Hill) or to set up some type of negotiation rather than taking these steps on their own.

The congressional budget resolution is expected to be adopted by April 15 each year. According to section 301(a) of the Congressional Budget Act, the budget resolution must specify:

1. The appropriate level of budget authority and outlays for the total budget;
2. The recommended level of revenues;
3. The surplus or deficit;
4. The level of budget authority and outlays for each budget function; and
5. The appropriate level of the public debt.[1]

Under GRH, the budget resolution only provided these levels for one year along with "planning levels" for the next two fiscal years. BEA changed this so that the budget resolution must show binding levels for the budget year and the "out years," that is, the following five years.

Congress has little discretion when it comes to most of the levels in the budget resolution. Because the amount that can be spent on appropriations (through the discretionary spending caps) is set by BEA, the only real discretion is in the amount that can be devoted to each of the functions.[2] While BEA provides an overall total, it does not allocate it in any way. In a nonevent year, therefore, this is the task likely to create the largest controversy, especially the split between National Defense and all other functions.

The congressional budget resolution is drafted by the budget committees after they review a number of sources of information, in particular the president's budget proposal. The budget committees also consider the views and estimates (see chapter 3), testimony from their own hearings, public support for or against presidential initiatives, and the wishes of their own members.[3]

The budget committees are required to consult with the other committees in compiling their versions of the congressional budget resolution. Many of the decisions are also based on information received informally from colleagues on other committees about their wants, needs, and intentions on budget-related matters. For example, the chairmen and ranking minority members of the budget committees and committee staff members discuss likely spending actions with their counterparts. These discussions are necessary because the budget committees cannot simply propose a budget as the president did: they must report a plan that will eventually be adopted by a majority of the House and Senate.[4]

To facilitate this acceptance and to avoid the appearance that the budget committees are usurping the substantive jurisdiction of the other committees, **the congressional budget resolution makes decisions only on the aggregate and functional totals: it makes no line-**

by-line or program decisions. The budget committees may make certain assumptions about a particular program as the budget resolution is being drafted, but those assumptions are in no way binding on the authorization, appropriations, and revenue committees.

This will not appear to be the case for anyone watching the budget committees debate and draft ("markup") the congressional budget resolution. Amendments will be offered, and individual programs and even parts of programs will be discussed. All these amendments and discussions, however, are based only on an expectation that the relevant committee ultimately will do what the budget committee is assuming. But, even if an amendment is offered and accepted on the assumption that the funds will go to or be cut from a certain program, only the appropriate aggregate and functional totals of the budget resolution will actually be affected. This is true even if the budget committee specifies its assumptions during the markup of the budget resolution, includes them in the report accompanying the resolution, discusses them during the debate on the floor of the House or Senate, and mentions them in the budget resolution conference report. The authorization, appropriation, and tax-writing committees are free to follow the assumptions if they wish or to ignore them entirely, as long as they stay within the overall totals allocated to them.

In the past, the House and Senate Budget Committees have often approached the job of marking up the budget resolution very differently. In the House, the chairman of the committee frequently has compiled a "chairman's mark," a document that usually contains recommendations for the budget as a whole and for each function.[5] A typical functional recommendation might show the amount recommended in the president's budget, the baseline, the issues on which the chair disagreed with the president, and the net total for the function after all the budget implications of the chair's recommendations had been added together. This total then becomes the starting point for the debate during the committee's markup, and members can offer amendments to it if they disagree with the chair.

The markup procedure in the House Budget Committee changed somewhat after GRH was enacted. The most important change was that amendments to the chairman's mark had to keep the deficit at or below the maximum deficit amount for the year. In budget terms, they had to be "deficit neutral."

The process in the Senate Budget Committee generally has been less detailed than the one used by the House Budget Committee, with the markup materials changing from year to year depending on the presentation the committee believed most suitable for the situation.

The procedures for debating a budget resolution once it has been reported to the full House and Senate for consideration are very specific. In the House, debate can begin no earlier than five days after the budget resolution has been reported, not including Saturdays, Sundays, and legal holidays.[6] No more than 10 hours of general debate on the resolution are allowed initially, after which amendments may be considered under the "five-minute" rule (each member is entitled to speak for only five minutes). A proposed amendment must be "mathematically consistent;" that is, all aggregate and functional totals it seeks to modify must be specified and added to or subtracted from properly.[7]

In the past, the House Budget Committee has often proposed ad hoc rules to expedite the floor debate. The most stringent of these rules placed limits on the amendments that could be offered by requiring them first to be approved by the House Rules Committee. Amendments have also been limited by a rule that prohibited amending a function that had already been amended during the debate unless the new amendment was "broader" in some way.[8] If the budget committee does propose such rules changes, the budget resolution must be referred to the rules committee before it goes to the House floor. The rules committee then reviews those proposed rules and, within five days (not counting days that the House is not in session), must report the budget resolution to the House floor with its recommendation as to whether they should be adopted.

The Senate has no specific layover period between presentation and consideration of the budget committee's report on the congressional budget resolution. A maximum of 50 hours of debate is allowed, with debate on any one amendment limited to two hours. Debate on an amendment to an amendment is limited to one hour. Mathematical consistency is again required.

The conference report on a congressional budget resolution can be debated by the Senate only after a three-day layover, and debate is limited to 10 hours. The House has a three-day layover, and debate is limited to five hours. The layover rules are often waived in both houses, however.

In addition to the compromise budget resolution language, the conferees from the House and Senate must also file an accompanying report known as the "joint statement of managers." Along with explaining the compromise between the House and Senate versions of the budget resolution, for the House the report must divide the total new budget authority, outlays, and entitlement authority among all House committees with jurisdiction over part of the budget.[9] For the

Senate, the report must divide the total new budget authority, outlays, and Social Security outlays among all Senate committees with jurisdiction over part of the budget. These allocations, known as the "section 602(a) allocations," are named for the part of the Congressional Budget Act that requires them to be made. BEA requires that the allocations cover all fiscal years through 1998 rather than just the budget year.

The committees that receive these allocations must further divide them according to section 602(b) of the Congressional Budget Act. The House and Senate Appropriations Committees must allocate the amount provided to them among their subcommittees. All other Senate committees *may* subdivide the amounts allocated to them either among their subcommittees or among the programs over which they have jurisdiction. Each committee is then required to report these suballocations back to its respective house "promptly."

In accordance with the Violent Crime Control and Law Enforcement Act of 1994 (P.L. 103-322), the appropriations committees' 602(b) allocations will also allocate spending to their subcommittees for programs covered by the Violent Crime Reduction Trust Fund (see chapter 2).

Under GRH, a committee could not bring a spending bill to the floor for consideration until it had reported its suballocations to its respective house. This meant that the committee had to wait for the budget resolution to be passed before the debate on appropriations could begin. In years when Congress had trouble passing a budget resolution by the April 15 deadline, this delayed the appropriations process and made it difficult for the bills to be enacted by the start of the fiscal year. A continuing resolution was then needed.

To deal with this problem, BEA changed the procedure. Under the new rules, if a budget resolution has not been adopted by April 15, the allocations to all committees are made based on the amounts included in the president's budget for total discretionary spending.[10]

Congress uses the suballocations to determine how close to the congressional budget resolution and BEA limits the different spending and revenue bills are when they are debated during the year. As explained in chapter 5, BEA put in place a number of procedural hurdles to the consideration of budget bills that exceed these suballocations.

Because the budget resolution is a concurrent resolution, it is effective as soon as the conference report is passed by both houses. It does not have to be signed by the president and, therefore, is not subject to a veto.

RECONCILIATION

Reconciliation is the process that is supposed to enable Congress to enforce the priorities and totals of a budget resolution. It can best be understood by reviewing two of the difficulties Congress faced before the 1974 legislation was passed.

First, Congress found itself unable to establish a fiscal policy. Second, even if a fiscal policy could have been set, Congress had no way of forcing its committees to comply with it. The fiscal policy problem was dealt with by requiring a budget resolution to be passed. Without an enforcement procedure, however, a budget resolution would have been meaningless because congressional committees would have been able to ignore it.

Reconciliation was designed to make sure this did not happen. Language in the budget resolution directs one or more committees to report new legislation that reduces spending or increases revenues as needed.[11] If the committees refuse or are unable to comply, the budget committees can be given authority to make the changes for them.

In the early years of the budget process, reconciliation was hardly discussed, let alone attempted. The primary reason was that the budget committees generally were unwilling to risk the future of the process by antagonizing the other committees, which were highly suspicious of intrusions into their legislative jurisdictions. The concern was that an early defeat of an attempted reconciliation might have had the same effect as not including these procedures in the Congressional Budget Act at all—committees would feel free to ignore a budget resolution.

As the deficit became an increasingly important issue in the early 1980s, however, reconciliation became not only worth the risk but the standard way of doing business.

In fact, GRH codified the practice of using reconciliation each year. Whereas Congress previously had the option of including reconciliation instructions in a budget resolution, GRH made such instructions mandatory. Every budget resolution had "to the extent necessary to effectuate the provisions and requirements of such resolution" to specify the amounts by which new budget authority, budget authority provided in previous years, new entitlement authority, and revenues had to be changed. It directed the committees in both houses to recommend changes in laws within their jurisdiction to accomplish these required changes.

The key was the phrase "to the extent necessary." If no changes were assumed in a budget resolution, reconciliation was not needed. The fiscal 1995 budget resolution, for example, did not assume any such changes; as a result there were no reconciliation directives and no reconciliation process.

This continues to be the essence of reconciliation under BEA. It is required, but only if Congress wants to make changes in mandatory spending programs and revenues. But because such changes are not required each year, it is up to Congress to decide whether it wants to cut the deficit further by reducing entitlements or increasing revenues. In effect, therefore, reconciliation is mandatory only in the sense that it is the procedure that must be used to implement a discretionary decision.

Reconciliation is also the process that Congress will probably use to implement the pay-as-you-go system. If a budget resolution assumes an increase in mandatory spending or a decrease in revenues, it most likely will also include reconciliation instructions to one or more committees to make offsetting spending cuts or tax increases.

Although reconciliation instructions are provided to specific committees and usually are based on assumptions about how the changes should be accomplished, the assumptions are not binding. The committees named in the reconciliation instructions may achieve the specified spending or revenue changes any way they wish.

In fact, some committees were given even more discretion by GRH as to how to comply with the reconciliation directives than they had before. Any committee that receives reconciliation instructions involving both revenue increases and spending reductions can now substitute up to 20 percent of its spending reductions for revenue increases and vice versa.[12]

The reconciliation procedures themselves are relatively simple. The budget resolution contains language that directs one or more committees to change existing law to comply with the resolution's spending ceilings and revenue floor or to offset a proposed mandatory spending increase or revenue reduction. In contrast to the budget resolution, which is organized by budget function, reconciliation instructions are organized by committee.[13] If only one committee is specified, it must report a reconciliation bill to its respective house with specific legislative language as to how the required spending cuts or tax increases are to be achieved. If more than one committee is involved, each must submit its recommendations to its respective budget committee, which assembles them into a single piece of legislation without making any substantive changes and then reports it to the floor for debate. Although the budget committee chairperson technically is manager of the debate, each section of the bill is usually managed by the chair of the committee that reported it.

Debate on a reconciliation bill in the Senate is limited to 20 hours and is governed by the same rules that apply to debate on a budget resolution (see above). The rules for House consideration are determined each year by the rules committee.

Most reconciliation efforts deal only with the authorization and tax-writing committees, which are instructed to make changes in permanent law—direct spending and revenues—to reconcile it with the budget resolution assumptions. Hence the name "reconciliation." These two types of committees should become even more prevalent players in reconciliation in the future because they are the ones that are covered by the pay-as-you-go rules.

In the past the emphasis on authorizations sometimes led to the inclusion of nonbudget items in reconciliation bills. For example, in 1989 the House Energy and Commerce Committee included in its reconciliation recommendations a restriction on consumers' access to so-called "dial-a-porn" services and a reinstatement of the broadcast fairness doctrine. These provisions might not have been considered had they been reviewed on their own in separate legislation. But because the budget process did not prevent these additions to a reconciliation bill, and because the budget committees are specifically prohibited from making any substantive changes in the recommendations from each committee, there have been few ways to stop this from occurring.

This has generally been more of a problem in the Senate than in the House, and so two specific rules that apply only in the Senate— the "Byrd rule" and the requirement that provisions in reconciliation bills be "germane"—were adopted.

Byrd Rule. The Byrd rule, which is named for its author, Senator Robert Byrd (D-WV), attempts to exclude extraneous provisions from a reconciliation bill by defining extraneous and establishing a procedure to remove such provisions once they have been so designated.

According to this rule, a provision is considered extraneous if it meets any one of five criteria:

1. It does not produce a change in outlays or revenues;
2. The net effect of the provisions reported by the committee is that the committee fails to reduce the deficit by the amount specified in its reconciliation instructions;

3. It is not within the jurisdiction of the committee that reported it;
4. It produces changes in outlays or revenues which are merely incidental to the nonbudgetary components of the provision; or
5. It increases outlays or decreases revenues in future years and the increases or decreases are greater than outlay reductions or revenue increases resulting from other provisions proposed by the committee.

The Byrd rule also specifies that a provision is not considered to be extraneous if:

1. It mitigates direct effects clearly attributable to provisions changing outlays or revenues, and both provisions together produce a net reduction in the deficit;
2. The provision results in a substantial reduction in outlays or an increase in revenues in future fiscal years;
3. A reduction in outlays or increase in revenues is likely to occur as a result of the provision in the event of new regulations authorized by the provision or likely to be proposed; court rulings or pending litigation; or relationships between economic indicators and statutory triggers pertaining to the provision other than the regulations, court rulings, or relationships currently projected by CBO;
4. It will probably produce a significant reduction in outlays or an increase in revenues, but due to insufficient data it cannot be estimated;
5. It is an integral part of another provision which, if introduced separately as a bill or resolution, would be referred to the same committee that included the original provision, and the original provision establishes the procedure to carry out or implement the substantive provisions that were reported; or
6. It states an exception to or a special application of the general provision of which it is a part and the general provision, if introduced as a separate bill or resolution, would be referred to the committee proposing the original reconciliation recommendation.

The Byrd rule has become an important deterrent to attempts to add nonbudget legislation to a reconciliation bill. It can only be waived by a three-fifths "super majority" vote. The super majority is also needed to appeal a ruling by the presiding officer that a particular reconciliation provision is extraneous.

Technically, the Byrd rule only applies to the Senate. However, because it also applies to reconciliation conference reports, it in effect applies to the House as well.

Germaneness. Senate rules require that any amendment to a reconciliation bill must be "germane" to the bill. An amendment is germane only if it:

1. proposes to strike an existing provision in the bill;
2. changes a number or date in the bill;
3. restricts the authority or scope of the bill without adding any new subject matters; or
4. states a sense of the Senate or a sense of Congress.

An amendment that is ruled by the chair to be not germane can only be debated if a super majority of 60 senators votes to allow it.

Under the BEA timetable, Congress is supposed to complete reconciliation by June 15, and the House is prohibited from adjourning for more than three consecutive days in July (and so cannot leave Washington for its July 4 recess unless it is an extremely short recess) until it has completed work on the reconciliation bill. This rule has never been enforced, however.

Notes

1. The budget resolution passed by the Senate must also include an estimate of the baseline outlays and revenues of the Old-age, Survivors, and Disability Insurance Program established under title II of the Social Security Act for the budget year and the succeeding four fiscal years.

2. For fiscal 1991–1995 BEA also set maximum deficit amounts, and the budget resolution could not propose a deficit that was higher than the limit.

3. In the past, the committees would also consult extensively with CBO to get alternative cost estimates and economic forecasts. Under BEA, however, the economic and technical assumptions in the president's budget are the ones that must be used by Congress because they are now locked in for the year once the president submits the budget.

4. The informal contacts are, of course, continual. The staffs of the budget committees and other committees regularly talk on an informal basis to compare spending estimates and to discuss and negotiate potential violations of budget process rules.

5. This was especially true when the White House and Congress were controlled by different political parties and the chairman's mark was used to distinguish one party's proposal from the other.

6. This requirement has often been waived in the past so that the budget resolution has sometimes been debated within hours of it being reported.

7. For example, an amendment that seeks to increase the budget authority and outlays for one function also must specify the additions to the aggregate totals of budget authority and outlays and must adjust the surplus or deficit accordingly. Similarly, an amendment to lower the deficit would have to specify the functional decreases that would constitute the change.

8. For example, if function 800, General Government, had been previously changed by an amendment that dealt only with it, a second amendment to increase or decrease the function would not be in order unless it included changes in at least one other function.

9. For example, if the conference report provides $10 billion in budget authority and outlays for a particular function, the joint statement of managers divides that amount among the committees with jurisdiction over the programs that make up that function. Each committee's total allocation equals the amount it receives from all functions in which one or more of its programs is located.

10. The reason that this procedure works is that the cap in the president's budget is the most that can be spent. There is, therefore, no reason to wait for the budget resolution.

11. The Congressional Budget Act actually does not specify "increases" or "decreases" but rather "changes." Therefore, reconciliation could be used to require a spending increase or revenue decrease.

12. In practice, this provision has only applied to the House Ways and Means Committee and Senate Finance Committee because they were the only ones with jurisdiction over both taxes and spending.

13. Appendix A is the fiscal 1994 budget resolution, including the reconciliation instructions.

Chapter Five

STAGE THREE: AUTHORIZATIONS AND APPROPRIATIONS

Deadline	Action
By April 15, 1995	Congress is supposed to complete action on the fiscal 1996 congressional budget resolution.
April 15	The House Appropriations Committee receives its 602(a) allocation based on the president's budget if the fiscal 1996 budget resolution has not been adopted.
May 15	The House may start to debate and pass fiscal 1996 appropriations even if the fiscal 1996 budget resolution has not been adopted.
By June 10	The House Appropriations Committee is supposed to report its version of all fiscal 1996 appropriations bills.
By June 30	The House is supposed to pass its version of all fiscal 1996 appropriations.
By October 1	All fiscal 1996 appropriations are supposed to be enacted.

Passage of the different authorization and appropriations bills is the first part of the congressional budget process that commits the federal government to conducting certain activities and spending money. Until this stage no funds actually are made available: the president's budget is only a proposal; the views and estimates do not bind the committees that submit them; the congressional budget resolution simply establishes aggregate and functional totals rather than requiring that funds be spent; and, if it has been used, reconciliation usually *reduces* program levels. The authorization and appropriation stage is different: the decisions commit the government to spend funds for specific purposes.

The Congressional Budget Act made few changes in the authorization and appropriation process. It merely imposed the budget process over it, and created a framework within which authorization and appropriation committees had to conduct their activities. Gramm–Rudman–Hollings then strengthened the framework by placing several additional and more stringent requirements on the committees, both to make it more likely that their legislation would be enacted by the start of the fiscal year and to make it more difficult for them to increase spending and reduce revenues more than the amounts assumed in the congressional budget resolution.

The Budget Enforcement Act provided even more stringent restrictions, principally through creation of the discretionary spending limits. This made it even harder for spending in excess of the approved amounts to be enacted.

Before 1974, the authorization and appropriations committees were given no guidelines as to when they had to act, and many conducted their activities with little or no regard for the start of the fiscal year, the need to pass authorizations before appropriations, or the work of the other committees. The Congressional Budget Act tried to impose some discipline by establishing a series of what were considered at the time to be stringent deadlines. However, while that budget act was in effect, these deadlines were routinely ignored or modified to suit political needs.

Under GRH, the authorization and appropriations committees were given far less discretion and were supposedly forced to act earlier in the year. In addition, two new deadlines were created specifically for appropriations bills. First, the House Appropriations Committee was supposed to "report"—complete its deliberations, vote on, and make a formal recommendation to the full House—all appropriations bills for the budget year by June 10. Second, the full House was supposed to pass its version of the 13 annual appropriations by June 30. To enforce this deadline, the House was not supposed to be able to adjourn for more than three consecutive days in July (and so could not leave Washington for the Independence Day recess) if it had not completed action on regular appropriations.

The reasons for these new deadlines were Congress's increasing inability to enact appropriations bills before the fiscal year began and its growing reliance on "continuing resolutions"—legislation that allows a federal department or agency to continue operations when its regular appropriation is not passed on time. Delayed appropriations were one of the principal problems the Congressional Budget Act had been created to solve. But during the time it was in effect all 13 annual appropriations were enacted by the start of the fiscal year only once—for fiscal 1976, the first year the new budget process was implemented. The continuing delay in the enactment of appropriations from 1976 to 1985 was a major reason why many people think the Congressional Budget Act was a failure.

The experience with the revised GRH timetable demonstrated that its tighter statutory deadlines did not necessarily compel Congress to act either. Not one of the fiscal 1987 or 1988 appropriations was enacted on time.

The 1989 appropriations process moved along rather steadily, however, with all of the 13 spending bills approved by the start of the fiscal year. One of the prime reasons for this relatively fast action was President Ronald Reagan's pledge in his January 1988 State of the Union address to veto a continuing resolution if Congress passed one. Congressional leaders were embarrassed by the president's theatrics on national television when he held up a photocopied version of the previous year's continuing resolution (copied only on one side of the page so that the bill appeared as large as possible) and then dropped it on the podium with an audible thud.

But a second, more hidden, and more important reason for the expedited action was that, because of the November 1987 budget summit agreement between Congress and the White House, there was little chance that sequestration would occur for fiscal 1989. This meant that appropriators could be certain that, if their bills were enacted by the start of the fiscal year, there would be no chance that additional reductions would occur later because of GRH.

This is not generally well understood. The threat of a GRH sequester was one of the main reasons that Congress adopted appropriations late. In retrospect, however, this is understandable. For example, suppose that a particular appropriation with a 10 percent overall cut was signed into law before the sequestration deadline, which at that time was October 15. If a 10 percent sequestration subsequently occurred because the other committees did not do what they were supposed to do to reduce the deficit, the effect would be a 19 percent overall cut in all of the programs in the one bill that had been enacted. If, however, the appropriators waited until the sequestration deadline passed, they could also wait to see if sequestration occurred before they made any final decisions on the programs within their jurisdiction. This prevented what in appropriations parlance is known as a "double hit."

BEA formalized this process in two ways and, therefore, made it somewhat more likely that appropriations will be enacted by the start of the fiscal year.[1] First, because of the creation of the cap for discretionary spending (see chapters 2 and 6), and the fact that a sequester can only occur *within* a category except in very limited circumstances, there is far less likelihood that a double hit can happen.

Second, and more importantly, the sequester deadline was changed from October 15 to 15 days after Congress adjourns. There is no way, therefore, to delay appropriations until after the deadline passes.

Less evident but more important than the timetable changes are the other limitations placed on the appropriations committees by the budget process. Before the Congressional Budget Act was passed, there was no way to determine whether estimated spending in proposed legislation was too high. That act made such comparison possible, and the appropriations committees often had to explain and justify any changes they were proposing from the congressional budget resolution. Now, however, increases above what is in the budget resolution (which is based on the BEA restrictions) are prohibited.

This strict comparison of spending bills with the congressional budget resolution is accomplished through use of the section 602(a) and section 602(b) allocations discussed briefly in chapter 3.

The House and Senate determine the allocations differently. For all committees except appropriations, the House determines the 602(a) allocations by dividing total new budget authority, total entitlement authority, and total outlays into two categories: the amount that will result from laws enacted in prior years and the amount to be provided in new legislation this year. For appropriations, total new budget authority, total entitlement authority, and total outlays are divided between mandatory and discretionary spending (see chapter 1). The appropriations committee then subdivides the 602(a) allocations by subcommittee to get its 602(b) allocations.

The Senate determines its 602(a) allocations by dividing total new budget authority, total outlays, and Social Security outlays among each committee that has any spending jurisdiction. The appropriations committee then divides these amounts among its subcommittees. All other Senate committees can decide whether to divide their allocations by subcommittee or by program.

In the House, legislation that violates a 602(b) allocation of budget authority is subject to a point of order. In the Senate, legislation that violates either the budget authority or outlay 602(b) allocation is subject to a point of order.

BEA also created a point of order in the Senate against any appropriation bill that would cause a discretionary spending cap to be breached. There is no similar point of order in the House.

It is important to keep in mind that the legislative process requires that the House and Senate pass exactly the same spending bills before they can be sent to the president for signature. In essence, therefore, the more rigorous Senate restrictions eventually will also apply to the House. In general, the House applies its more lenient enforcement procedures to spending bills when they are first considered and passed. However, any conference agreement between the two houses must be judged by the tougher Senate standards because the Senate is not supposed to consider any spending legislation that would cause its 602(b) allocations to be violated. This prohibition can only be waived by a three-fifths vote.[2]

The authorization and appropriations committees must include specific budget information in the reports accompanying their bills. The report accompanying any proposed bill in either the House or Senate providing new budget authority or outlays or any legislation providing new or increased tax expenditures must contain (1) an estimate of how the bill compares with the section 602(b) allocation; (2) a CBO projection of how the bill will affect the levels of budget authority, outlays, spending authority, and revenues for the next five years; and (3) a CBO estimate of the new budget authority provided as aid to state and local governments.

It is the budget committees' responsibility to let their respective houses know how close each spending bill is to the 602(b) allocations. The budget committees generally enforce these allocations through behind-the-scenes activities, with negotiations often conducted long before a bill reaches the floor for debate. When these discussions are not successful, the budget committees sometimes try more formally during floor debate to explain the budget implications of the bills being considered. The budget committees have always been severely hampered in this role because all they can do is advise their respective houses about excessive spending. The threat of a point of order being raised, however, does give the budget committees some additional leverage to influence the spending levels in any bill.

The budget committees and Congress in general must use the spending estimates provided by CBO during the legislative process. However, BEA requires that OMB provide its own cost estimate within five days of the enactment of any appropriation bill and that this estimate be used to determine whether a bill has caused the discretionary cap to be breached.[3]

This gives OMB and the White House tremendous additional influence in the appropriations process that they did not have before BEA was enacted. OMB does not, for example, have to wait for the bill to be enacted before providing its cost estimate. Announcing the estimate early could have a substantial impact on what is appropriated. Even if CBO says that an appropriation will not cause the discretionary spending cap to be breached, a preliminary determination by OMB that it will be breached could force Congress to revise the bill in some way so that it is more to the administration's liking. This could, therefore, allow an active administration to influence the appropriations process in ways other than simply threatening a presidential veto.

A threatened sequester could actually be a much more effective tool for the president than a threatened veto for several reasons.

First, the White House will be able to get involved much earlier in the legislative process. This will give it access to legislative markup sessions and other congressional events in which it previously might not have been a key player. What committee, for example, would not want to know OMB's cost estimate as early as possible?

Second, the president will not have to veto a bill and so will not have to antagonize any particular group that would benefit by the bill's passage. He or she could simply sign the bill and then impose a sequester later in the year if Congress does not fix the BEA problem. This means that it will be Congress that will risk antagonizing the constituency.

Third, the cost estimating process can be classified by the White House as technical rather than political. This will strengthen the president's hand because he can say that he is only applying the best methodology rather than playing politics.

The overall impact of the Congressional Budget Act, GRH, and BEA on this stage of the budget process has been to make it much more visible. The authorization and appropriations committees are supposed to do their work within a specified period and in such a way that Congress and the White House can judge how well that work carries out the fiscal policy and spending priorities of BEA and the most recent congressional budget resolution.

This stage must be considered crucial to the overall outcome of the budget process because actual spending decisions are made during it. It is also important because it again allows the president to influence directly the spending decisions made by Congress. The congressional budget resolution does not require the president's signature, and the views and estimates are internal congressional documents. In contrast, authorization and appropriations bills will be officially estimated by OMB and subject to a veto.

The president is required to prepare a budget report during this period. The mid-session review—which is required to be submitted by July 15 but has often been late[4]—is generally an updated version of the president's budget submission which incorporates the most up-to-date estimates available as well as the final spending and revenue totals for the previous year.

BEA has made the mid-session review far less important than it was under GRH, however. The reason is that the economic forecast included in the mid-session review previously was the one used to determine whether sequestration was needed. Under BEA, however, the forecast in the president's budget is locked in for the rest of the year. Therefore, the only things of interest in the mid-session review are likely to be updated deficit forecasts, an interim sequestration status report, and any revisions in the discretionary caps that have occurred since the sequester preview report was issued.[5]

The next formal status report will be issued in August, as is described in the next chapter.

Notes

1. All 13 of the fiscal 1995 appropriations were passed by Congress before the start of the fiscal year.

2. This point of order is not, however, automatic. If a senator does not raise the point of order when the conference report is debated, the prohibition is not enforced and a waiver is not needed.

3. House Democrats adopted a House rule in early December 1990 that tried to change this situation. The rule required that OMB use CBO spending estimates for all direct-spending legislation. The rule was never adopted by the Senate, however, so it was never implemented.

4. The Clinton fiscal 1995 mid-session review was sent to Congress on July 14, 1994, one day early. The Clinton 1994 mid-session budget review was not sent to Capitol Hill until September 1, 1993. The White House decided to wait until Congress adopted the fiscal 1994 reconciliation bill, which included the Clinton deficit reduction plan, so that the updated numbers could be displayed. OMB Director Panetta sent Congress a letter with preliminary updated estimates on July 15, 1993, in response to congressional criticism that the mid-session review would be too late to have any impact.

5. The 1993 mid-session report was controversial for another reason—OMB Director Richard Darman transformed it into an almost purely political document by restating the president's budget plans in blatantly partisan terms that openly criticized Congress. As a result, what in prior years was a 50-page document turned into a 421-page document. See Office of Management and Budget, *Mid-Session Review: The President's Budget and Economic Growth Agenda*, July 24, 1992.

Chapter Six

STAGE FOUR: SEQUESTRATION

Deadline	Action
Five days before the president submits the fiscal 1996 budget to Congress	The Congressional Budget Office (CBO) issues its fiscal 1996 sequestration preview report.
The same day the president submits the fiscal 1996 budget to Congress	The Office of Management and Budget (OMB) issues its fiscal 1996 sequestration preview report.
By August 10	The president must notify Congress if and how he plans to exempt military uniformed personnel from sequestration.
August 15	CBO issues its sequestration update report.
August 20	OMB issues its sequestration update report.
Ten days after Congress adjourns	CBO issues its final sequestration report.
Fifteen days after Congress adjourns	OMB issues its final sequestration report and the president issues a sequestration order to all federal departments and agencies, which is effective immediately.

The most innovative, far-reaching, and controversial change in the congressional budget process that was created by Gramm–Rudman–Hollings was sequestration. The Budget Enforcement Act not only retained sequestration, it greatly expanded its application. The sequestration process was so enhanced that the BEA system bears only a limited resemblance to the one put in place by GRH.

The original idea behind sequestration was straightforward. If the president and Congress did not reduce the deficit to the maximum amount allowed in the budget year, spending would be cut automatically according to a preset formula by whatever amount was needed to reach the target. This was supposed to do two things: (1) provide additional pressure on all participants in the budget debate to compromise their differences over how the deficit should be reduced, and (2) guarantee that the deficit would be reduced even if there was no compromise.

BEA changed sequestration in the following ways.

1. Under GRH, the deficit was the sole target. Under BEA, the deficit is no longer the only concern and sequestration is no longer aimed at keeping the deficit down. Maintaining mandatory spending at its baseline levels, discretionary spending at or below the cap, and revenues at or above the baseline are now the main reasons that sequestration occurs.
2. Under GRH there was only one type of sequester. BEA has created two additional types to go along with the previous one and has made the two new ones more important than the original.
3. Under GRH a sequester could only occur once a year, on October 15. Under BEA the basic sequester now occurs 15 days after Congress adjourns. More importantly, the sequestration process is now continuous; sequesters can occur throughout the year.

It is important to emphasize the first point. For fiscal 1991–1995, BEA was not as concerned with reducing the deficit as was GRH. This means that it is no longer enough for Congress and the president to meet a deficit maximum by raising revenues to pay for higher discretionary spending. Although this would have been allowed (and perhaps even encouraged) under GRH, a sequester will now be required under BEA because of the probable violations of the discretionary cap.

Therefore, BEA instead starts with the assumption that keeping discretionary spending at or below the established limits, keeping mandatory spending at or below the baseline, and maintaining revenues at or above the baseline are the most important priorities in federal budgeting.

THREE TYPES OF BUDGET ENFORCEMENT ACT SEQUESTERS

Type 1: Discretionary Spending

The key to understanding this sequester is the limit that BEA establishes for discretionary spending.[1]

For fiscal years 1991–1993, BEA divided all discretionary spending into three categories—defense, international, and domestic. As table 12 (table 9 repeated for convenience) shows, for fiscal 1994 through 1998, the three categories were combined into a single category that includes all discretionary programs. The only exceptions are the programs funded by the Violent Crime Reduction Trust Fund that was created by the Violent Crime Control and Law Enforcement Act of 1994 (see chapter 2).

A discretionary spending sequester will occur if either the budget authority or outlays cap is breached.[2] In fact, there can be two separate sequesters if both the budget authority and outlay levels are breached at the same time. The first would reduce budget authority by whatever amount is needed and outlays would be reduced appropriately. If outlays were still above the cap even after this sequester, a separate outlay sequester would be necessary.

Congress and the president can, of course, always enact legislation that revises the caps any time they see fit.[3] However, BEA already provides a number of ways for the caps to be revised without legislation. The possible revisions can be divided into three categories.

1. *Automatic.* The caps will be revised automatically each year when the president submits the budget to Congress to take into account changes in "concepts and definitions,"[4] and inflation.[5]
2. *As Used.* BEA allows the caps to be increased to the extent that Congress and the president enact additional funding for the Internal Revenue Service, additional funding for the International Monetary Fund, and emergencies.[6]
3. *Allowances.* This category is roughly equivalent to the margin for error that existed in GRH between the deficit maximums and the level that would trigger a sequester. The purpose of that margin

Table 12 BEA DISCRETIONARY SPENDING CAPS 1994–1998 (billions of dollars)

	1994	1995	1996	1997	1998
Total Discretionary					
Budget Authority	524.1	515.9	514.3	522.6	524.6
Outlays	547.2	544.8	547.1	544.1	542.3

Source: Office of Management and Budget, "OMB Sequestration Update Report to the President and Congress," August 19, 1994, p. 6, and Violent Crime Control and Law Enforcement Act of 1994 (P.L. 103-322).
NOTE: The numbers for fiscal 1996–1998 will be revised in the 1996 budget submitted by the president to Congress.

was to provide a cushion so that estimating differences would not automatically cause a sequester.

The basic purpose of the allowances is to provide a small cushion between CBO's cost estimates, which will be used by Congress during the legislative process, and OMB's, which will be used by the White House to determine whether a sequester is necessary. If, for example, Congress believes that spending is at or just below a cap but OMB believes that spending has exceeded the cap by a small amount, the allowance could prevent a sequester from occurring. This recognizes the fact that CBO and OMB sometimes differ on their estimates.

Table 13 shows the adjustments to the spending caps that were made by OMB when it issued the sequestration update report for fiscal 1995.

There are three discretionary spending sequesters.

End-of-Session. If necessary, the "end-of-session" sequester occurs 15 days after Congress adjourns, regardless of when that happens. The

Table 13 DISCRETIONARY SPENDING LIMITS
(In millions of dollars)

		1994	1995	1996	1997	1998
Total discretionary spending limits, February 7, 1994 Preview Report	BA	513,363	515,178	518,631	527,555	530,092
	OL	542,708	539,636	547,318	546,879	547,055
Adjustments:						
Emergency supplemental appropriations (P.L. 103–211)	BA	9,069	....	....	....	....
	OL	3,536	3,700	1,143	609	41
Contingent emergency appropriations released	BA	1,643	....	....	....	....
	OL	905	502	145	73	14
Subtotal, adjustments	BA	10,712	....	....	....	....
	OL	4,441	4,202	1,288	682	55
Update Report discretionary limits	BA	524,075	515,178	518,631	527,555	530,092
	OL	547,149	543,838	548,606	547,561	547,110
Anticipated further adjustments for the Final Sequestration Report:						
IRS funding	BA	....	188	....	....	....
	OL	....	184	....	....	....
Special allowances	BA	....	2,880	....	....	....
	OL	....	1,438	753	396	134
Estimated discretionary spending limits for the Final Sequestration Report	BA	524,075	518,246	518,631	527,555	530,092
	OL	547,149	545,460	549,359	547,957	547,244

Source: Office of Management and Budget, "OMB Sequestration Update OMB Report to the President and Congress," August 19, 1994, p. 6.

sequester is determined by OMB based on the appropriations that have been enacted during the just-completed session of Congress plus previously enacted advance appropriations[7] and outlays from prior-year budget authority (see chapter 1). Spending that causes the cap for either budget authority or outlays to be exceeded will cause all discretionary spending to be cut by whatever percentage will bring it back to the limit.

For example, on November 9, 1990, 15 days after the House and Senate adjourned at the end of the second session of the 101st Congress, OMB determined that budget authority for the international category breached the cap by $395 million. Because the total amount of new budget authority provided for the category was estimated to be $20,495 million, all programs had to be cut by 1.9 percent (395/20,495) to reduce budget authority to the cap.

Figure 2 is the final sequester order for fiscal 1991 that was issued by the president on November 9, 1990.

Within-Session. The second discretionary spending sequester occurs after Congress convenes following the previous end-of-session sequester (if any) but before July 1. If, during that period, legislation is enacted that breaches a cap *for the current fiscal year* (the fiscal year currently underway), then a sequester will occur 15 days after the president signs the bill. The sequester will be exactly the same as the end-of-session sequester; that is, current-year discretionary budget authority and outlays will be reduced by the percentage necessary to reduce spending to the cap.

Look-Back. The third discretionary spending sequester occurs if a spending bill *for the current fiscal year* is enacted after June 30 but before the end of the fiscal year on September 30 and it breaches a cap. In this case the current-year spending limit will be unaffected. However, the budget year cap, that is, the cap for the year that will start on October 1, will be lowered by the amount of the breach.

For example, suppose that Congress passes a fiscal 1995 supplemental appropriation in July 1995 that increases fiscal 1995 budget authority above the cap by $10 billion, fiscal 1995 outlays above the cap by $6 billion, and fiscal 1996 outlays by $4 billion. Because the appropriation was enacted after July 1, there would be no fiscal 1995 sequester. The fiscal 1996 cap, however, would be lowered by $10 billion in budget authority and $6 billion in outlays. The additional $4 billion in 1996 outlays provided by the 1995 supplemental would count against the new 1996 cap.

Figure 2 FINAL PRESIDENTIAL SEQUESTER ORDER FOR FISCAL 1991

THE WHITE HOUSE

Office of the Press Secretary

For Immediate Release   November 9, 1990

FINAL SEQUESTER ORDER

By the authority vested in me as President by the statutes of the United States of America, including section 254 of the Balanced Budget and Emergency Deficit Control Act of 1985 (Public Law 99-177), as amended by the Balanced Budget and Emergency Deficit Control Reaffirmation Act of 1987 (Public Law 100-119) and Title XIII of the Omnibus Reconciliation Act of 1990 (Public Law 101-508) (hereafter referred to as "the Act"), I hereby order that the following actions be taken immediately to implement the sequestrations and reductions determined by the Director of the Office of Management and Budget as set forth in his report dated November 9, 1990, under sections 251 and 254 of the Act:

(1) Budgetary resources for each non-exempt account within the international category of discretionary spending shall be reduced as specified by the Director of the Office of Management and Budget in his report of November 9, 1990.

(2) Pursuant to sections 250(c)(6) and 251, budgetary resources subject to sequestration shall be new budget authority; new loan guarantee commitments or limitations; new direct loan obligations, commitments, or limitations; and obligation limitations.

(3) For accounts making commitments for guaranteed loans as authorized by substantive law, the head of each Department or agency is directed to reduce the level of such commitments or obligations to the extent necessary to conform to the limitations established by the Act and specified by the Director of the Office of Management and Budget in his report of November 9, 1990.

All sequestrations shall be made in strict accordance with the specifications of the November 9th report of the Director of the Office of Management and Budget and the requirements of sections 251 and 254.

GEORGE BUSH

THE WHITE HOUSE,
    November 9, 1990.

Type 2: Pay-As-You-Go

The pay-as-you-go or PAYGO sequester deals with mandatory spending and revenues. The key to understanding it is the baseline.

The baseline is the amount of spending that will occur and the amount of revenue that will be raised under existing law.[8] The pay-as-you-go rules require that the net effect of all mandatory spending and tax legislation not increase the deficit in any year. If it does, then a PAYGO sequester will occur that will cut eligible mandatory programs by whatever percentage is necessary to offset the increase. The pay-as-you-go rules do not, therefore, require that every bill dealing with mandatory spending or revenues be deficit-neutral, only that the sum of all such legislation enacted during that session of Congress be deficit-neutral.

This means that PAYGO is different from the discretionary spending rules in one very important sense. An increase in discretionary spending cannot be offset by an increase in revenues because the cap established by BEA would still be breached. However, an increase in mandatory spending can be offset with an increase in revenues because the two will be summed to determined whether a sequester is necessary.

If needed, the basic PAYGO sequester occurs 15 days after Congress adjourns, the same day that the end-of-session discretionary sequester occurs. In the same report that deals with discretionary spending, OMB will determine how much revenues and mandatory spending differ from the baseline and, therefore, whether a sequester is needed.

If a sequester is needed, only eligible mandatory programs will be cut by the across-the-board percentage; there is no automatic increase in revenues. This means that spending could potentially be cut to pay for a reduction in taxes.

However, there is only a limited amount of mandatory spending that is eligible to be cut if a PAYGO sequester occurs. The first cut will be achieved by cancelling the automatic spending increase slated for several small programs. This will create a small amount—$50 million to $100 million—in savings. If spending needs to be cut further, several other programs—Federal Family Education Loan Program (formerly Guaranteed Student Loans) and Foster Care and Adoption Assistance—will be cut according to special rules. This too will create relatively small savings—about $50 million.

If additional spending reductions are still required, then Medicare payments to providers will be cut by a maximum of 4 percent[9] and several other health programs by a maximum of 2 percent. In fiscal 1994 this would have produced about $4.0 billion.

Finally, if further spending reductions are still needed for a PAYGO sequester, all remaining eligible mandatory programs ($25 billion to $30 billion) will be cut by whatever across-the-board percentage is needed.

As with the discretionary spending caps, BEA allows several adjustments to be made to the baseline. First, any increase in deposit insurance[10] is not considered an increase in the baseline. Similarly, a decrease in deposit insurance is not considered as creating savings. Second, BEA allows the president to adjust the baseline for "emergency" mandatory spending or revenues.

Several examples are useful to demonstrate how PAYGO is supposed to work.

Suppose that legislation is enacted that will increase mandatory spending or reduce revenues by $1 billion in fiscal 1996 and by $500 million in fiscal 1997 compared to the baseline, and that these increases in the deficit are not offset. According to the PAYGO rules, a sequester would be needed 15 days after Congress adjourns that would cut mandatory spending by $1 billion. The next session of Congress would then begin with the White House and Congress knowing that they must find $500 million in offsets for the amount that has already been spent. Otherwise, they would face another sequester, this time for fiscal 1997, after the next session ends.

As a second example, suppose that, in addition to the legislation noted in example 1, a second bill is enacted that raises the fiscal 1997 deficit by an additional $100 million because of a mandatory spending increase or tax cut. In this case a $1 billion PAYGO sequester would be needed for fiscal 1996, and a $600 million PAYGO sequester would be needed for fiscal 1997. Example 2 is depicted in table 14.

As a third example, suppose that mandatory spending and revenue bills would increase the deficit by $990 million in fiscal 1996 and by $590 million in fiscal 1997. As a result, a fiscal 1996 PAYGO sequester occurs that offsets the 1996 increase completely and reduces the deficit by $50 billion in 1997. As table 15 shows, this would still leave $540 billion to be offset in 1997 and either Congress and the president

Table 14 PAYGO SEQUESTER—EXAMPLE 2 (millions of dollars)

	1996	1997
Bill #1	+ 1000	+ 500
Bill #2	0	+ 100

Table 15 PAYGO SEQUESTER—EXAMPLE 3 (millions of dollars)

	1996	1997
All Bills	+990	+590
FY96 Sequester	−990	−50
Net Impact	0	+540

would have to enact legislation that would do so or a PAYGO sequester would occur.

Although the basic PAYGO sequester takes place 15 days after Congress adjourns, there is also a look-back PAYGO sequester in the event that a mandatory spending increase or revenue decrease is enacted after the basic PAYGO sequester occurs but before the start of the next fiscal year and is effective immediately, that is, in the current budget year. For example, suppose that legislation is enacted in May 1995 that reduces revenues in fiscal 1995 (the current year) by $200 million and in fiscal 1996 (the budget year) by $300 million. As table 16 shows, in this case there would be no fiscal 1995 PAYGO sequester. There would, however, be a $500 million fiscal 1997 PAYGO sequester to offset both increases.[11]

Table 16 PAYGO SEQUESTER—EXAMPLE 4 (millions of dollars)

	1996	1997
Bill enacted May 1995	+200	+300
Potential FY95 Sequester	0	−500

Type 3: Excess-Deficit

In its purest form, the excess-deficit sequester was supposed to be the same type of sequester that occurred under GRH. Its purpose was to reduce the deficit to the BEA maximum if OMB projected that it would be exceeded. Unlike the GRH timetable, however, an excess-deficit sequester under BEA was to occur 15 days after Congress adjourns, the same date as the discretionary spending and PAYGO sequesters.

The BEA maximum deficit amounts for fiscal 1991–1995 are shown in table 17.

An excess-deficit sequester did not occur for fiscal 1991–1995 for two reasons:

1. BEA specifically cancelled the excess-deficit sequester for 1991.

Table 17 BEA DEFICIT MAXIMUMS (billions of dollars)

1991	1992	1993	1994	1995
327[a]	360[b]	428[b]	324[c]	243[d]

[a]Section 601(a)(1) of Public law 93-344 (as amended).
[b]Office of Management and Budget. "OMB Sequestration Update Report to the President and Congress," August 20, 1991, p. 11.
[c]Office of Management and Budget. "OMB Sequestration Update Report to the President and Congress," August 20, 1993, p. 13.
[d]Office of Management and Budget. "OMB Sequestration Update Report to the President and Congress," August 19, 1994, p. 15.

2. Even though they were scheduled to happen on the same day, BEA required that the discretionary spending and PAYGO sequesters occur before the excess-deficit sequester. Therefore, discretionary spending was already no higher than the caps and mandatory spending and revenues were already at the baseline. This meant that any increase in the deficit over the maximum must have been the result of a changed economic forecast. But BEA specifically required that the economic forecast not be revised until the president submitted the next budget to Congress the following year. Therefore, even though the actual deficit might have been projected to be over the maximum, the theoretical deficit created by the use of the president's economic assumptions would still be low.

The BEA deficit maximums were not extended past fiscal 1995 by the Omnibus Budget Reconciliation Act of 1993 (P.L. 103-66), which extended the caps on discretionary spending and pay-as-you-go rules. As a result, BEA no longer has deficit maximums and there is no chance of an excess-deficit sequester occurring.

GRH allowed for suspension of its major provisions in two circumstances, and these were not changed by BEA. The first is a formal declaration of war by Congress, when the provisions pertaining to sequestration are automatically suspended. The suspension continues until the first fiscal year that begins after the Senate ratifies the treaty formally ending the hostilities.

The second is a recession. BEA defines a recession as one of two things:

1. The Department of Commerce reports that, for this quarter of the current fiscal year and the one immediately preceding it, the rate of real economic growth is less than one percent.

2. OMB or CBO projects that there will be two consecutive quarters of negative economic growth, as measured by gross national product (GNP), "during the period consisting of the quarter in which such notification is given, the quarter preceding such notification, and the 4 quarters following such notification."

In either event, the CBO director must notify Congress and the majority leader in the Senate must introduce a joint resolution that suspends the sequestration provisions through the fiscal year that begins at least 12 months later, as long as the recession is projected to be over by that time. The majority leader in the House "may" introduce such a resolution if he or she chooses to do so.

The joint resolution is considered under expedited procedures in both houses. If it is enacted, the sequestration provisions are suspended.

During the debate on the fiscal 1992 budget, the Senate voted three times on a BEA suspension due to slow economic growth. The legislation was defeated in all three cases.

Notes

1. See chapter 1 and the glossary for an explanation of discretionary spending.

2. This is a fundamental change from GRH which, because it was only concerned with the deficit, addressed only outlays. This led many committees to propose legislation that would have only a limited outlay impact in the first year but, because of the budget authority that was provided, a large outlay impact in future years.

3. During consideration of the fiscal 1993 budget, the House and Senate tried to combine the separate caps for defense, international, and domestic discretionary spending into one cap that would have covered all discretionary spending. Essentially, this would have accelerated the combination of the categories that BEA required for fiscal 1994 and 1995. The House and Senate both failed to pass the legislation, however, so the separate caps remained in effect. Even if Congress had passed the change, President Bush most likely would have vetoed it.

As part of the fiscal 1995 congressional budget resolution, Congress voted to keep spending below the caps as a result of an amendment offered by Senators James Exon (D-NE) and Charles Grassley (R-IA) during the Senate Budget Committee's markup. Because this decision was in the budget resolution, and because the budget resolution is a "concurrent resolution" that does not change a statute, the caps were not reduced formally. Congress could still enforce the lower figures if it chooses, however.

4. There is no description in BEA of what constitutes a change in a concept or definition. The assumption is that it covers technical changes, such as the definition of budget authority, leases, or credit programs. OMB will make the final decision as to what fits in this category.

5. If inflation is higher or lower than anticipated the previous year, the cap will be adjusted accordingly.

6. Except for the costs for Operation Desert Shield/Storm, which were automatically classified as an emergency, BEA does not define "emergency." Any spending can qualify; the only thing that is required is for the president to sign legislation that states that the funds are needed for emergency purposes.

This means that both congressional and White House approval is needed. A presidential request for funds for a supposed emergency that is not approved by Congress in legislation would not qualify as an emergency. If the funds were approved without the emergency designation, they would have to fit within the relevant cap. Similarly, legislation passed by Congress designating funds for an emergency that is vetoed and then not overridden would also not qualify.

In 1991, OMB provided unofficial guidelines on what it would consider to be an emergency. It said that the appropriation would have to be:

- **a necessary expenditure**—an essential or vital expenditure, not one that is merely useful or beneficial;
- **sudden**—quickly coming into being, not building up over time;
- **urgent**—a pressing and compelling need requiring immediate action;
- **unforeseen**—not predictable or seen beforehand as a coming need (an emergency that is part of an aggregate level of anticipated emergencies, particularly when normally estimated in advance would not be "unforeseen"); and
- **not permanent**—the need is temporary in nature.

In addition, the classification of certain spending as an "emergency" depends on common sense judgement made on a case-by-case basis, about whether the totality of facts and circumstances indicate a true emergency, and about whether the needs can be absorbed within the existing level of resources available.

Source: Office of Management and Budget. "Selected Pending Proposals to Expand the Definition of Emergency and Escape BEA Provisions Discipline," July 16, 1991, p. 29.

7. See the glossary for a definition of advance appropriations.

8. The conference report on the Budget Enforcement Act of 1990, House Report 101-964, includes a complete list of all mandatory programs.

9. This was a change from GRH, which limited the cut to 2 percent.

10. BEA defines deposit insurance as the expenses of the Federal Deposit Insurance Corporation and the funds it incorporates, the Resolution Trust Corporation, the National Credit Union Administration and the funds it incorporates, the Office of Thrift Supervision, the Comptroller of the Currency Assessment Fund, and the Resolution Trust Corporation Office of Inspector General.

11. If a bill were enacted in May that decreased revenues or increased spending in the current year but increased revenues or reduced spending by the same amount in the budget year, there would not need to be a look-back PAYGO sequester in the second year because the bill would have no net impact on the deficit.

Chapter Seven

IMPOUNDMENTS

The president is expected to spend the appropriations that Congress passes in a timely manner and according to the priorities that Congress expresses. Theoretically, a president who disagrees with the level of spending or the priorities being proposed has only one option: to veto the bill in its entirety. No individual item within an appropriation can be vetoed,[1] and if two-thirds of each house, voting separately, vote to override a presidential veto, the money must be spent as originally intended.

Despite these provisions, Congress generally has assumed that the president does have some spending discretion, for any other interpretation would change the nature of the presidency from "Chief Executive to Chief Clerk."[2] Congress has permitted the president to refuse to spend funds for three reasons: to increase the government's efficiency; to comply with statutory language that allows such discretion; and to fulfill other constitutionally granted powers, particularly those that pertain to the president's role as commander in chief.[3] Decisions not to spend appropriated funds in these circumstances have been relatively noncontroversial and have been made by almost every president.

A fourth reason for presidential impoundments—disagreement with congressional budget policy and spending priorities—has, however, been extraordinarily controversial. Richard Nixon's unprecedented refusal to spend congressionally approved appropriations because he disagreed with the policies they embodied provided the initial impetus and continued momentum necessary for Congress to create not just impoundment control procedures but the entire congressional budget process enacted in 1974. Congress found itself without any procedure for dealing with Nixon's continued intransigence on impoundments. The only remedy available was to sue the appropriate cabinet official to force the appropriations to be spent, a tactic most representatives and senators found cumbersome, time-consuming, and unsatisfactory.

The impoundment control procedures Congress created not only provided a means to review presidential actions but required such a review. They probably are the most successful of all the provisions of the Congressional Budget Act—so much so in fact, that for the most part, impoundments have ceased to be a significant issue.

In 1986, however, several members of Congress and a number of cities successfully challenged the constitutionality of one of the two types of presidential impoundments established by the Congressional Budget and Impoundment Control Act. That suit, *City of New Haven v. United States*,[4] addressed "deferrals"—a proposed presidential action that would temporarily withhold or otherwise delay the obligation or spending of some or all of the budget authority provided in an appropriations bill.

The *City of New Haven* suit was based on another case decided in 1983—*INS v. Chadha*[5]—which declared one-house vetoes of proposed presidential actions to be unconstitutional. Although the Congressional Budget Act was not the law challenged in the *Chadha* decision, it was affected because the procedure for Congress to review proposed deferrals is a one-house legislative veto. The result of the decision was that the president was able to propose deferrals but Congress had no way to review and, if it chose, disapprove them. This was similar to the situation that existed in the early 1970s which led to the passage of the Congressional Budget Act in the first place.

This was not much of a problem until the Reagan fiscal 1987 budget was submitted to Congress in February 1986. That budget included billions of dollars in proposed deferrals, much of which was for programs directly benefiting cities. The *City of New Haven* lawsuit against deferrals claimed that Congress would not have given the president the ability to propose them if it had not also established a procedure that allowed them to be reviewed. The plaintiffs said that the effect of the *Chadha* decision, therefore, should be to declare illegal not only the congressional review procedure but also the president's ability to propose deferrals in the first place.

In May 1986 a U.S. district court agreed and declared the president's authority to propose deferrals for policy reasons to be unconstitutional. Eight months later, in January 1987, that decision was unanimously affirmed by a U.S. court of appeals.

Congress decided in GRH II to codify the ruling in the *City of New Haven* decision. It specifically prohibited policy deferrals and provides that deferrals are allowed under only three circumstances:

1. for contingencies,

2. for emergencies, and
3. as specifically provided by law.

These so-called "programmatic" deferrals must be reported by the president to Congress and the comptroller general in a special message that must include a full explanation and justification. Deferrals can be proposed for any length of time, but they cannot extend beyond the end of the fiscal year. The message must include the estimated fiscal, economic, and budgetary effects of the proposed action.

The comptroller general is required to submit a separate report on the proposed deferral to Congress. Besides making an independent judgment on the information submitted by the president, the comptroller general has the power to reclassify a deferral message as a rescission (or vice versa) if it is found to be incorrectly labeled. Furthermore, if the comptroller general determines that the president is attempting a deferral without notifying Congress, he or she may send a message to Capitol Hill, and Congress will treat it as if it was a special deferral message submitted by the president.

A proposed deferral is automatically considered to be approved until either house of Congress specifically votes to disapprove it.

The other type of impoundment is a "rescission," an executive action not to spend part or all of the budget authority provided in an appropriation. When proposing a rescission, the president must send a message to the House, the Senate, and the comptroller general explaining the proposal in detail, including the amount of budget authority to be rescinded, the department or agency to which the budget authority has been allocated, the specific project for which the budget authority is intended, and the reasons for the action. The message must also include the estimated fiscal, economic, and budgetary impact of the action and all other pertinent information.

A rescission message is treated by the comptroller general the same way that a deferral message is treated.

A rescission must be specifically approved by both houses of Congress within 45 legislative days after the message is received from the president. If either the House or Senate votes to disapprove the proposal *or takes no action within this period,* the president must spend the funds as originally intended. If the president continues to refuse to spend the funds, the comptroller general may sue in federal court to require the money to be spent.

In recent years there have been renewed calls for changing the rescission process. Most suggested reforms would force Congress to take some action to disapprove a proposed rescission instead of disapproving it by taking no action whatsoever and would shorten the length of time within which Congress must act.[6] Although there have been a number of different "enhanced" or "expedited" rescission proposals, all would give the president the upper hand by allowing a proposed rescission to take effect either immediately or within a very short period of time (10 days, for example) unless both houses of Congress specifically voted to disapprove it. This is the opposite of the current situation, where the proposed rescission is only approved if the House and Senate specifically vote in favor of the president's proposal.

In 1992, President Bush briefly created a new rescission controversy when he proposed billions of dollars in rescissions and then, through the use of a little-known and previously untried provision of the impoundment control provisions of the Congressional Budget Act, threatened to force Congress to vote on a different rescission bill every week.

Under section 1017 of the act, a member of Congress can introduce legislation that embodies one or more of the president's proposed rescissions. Each bill is then referred to the appropriations committee in the House and the appropriations, budget, and relevant authorizing committees in the Senate. A 25-day period (including weekends and holidays but not including any time that Congress is in recess for more than three days) then starts, during which the bill (or bills) is supposed to be reported by the committee(s) to which it has been referred. If it is not reported during this period, any representative or senator can move on the House or Senate floor to discharge the committee from further consideration as long as he or she is supported by one-fifth of the members of their house.

If the discharge motion is approved, the rescission bill is brought to the floor and debated under expedited procedures that limit discussion and the types of amendments that can be offered.

The current deferral and rescission processes take much of the discretion away from the executive branch on impoundments. The president must notify Congress of all proposed actions and, if he or she neglects to do so, the comptroller general may inform Congress instead. All actions must receive either the explicit or implicit approval of both the House and Senate or the president is forced to spend the funds as Congress intended. Finally, the comptroller general is given the authority to bring a legal action if the president continues to refuse to spend the funds after a rescission or deferral is disapproved.

Rescission messages are handled jointly by the budget and appropriations committees in the Senate but only by the appropriations committee in the House. Floor consideration in the Senate on a rescission bill is limited to 10 hours of debate, with debate on any amendment limited to two hours. Debate in the House is limited to two hours, with amendments considered under the five-minute rule.

The impoundment control procedures provide both the president and Congress with the opportunity to make adjustments in the budget after it has been approved if events occur that differ from the economic, political, programmatic, and technical assumptions on which the budget was based. Therefore, the new procedures have eliminated the president's ability to act unilaterally in these matters but not the ability to propose changes.

Appendix E is the fiscal 1994 rescission message sent by President Clinton to Congress on November 1, 1993.

Notes

1. This would be a "line-item" veto. Every recent president has asked that this be given to him in some form.

2. Louis Fisher, *Presidential Spending Power* (Princeton, New Jersey: Princeton University Press, 1975), p. 158.

3. Ibid., p. 148.

4. *City of New Haven v. United States*, 809 F.2nd 900 (D.C. Cir. 1987).

5. *INS v. Chadha*, 454 U.S. 812, 102 S.Ct. 87 (1983).

6. In 1994, the House passed legislation (H.R. 4600) that would have created an expedited rescission procedure. The Senate took no action on the bill, however.

Part Two

THE FEDERAL BUDGET

Chapter Eight

OVERVIEW

This section describes the documents the president uses to submit his or her proposed budget to Congress and explains how to read and interpret the major tables they contain.

The president's budget, which is produced by the Office of Management and Budget, is clearly partisan and is intended to put the administration's program in the best possible light. If used carefully and correctly, however, it can also serve as a source of objective information on federal spending and taxing. The president's budget includes some of the most detailed information available to the public on federal activities. As noted in chapter 3, Congress generally uses the president's budget more than any other source of budget data, and that budget usually serves as the starting point for most congressional deliberations.

Until the fiscal 1991 edition, the president's budget consisted of seven documents.[1]

1. *Budget of the United States Government.* This was the basic budget document. It included the president's budget message, an explanation of the administration's economic policy and the projections on which the budget was based, descriptions of the spending and taxing proposals by both function and department, and summary tables that presented the budget historically and according to certain accounting and budget principals.
2. *The United States Budget in Brief.* This was a less technical presentation of the basic *Budget of the United States Government.* Although it provided summary and historical tables and graphs, it was designed for the non-expert reader and so was not detailed enough to permit much independent analysis.
3. *Budget of the United States Government, Appendix.* The Appendix was the most detailed of all the budget documents. It listed, by department, the proposed text of appropriations language and the activities and financing of each program under the jurisdiction of

that department. The Appendix was the size of a large city telephone directory with print almost as small and the detail it contained was not appropriate for most budget users. The Appendix
was the only suitable document to consult for individual line-
items, however.

4. *Special Analyses, Budget of the United States Government.* Special
Analyses generally contained separate reports that looked at federal spending in ways that cut across several budget functions or
involved more than one department. It also generally contained a
number of "alternative views" of the budget, including the current
services estimates and national income and product accounts.

5. *Historical Tables.* Historical Tables provided budget information
for periods longer than those included in the other budget books.
In some cases the data were included for periods dating back to
the mid-1930s.

6. *Major Policy Initiatives.* This was the most partisan of all the presidential budget documents. It described the administration's
spending and revenues proposals in the way that best suited the
White House's aims.

7. *Management of the United States Government.* This document described the president's nonbudgetary proposals to make the government operate more efficiently (and, presumably, less expen-
sively).[2] This too was a highly partisan document that had to be
used carefully.

These seven documents were combined into a single document
when President Bush submitted his fiscal 1991 and 1992 budgets to
Congress.

The fiscal 1993 Bush budget was submitted in two documents. The
basic *Budget of the United States Government* included the vast majority of the materials that were in the 1991 and 1992 single volumes.
About three weeks later a "supplement" was submitted that provided
a variety of additional materials.

There are many possible reasons why the Bush Administration
changed the format of the president's budget. The administration itself
said the seven documents were too long, too confusing, and too
expensive[3] to be of much use to the average user. Some thought it was
an attempt by OMB Director Richard Darman to present the information in the way that best suited his, and the president's, purposes.
Others thought it was a way for the administration to make it more
difficult for anyone who might oppose the president's proposals to
analyze them. There were also some who thought it was a way for the

White House to control the early debate on the president's budget because the only information available in the first few days was what the administration released.

Regardless of the reason, the presentation of the president's budget was changed radically. Some (although only a small amount) of the information presented in prior budgets was dropped entirely. The bulk of what was previously presented could still be found, although it was often in a different place and/or in a radically different form. The reason that this was possible is that most of the information in the president's budget is required by either the Budget and Accounting Act, the Congressional Budget and Impoundment Control Act, the Balanced Budget and Emergency Deficit Control Act, the Balanced Budget and Emergency Deficit Control Reaffirmation Act, or BEA. The tables and the data they require should, therefore, always be available somewhere.

Because of the change in presidents, the fiscal 1994 presidential budget was something of a hybrid document, with one book submitted by the outgoing Bush Administration and two others submitted by the incoming Clinton Administration.

President Bush sent *Budget Baselines, Historical Data, and Alternatives for the Future* to Congress on January 6, 1993, two weeks before the end of his administration. As its name suggests, this document contained much of the historical and baseline information that is usually included in the president's budget. It did not, however, include any policy choices. As the president said in the transmittal message, the document was intended "to provide a perspective from which to evaluate choices and actions . . ."[4]

The first Clinton budget document, *A Vision of Change for America*, was sent to Congress on February 17, 1993, slightly less than one month after the new president had been inaugurated. Although it contained the administration's deficit reduction and economic stimulus plans, it was not the budget for fiscal 1994. That document, *Budget of the United States Government, Fiscal 1994*, was sent to Congress on April 8, 1993.

How was it possible for the president's budget to be submitted so late? The reason was that inauguration day—January 20, 1993—fell in the middle of the one-month period between the first Monday in January and the first Monday in February during which the president's budget is required to be sent to Congress. The Bush Administration could have prepared a budget while it was still in office, but it decided not to do so claiming that BEA was intended to require the new president to submit the budget. However, the Clinton Administration indicated that it thought the law did apply to the outgoing president because the incoming president could not possibly prepare a budget in the very short time between noon on January 20 and the first Monday in February.

The budget that President Clinton did submit for fiscal 1994 was similar in many respects to the one-book approach that President Bush began several years earlier. Its major difference was that it did not include the historical tables and summary information that had been included by the Bush Administration in its January document.

The Clinton Administration's fiscal 1995 budget was a complete departure from both the one-book approach used during most of the Bush Administration and the two-book format used for fiscal 1994. In fact, the fiscal 1995 Clinton budget was something of a throwback to the budgets that presidents used to send to Congress.

The Clinton fiscal 1995 budget was presented in four documents.

Budget of the United States Government was a combination of both the basic budget and the major policy initiatives documents that existed prior to the Bush Administration.

Budget of the United States Government, Appendix returned to the way it was in the years before 1991—a straightforward, detailed, nonrhetorical presentation of the entire budget on a program-by-program, department-by-department basis.

Budget of the United States Government, Analytical Perspectives was a combination of materials that in prior years was included in both the basic budget document and the Special Analyses.

Finally, *Budget of the United States Government, Historical Tables* returned to its previous status as a stand-alone document. As before, it provided longer-term views of the budget, federal finances, and the impact of the Clinton proposals.

Each of these documents is described in detail in the chapters that follow.

Notes

1. Not all documents were produced in all years. In some years, new documents were created or two documents were combined into one new book. This can happen because, while the president is required to provide certain information, he or she generally is not required to use a particular format.

2. A typical proposal might, for example, deal with enhanced inspectors general, privatization, or better coordination of computers within the government.

3. In total, the seven fiscal 1990 documents cost $94.50.

4. Office of Management and Budget, *Budget Baselines, Historical Data, and Alternatives for the Future, January 1993* (Washington, D.C.: U.S. Government Printing Office, 1993), p. 5.

Chapter Nine

BUDGET OF
THE UNITED STATES GOVERNMENT

This first document of the Clinton fiscal 1995 budget included material that in previous years had been displayed in a variety of ways and with varying degrees of emphasis.

In many ways, this document resembled most closely the *Major Policy Initiatives* document from previous administrations. In fact, most of this document presented the president's budget in a rhetorical format that put the Clinton program in the best possible light without necessarily providing information that allowed the reader to verify the claims. This document was, therefore, very similar to the first fiscal 1994 Clinton budget document—*A Vision of Change for America*—which primarily presented the president's budget stylistically. Documents like this should always be used carefully.

After the "Budget Message of the President," the document provided a 20-page summary of the Clinton fiscal 1995 budget proposal, including straightforward tables summarizing the outlook for outlays, receipts, and the deficit through fiscal 1999; the economic forecast; and discretionary spending by agency. The document then provided tables with an "illustrative" list of proposed program terminations and reductions, additional spending (termed "investments"), and an overall review of mandatory spending and receipts based on the Clinton economic forecast and budget proposals.

The rest of the document was divided into three sections.

"The Record Thus Far" provided a discussion of how much the Clinton Administration believed it had accomplished on the budget in its first year in office and the situation it inherited from the Bush Administration in 1993. As with other such narrative discussions from previous years' budgets, ones like this should always be used carefully because the information and conclusions are not necessarily evenly balanced.

"The Agenda Remaining" presented the Clinton program at length in narrative form. As might be expected, this part of the budget was highly subjective. Although many tables were used to illustrate the points being made, they should be used as carefully as the narrative they accompany. For example, the section "Investing in Know How" displayed a table called "Funding for Science and Technology *Highlights*" (emphasis added), and there is no way to know what proposals or programs are not included. Spending cuts in this area may not have been shown.

The most important part of this document for most users was the series of summary tables at the end, all of which are included somewhere in most presidential budgets.

The first table (table 18) divided all outlays in the budget into discretionary, mandatory, and interest. This table is extremely useful when determining the amount of spending each year that is "controllable" and "uncontrollable" (see chapter 1 and the glossary). Moreover, because the table divides discretionary and mandatory spending into their major components, it provides an excellent look at the political difficulty in cutting spending each year. Several points about this table should be noted.

1. The table was in billions of dollars.
2. The first column (1993) was the actual amount that was spent in fiscal 1993, the second column (1994) was the amount expected to

Table 18 BUDGET OUTLAYS BY CATEGORY (In billions of dollars)

	1993 Actual	Estimate					
		1994	1995	1996	1997	1998	1999
Discretionary:							
Defense discretionary	292.4	280.6	271.1	261.6	257.0	257.1	258.1
Nondefense discretionary	250.0	269.5	271.3	282.3	287.3	291.0	296.3
Discretionary health care reform	.....	.....	.....	2.2	3.4	-3.7	-6.1
Subtotal, discretionary	542.5	550.1	542.4	546.1	547.8	544.4	548.3
Mandatory:							
Social Security benefits	302.0	317.7	334.5	353.7	369.5	389.6	410.8
Federal retirement benefits [1]	59.8	63.0	65.2	67.9	71.3	74.6	78.9
Medicare	127.8	140.8	153.3	173.1	192.9	202.2	215.0
Medicaid	75.8	87.2	96.4	104.6	109.7	105.9	100.9
Unemployment benefits	35.5	26.7	23.0	23.5	23.9	24.0	25.1
Means-tested entitlements benefits [2]	80.8	89.4	96.7	102.4	109.9	116.6	124.0
Deposit insurance	-28.0	-3.3	-11.1	-11.3	-6.1	-4.9	-3.3
Health care allowances [3]	.....	.....	3.0	16.4	39.9	83.3	101.8
Undistributed offsetting receipts	-37.4	-37.9	-42.5	-41.6	-39.4	-41.4	-40.5
Other	50.7	46.7	45.2	37.9	38.1	38.3	38.7
Subtotal, mandatory	666.9	730.3	763.7	826.6	909.7	988.3	1,051.3
Net interest	198.8	203.4	212.8	224.2	234.0	244.6	254.4
Total outlays	1,408.2	1,483.8	1,518.9	1,596.9	1,691.4	1,777.4	1,854.0

Reprinted from Office of Management and Budget, *Budget of the United States Government, Fiscal Year 1995* (Washington, D.C.: U.S. Government Printing Office, 1994), p. 235.

be spent in the fiscal year that was underway when the Clinton fiscal 1995 budget was submitted to Congress, the third column (1995) was the amount expected to be spent based on the Clinton proposals in this budget, and the fourth through seventh columns (1996–1999) were forecasts based on the assumption that the president's fiscal 1995 proposals would be enacted.
3. These amounts were based on the assumption that the Clinton health care reform proposal would be enacted.

Receipts by Source. Besides providing the aggregate level of revenues, the second table (table 19) divided each year's total into their various sources. The following points should be noted.

1. The table was in billions of dollars.
2. The first column (1993 actual) was the actual figures for the year just completed when the budget was submitted to Congress. The second column (1994) was an estimate based on existing law as changed by the administration's proposals for that year. The third column (1995) included changes that already had been enacted into law and the estimated impact of all new administration revenue proposals for the budget year. The fourth through seventh columns (1996–1999) were estimates of the revenues from current law plus the effects of the revenue changes in those years from the administration's proposals for fiscal 1995.

Table 19 RECEIPTS BY SOURCE—SUMMARY (In billions of dollars) **1**

Source	**2** 1993 Actual	Estimate					
		1994	1995	1996	1997	1998	1999
Individual income taxes	509.7	549.9	595.0	627.7	664.1	701.6	745.1
Corporation income taxes	117.5	130.7	140.4	145.8	149.8	152.5	157.2
Social insurance taxes and contributions	428.3	461.9	490.4	518.3	548.5	580.0	610.2
(On-budget)	(116.4)	(125.7)	(135.2)	(143.6)	(151.0)	(158.6)	(165.0)
(Off-budget)	(311.9)	(336.2)	(355.2)	(374.7)	(397.5)	(421.4)	(445.1)
Excise taxes	48.1	54.6	71.9	71.7	72.7	73.6	74.9
Estate and gift taxes	12.6	12.7	13.9	15.0	16.1	17.3	18.5
Customs duties	18.8	19.2	20.9	21.3	22.2	23.1	24.0
Miscellaneous receipts	18.6	20.0	21.3	27.6	31.6	38.7	43.1
Total receipts	**1,153.5**	**1,249.1**	**1,353.8**	**1,427.3**	**1,505.1**	**1,586.9**	**1,672.9**
(On-budget)	(841.6)	(912.9)	(998.6)	(1,052.6)	(1,107.6)	(1,165.5)	(1,227.8)
(Off-budget)	(311.9)	(336.2)	(355.2)	(374.7)	(397.5)	(421.4)	(445.1)

Reprinted from Office of Management and Budget, *Budget of the United States Government, Fiscal Year 1995* (Washington, D.C.: U.S. Government Printing Office, 1994), p. 236.

Discretionary Budget Authority and Outlays by Agency. These tables (tables 20 and 21) showed the amounts that either had been or would be appropriated to each department or agency based on the president's proposals. This is an easy way to see which part of the federal government will be increased or decreased as a result of the president's budget. Several points should be noted in both tables.

1. The tables were in millions of dollars.
2. The first column (1993) was the actual amount that was spent in the fiscal year that had just been completed when the budget was submitted to Congress. The second column (1994) was the amount expected to be spent in the fiscal year that was underway when the fiscal 1995 budget was submitted to Congress. The third column (1995) was the amount expected to be spent in the budget year based on the proposals in the president's budget. The fourth through seventh columns (1996–1999) were forecasts based on the assumption that the president's fiscal 1995 proposals would be enacted.
3. This amount on the outlays table (table 21) is equal to the "Subtotal, discretionary" line on table 18.

Discretionary Proposals by Appropriations Subcommittee. This table (table 22) displayed all of the information shown on the previous two tables according to the House and Senate Appropriations Committee subcommittee that was expected to have jurisdiction over a portion of the total to be appropriated. Therefore, the table showed the administration's assumption of the 602(b) allocations that would be made by the appropriations committees themselves later in the budget process (see chapter five). The following points should be noted.

1. The table is in billions of dollars.
2. Both budget authority and outlays are displayed.
3. The amounts on this line are equal to the "Total" lines on the previous two tables.

Mandatory and Receipts PAYGO Proposals. The "pay-as-you-go" rules established by the Budget Enforcement Act require that any enacted increases in mandatory spending or decreases in revenue not increase the deficit (see chapter 2). This table (table 23) listed all of the administration's proposals that would have a PAYGO impact. The following points should be noted.

Table 20 DISCRETIONARY BUDGET AUTHORITY BY AGENCY
(In millions of dollars) **1**

Agency **2**	1993 Actual	Estimate					
		1994	1995	1996	1997	1998	1999
Cabinet Agencies:							
Agriculture (excluding International Programs)	14,052	15,018	14,170	14,241	14,402	14,436	14,595
Commerce	3,216	3,632	4,187	4,502	4,742	4,973	5,962
Defense	262,617	249,979	252,850	244,200	241,000	247,500	253,800
Education	23,696	24,354	26,060	26,305	26,539	26,747	26,935
Energy	19,262	18,614	18,010	18,282	18,278	18,580	19,021
Health and Human Services	31,608	34,318	35,414	36,193	37,957	39,304	41,179
Housing and Urban Development	25,524	25,105	26,064	33,537	35,152	37,544	38,785
Interior	7,078	7,512	7,231	7,346	7,380	7,433	7,491
Justice	9,315	9,376	12,144	14,343	15,240	16,000	17,255
Labor	9,920	10,561	11,694	11,987	12,492	12,517	12,625
State	4,928	5,289	4,860	4,713	4,807	4,847	4,960
Transportation	13,514	11,186	13,543	13,194	12,364	13,175	13,187
Treasury	10,082	10,339	10,350	10,790	10,649	10,381	10,094
Veterans Affairs	16,701	17,584	17,812	18,281	18,941	18,866	18,866
Major Agencies:							
Appalachian Regional Commission	190	249	187	187	187	187	187
Community Development Financial Institutions	....	....	144	144	111	101	....
Corporation for Public Broadcasting	319	275	293	312	293	293	293
Corps of Engineers	3,842	3,915	3,315	3,724	3,451	3,821	3,561
District of Columbia	688	700	722	722	722	722	722
Environmental Protection Agency	6,923	6,659	7,163	7,395	7,678	7,876	8,188
Executive Office of the President	236	185	190	190	191	191	192
Equal Employment Opportunity Commission	222	230	246	246	246	246	246
Federal Emergency Management Agency	2,573	800	704	704	704	704	704
General Services Administration	275	522	1,600	172	177	177	177
International Programs (other than the State Department)	16,266	15,528	16,001	15,917	15,839	15,804	15,710
Legal Services Corporation	357	400	500	500	500	500	500
National Aeronautics and Space Admin.	14,309	14,466	14,300	14,400	14,500	14,600	14,600
National Archives and Records Admin.	168	192	197	197	197	197	197
National Endowment for the Arts	174	170	170	170	170	170	170
National Endowment for the Humanities	177	177	177	177	177	177	177
National Labor Relations Board	170	171	175	175	175	175	175
National Science Foundation	2,734	3,018	3,200	3,234	3,300	3,400	3,500
National Service Initiative	279	575	850	1,359	1,587	1,860	2,185
Office of Personnel Management	123	123	117	114	116	118	121
Postal Service	122	91	92	92	92	92	92
Railroad Retirement Board	395	378	362	348	333	318	303
Securities and Exchange Commission	127	58	306	319	333	348	364
Small Business Administration	925	740	806	798	824	848	870
Smithsonian Institution	405	403	487	458	458	458	458
Tennessee Valley Authority	135	140	140	140	140	140	140
Allowances	....	....	-1,155	818	1,036	-6,831	-9,884
All Other Agencies	1,297	921	1,134	1,164	1,155	1,162	1,178
Judicial Branch	2,367	2,556	2,893	2,893	2,893	2,893	2,894
Legislative Branch	2,313	2,307	2,545	2,699	2,803	2,917	2,994
Total	**509,624**	**498,816**	**512,250**	**517,682**	**520,331**	**525,967**	**535,769**

Reprinted from Office of Management and Budget, *Budget of the United States Government, Fiscal Year 1995* (Washington, D.C.: U.S. Government Printing Office, 1994), p. 237.

Table 21 DISCRETIONARY OUTLAYS BY AGENCY (In millions of dollars) **1**

Agency	1993 Actual	Estimate					
		1994	1995	1996	1997	1998	1999
Cabinet Agencies:							
Agriculture (excluding International Programs)	13,095	14,572	14,398	14,195	14,371	14,483	14,671
Commerce	2,889	3,374	3,649	4,311	4,652	4,926	5,481
Defense	280,101	268,423	259,855	249,858	245,358	245,466	246,286
Education	23,017	24,457	24,046	25,769	26,261	26,520	26,723
Energy	18,022	18,971	17,877	18,561	18,415	18,556	18,931
Health and Human Services	32,020	36,641	36,805	38,846	40,416	42,288	43,982
Housing and Urban Development	24,965	27,498	29,477	30,514	31,183	31,163	31,892
Interior	7,118	7,275	7,363	7,447	7,506	7,461	7,525
Justice	9,153	9,705	10,614	12,943	14,332	15,521	17,068
Labor	9,502	9,981	10,421	11,317	11,787	12,264	12,405
State	4,946	5,378	4,954	4,795	4,892	4,925	5,009
Transportation	34,129	36,237	36,821	38,026	38,237	38,425	38,595
Treasury	9,936	10,410	10,322	10,695	10,594	10,340	10,154
Veterans Affairs	16,292	17,413	18,030	18,449	18,839	18,861	18,863
Major Agencies:							
Appalachian Regional Commission	145	149	180	205	198	195	193
Community Development Financial Institutions	....	....	86	144	124	105	40
Corporation for Public Broadcasting	319	275	293	312	293	293	293
Corps of Engineers	3,377	4,297	3,589	3,587	3,586	3,687	3,687
District of Columbia	698	698	722	722	722	722	722
Environmental Protection Agency	6,112	6,762	6,909	7,110	7,410	7,633	7,809
Executive Office of the President	195	191	188	188	190	191	193
Equal Employment Opportunity Commission	218	228	243	247	245	245	245
Federal Emergency Management Agency	2,855	2,566	1,844	967	836	704	704
General Services Administration	449	1,018	884	1,679	1,002	306	-206
International Programs (other than the State Department	16,624	16,462	15,834	16,372	16,377	16,303	16,247
Legal Services Corporation	389	393	483	500	500	500	500
National Aeronautics and Space Administration	14,304	14,182	14,410	14,375	14,399	14,529	14,592
National Archives and Records Administration	270	282	190	190	190	190	190
National Endowment for the Arts	173	173	172	173	170	170	170
National Endowment for the Humanities	168	190	180	179	178	178	178
National Labor Relations Board	171	173	174	175	175	175	175
National Science Foundation	2,442	2,814	2,858	3,039	3,187	3,266	3,361
National Service Initiative	219	436	601	941	1,344	1,625	1,904
Office of Personnel Management	222	214	214	217	224	226	231
Postal Service	122	91	92	92	92	92	92
Railroad Retirement Board	390	378	362	348	333	318	303
Securities and Exchange Commission	99	65	295	319	333	347	363
Small Business Administration	1,111	1,119	901	815	816	839	861
Smithsonian Institution	395	403	476	499	475	474	473
Tennessee Valley Authority	143	139	133	133	133	133	133
Allowances	....	....	-1,074	136	595	-7,093	-9,736
All Other Agencies	926	1,136	1,134	1,199	1,192	1,189	1,201
Judicial Branch	2,414	2,573	2,812	2,815	2,814	2,814	2,815
Legislative Branch	2,315	2,367	2,546	2,681	2,783	2,894	2,968
Total **3**	542,450	550,109	542,363	546,085	547,759	544,449	548,286

Reprinted from Office of Management and Budget, *Budget of the United States Government, Fiscal Year 1995* (Washington, D.C.: U.S. Government Printing Office, 1994), p. 238.

Table 22 DISCRETIONARY PROPOSALS BY APPROPRIATIONS SUBCOMMITTEE
(In billions of dollars) **1**

Appropriations Subcommittee	1994 Enacted		1994 Proposed [1]		1995 Proposed		Change: 1994 Enacted to 1995 Proposed	
2	BA	Outlays	BA	Outlays	BA	Outlays	BA	Outlays
Agriculture and Rural Development	14.9	14.9	15.0	14.9	13.7	14.2	−1.2	−0.7
Commerce, Justice, State and the Judiciary	23.0	24.0	23.7	24.6	27.4	25.6	4.3	1.6
Defense	239.8	259.0	240.7	259.9	244.6	251.4	4.8	−7.6
District of Columbia	0.7	0.7	0.7	0.7	0.7	0.7		
Energy and Water Development	22.3	23.0	21.9	22.7	20.6	20.6	−1.7	−2.4
Foreign Operations	13.7	14.1	13.4	14.0	13.9	13.7	0.2	−0.4
Interior and Related Agencies	13.8	13.5	13.8	13.5	13.5	13.8	−0.3	0.3
Labor, HHS, and Education	67.3	69.3	67.3	69.3	71.9	69.9	4.7	0.6
Legislative	2.3	2.3	2.3	2.3	2.5	2.5	0.2	0.2
Military Construction	10.1	8.7	9.5	8.6	8.4	8.5	−1.7	−0.1
Transportation and Related Agencies	13.3	35.6	10.9	35.6	13.3	36.3	−0.1	0.6
Treasury-Postal Service, and General Government	11.7	12.3	11.6	12.3	12.8	12.0	1.0	−0.3
Veterans Affairs, HUD, Independent Agencies	68.6	71.7	68.2	71.7	70.2	74.2	1.6	2.5
Allowances					−1.2	−1.1	−1.2	−1.1
Total Discretionary **3**	501.5	549.1	498.8	550.1	512.2	542.4	10.8	−6.8

1. The table was in millions of dollars.
2. The table showed the "deficit impact" of each proposal. Spending cuts and revenue increases were shown with minus signs because they reduce the deficit. Spending increases and revenue reductions are shown with plus signs because they increase the deficit.

Effect of Proposals on Receipts. This table (table 24) showed the revenue impact of all the receipts proposals that were included in the budget. The following points should be noted.

1. The table was in billions of dollars.
2. The totals in the first column (1994) showed the impact of the proposals included in the fiscal 1995 budget on the then current fiscal year. There was virtually no assumed impact because fiscal 1994 was already underway when the 1995 budget was submitted to Congress and was likely to be further along by the time the administration's proposal was enacted.
3. The totals in the remaining columns (1995–1999) showed the impact of the proposals in each of the next five fiscal years.

Proposed Investments. This table (an excerpt of which is displayed in table 25) showed all of the increased spending that the administra-

Table 23 MANDATORY AND RECEIPTS PAYGO PROPOSALS
2 (Deficit impact in millions of dollars) **1**

		1994	1995	1996	1997	1998	1999
PAYGO PROPOSALS (EXCLUDING HEALTH CARE REFORM)							
Agriculture:							
Comprehensive reform of Federal Crop Insurance program:							
Increase insurance program	O	—	168	701	877	977	1,159
Eliminate ad-hoc disaster payments	O	—	–500	–1,000	–1,000	–1,000	–1,000
Deficit impact, comprehensive crop reform		—	–332	–299	–123	–23	159
Energy/USEC:							
Propose to amend the Nuclear Waste Policy Act to allow for permanent appropriation of funds by the the Nuclear Waste Fund, starting 1995. Would allow the permanent use of 50% of the annual available balances of the NW for site characterization at Yucca Mountain	O	—	74	192	257	288	301
Achieve savings in uranium enrichment operations	O	—	–105	–261	–248	–314	–350
Allow private parties to bid for the right to upgrade electric power generation capacity at Federal dams and sell the resulting increment in hydroelectric power at market prices. Affects several agencies	O	—	—	—	—	–160	–160
Health and Human Services:							
Enhance debt collection authority (SSI program)—consistent with HR3400	O	—	–18	–13	–9	–9	–9
Housing and Urban Development:							
Reform disposition of multifamily housing properties[1]	O	–520	—	—	—	—	—
Interior:[2]							
Implement NPR recommendation to increase park fees to enhance park facilities and make 15 percent of estimated receipts available for fee collection costs. Create a new National Park Renewal Fund to expend 50 percent of net new receipts and return them to the collection park	U	—	–1	–4	–4	–3	–2
Impose 8% royalty on hardrock minerals removed from Federal lands—consistent with HR322	U	—	—	–16	–112	–110	–108
Establish hardrock reclamation fund to reclaim abandoned mine sites on federal lands	O	—	—	—	1	29	49
Justice:							
Create enforceable 15% surcharge against debtors	G	—	–39	–39	–39	–39	–39
Labor/PBGC:							
Strengthen PBGC requirements for underfunded pension plans, increase premiums for risky plans, enhance PBGC enforcement authority:							
Receipt effect	G	–36	–56	371	448	479	356
Outlay effect	O	4	–74	–259	–472	–526	–1,314
Deficit impact, PBGC		–32	–130	112	–24	–47	–958
Reduce overpayment of special benefits through (1) a review of payment rolls, (2) subsidized reemployment of some beneficiaries, and (3) cutting off benefits to people in jail and those convicted of defrauding the program—Consistent with H.R.3400	O	—	–2	–3	–3	–3	–3
Transportation:							
Maritime Reform:							
Increase customs tonnage duty fees by 150%	U	—	–100	–100	–100	–100	–100
Provide subsidies for operation of up to 52 merchant marine ships	O	—	80	98	110	104	104
Extend railroad safety user fees	U	—	—	–39	–40	–42	–43
Treasury:							
Impose Bureau of Alcohol, Tobacco and Firearms fees	G	—	–40	–40	–38	–38	–38
Veterans' Affairs:							
Allow Chairman of Board of Veterans Appeals, in limited instances, to overturn benefit denial decisions made by the Board	O	—	•	•	•	•	•
Environmental Protection Agency:							
Increase/extend pesticide reregistration fees on manufacturers	U	—	–1	–*	–*	–2	–1
Various:							
Adjust civil monetary penalties for inflation	G	—	–17	–17	–17	–17	–24

Reprinted from Office of Management and Budget, *Budget of the United States Government, Fiscal Year 1995* (Washington, D.C.: U.S. Government Printing Office, 1994), p. 240.

Table 24 EFFECT OF PROPOSALS ON RECEIPTS (In billions of dollars) 1

		Estimate				
	1994	1995	1996	1997	1998	1999
Health Security Act:						
Increase tax on tobacco products [1]	....	12.0	11.3	11.2	11.1	11.0
Levy assessment on corporate alliance employers [1]	....	....	3.8	5.0	5.1	5.1
Increase deduction for health insurance costs of the self-employed	−0.1	−0.5	−0.6	−0.9	−1.7	−2.5
Limit exclusion of employer-provided health coverage .	....	....	....	5.3	8.1	8.7
Provide deduction for qualified long-term care services	....	....	−0.1	−0.2	−0.2	−0.2
Modify tax treatment of long-term care insurance premiums and benefits	....	....	−0.1	−0.2	−0.3	−0.4
Modify tax treatment of accelerated death benefits	−*	−*	−*	−*	−*	−*
Provide tax credit for cost of personal assistance services	....	....	−*	−0.1	−0.1	−0.1
Provide tax credit for health service providers in shortage areas	....	....	−*	−*	−*	−*
Increase expensing limit for medical equipment in shortage areas	....	−*	−*	−*	−*	−*
Modify self-employment tax treatment of certain S corporation shareholders and partners	....	....	0.2	0.5	0.5	0.5
Modify penalty for failure to report payments to independent contractors	....	0.1	0.1	0.1	0.1	0.1
Modify tax treatment of health care organizations	....	....	....	0.1	0.2	0.2
Relate early retiree health premium discounts to income	....	....	....	*	*	0.1
Levy assessments on employers to pay for early retirees [1]	....	....	....	....	2.4	4.3
Modify employer contributions to post-retirement medical and life insurance reserves and retiree health accounts	....	*	*	*	*	0.1
Recapture medicare Part B subsidies	....	....	0.2	0.9	0.8	0.9
Extend medicare coverage to all State and local government employee [1]	....	....	1.6	1.6	1.5	1.5
Levy assessment on premiums for health coverage purchased through regional alliances [1]	....	....	0.5	1.6	4.3	5.5
Effect of employer mandate, cost containment, and subsidies on individual income and payroll taxes	....	....	0.1	0.9	4.4	9.3
Subtotal, Health Security Act [1]	**−0.1**	**11.6**	**16.9**	**25.6**	**36.2**	**44.0**
Other proposals:						
Modify Federal pay raise (receipt effect)	....	−0.1	−0.1	−0.2	−0.3	−0.4
Levy surcharge on civil judgements	....	*	*	*	*	*
Reform PBGC funding (receipt effect)	*	0.1	−0.4	−0.4	−0.5	−0.4
Reallocate old age survivors (OASI) and disability (DI) tax rates	....	....	....	....	....	....
Adjust civil monetary penalties for inflation	....	*	*	*	*	*
Increase or establish new BATF fees [1]	....	0.1	0.1	*	*	*
Increase or expand fees collected under securities laws	....	0.4	0.4	0.4	0.4	0.4
Levy fees on users of Federal fisheries [1]	....	0.1	0.1	0.1	0.1	0.1
Subtotal, other proposals [1]	*	**0.5**	*	**−0.2**	**−0.3**	**−0.2**
Total effect of proposals [1]	**−0.1**	**12.2**	**16.9**	**25.5**	**35.9**	**43.7**

* $50 million or less.
[1] Net of income offsets.

Reprinted from Office of Management and Budget, *Budget of the United States Government, Fiscal Year 1995* (Washington, D.C.: U.S. Government Printing Office, 1994), p. 242.

Table 25 PROPOSED INVESTMENTS (In millions of dollars)

		1993 Enacted	Estimate 1994	Estimate 1995	Change: 1994 to 1995	1996	1997	1998	1999
Climate change action plan	BA	....	2	12	10	17	24	30	30
	OL	....	2	11	9	15	23	27	30
Pacific Northwest Forest Plan implementation	BA	....	60	97	37	97	97	97	97
	OL	....	48	77	29	97	97	97	97
Commerce Department:									
Economic Development Administration, Defense conversion	BA	....	80	140	60	140	140	140	140
	OL	....	8	39	31	82	116	133	139
National Institute of Standards and Technology (NIST) growth, NIST high performance computing, and NIST NSTC	BA	381	520	935	415	1,089	1,379	1,407	1,422
	OL	252	370	527	157	781	1,057	1,257	1,356
Information highways	BA	....	26	100	74	150	150	150	150
	OL	....	1	18	17	61	103	136	150
NOAA: rebuild US fisheries	BA	232	231	280	49	280	280	280	280
	OL	227	221	261	40	266	277	280	280
NOAA NSTC	BA	47	64	106	42	142	142	142	142
	OL	46	62	100	38	134	140	142	142
Defense Department:									
ARPA technology reinvestment project	BA	472	554	625	71	650	675	700	725
	OL	223	445	557	112	611	648	676	703
Office of Economic Adjustment	BA	30	39	39	....	40	41	43	44
	OL	23	35	38	3	39	40	42	43
Education Department:									
School-to-work (Education Department share)	BA	....	50	150	100	200	200	165	110
	OL	....	6	52	46	135	188	195	165
Goals 2000	BA	....	105	700	595	1,000	1,000	1,000	1,000
	OL	....	13	154	141	618	929	994	1,000
Title I, education for the disadvantaged	BA	6,696	6,912	7,579	667	7,821	8,064	8,309	8,554
	OL	6,601	6,889	6,918	29	7,472	7,788	8,040	8,284
Safe and drug-free schools	BA	582	472	660	188	660	580	580	580
	OL	774	613	521	-92	620	647	596	581
Energy Department:									
Alternative fuels vehicles	BA	28	44	69	25	66	66	66	66
	OL	20	31	49	18	63	66	66	66
Conservation R&D/EPAct	BA	349	436	654	218	679	738	819	844
	OL	303	367	488	121	629	693	753	814
Conservation: weatherization assistance grants	BA	185	207	250	43	240	247	255	262
	OL	192	193	216	23	240	244	248	256
Federal facility energy efficiency (FFEE)	BA	5	16	37	21	49	49	49	49
	OL	19	11	21	10	37	48	49	49
Renewable energy programs	BA	251	341	393	52	426	454	483	512
	OL	238	295	354	59	408	435	463	492
Cooperative R&D agreements	BA	151	262	275	13	300	325	350	375
	OL	100	258	264	6	291	318	342	367
Advanced neutron source	BA	12	17	40	23	120	204	403	642
	OL	5	12	27	15	73	146	281	481
Linear accelerator "B-Factory"	BA	....	36	44	8	52	45	....	....
	OL	....	27	42	15	50	47	11	....
Climate change action plan	BA	....	17	208	191	233	235	213	211
	OL	....	6	83	77	183	225	221	212
Health and Human Services:									
Head Start	BA	2,776	3,326	4,026	700	4,726	5,426	6,126	6,826
	OL	2,567	3,066	3,529	463	4,270	4,938	5,633	6,332
Public Health Service:									
NIH	BA	10,326	10,956	11,473	517	11,955	12,457	12,980	13,525
	OL	9,533	10,251	11,009	758	11,680	12,369	13,071	13,594
Ryan White Act AIDS treatment	BA	348	579	672	93	773	889	1,022	1,175
	OL	316	510	627	117	739	862	999	1,152
Immunizations	BA	341	528	888	360	917	937	967	998
	OL	304	446	901	455	911	926	955	985
High performance computing	BA	47	58	82	24	85	89	92	96
	OL	41	53	79	26	83	86	90	93
Drug treatment	BA	717	755	1,040	285	1,071	1,104	1,139	1,174
	OL	601	704	862	158	1,009	1,069	1,110	1,146

Reprinted from Office of Management and Budget, *Budget of the United States Government, Fiscal Year 1995* (Washington, D.C.: U.S. Government Printing Office, 1994), p. 243.

tion was proposing in its budget. The following points should be noted.

1. The table was in millions of dollars.
2. Budget authority and outlays were both displayed.
3. The first column (1993) showed the actual numbers from the fiscal year that had just been completed when the budget was submitted to Congress. The second column (1994) showed the amount that was expected to be spent in the fiscal year underway when the budget was submitted. The third column (1995) was the president's proposal. The fifth through eighth columns were projections of the amounts that would be spent in those years assuming that the president's proposals were enacted.

Federal Employment in the Executive Branch. This table (table 26) showed the number of employees in every executive branch department and agency. The following points should be noted.

1. The table is in thousands of "full-time equivalents," or FTEs. An FTE is one full year of work regardless of the number of people who actually do it. Therefore, an FTE is not necessarily the same as the number of employees. In FTE terms, two part-time workers (whose combined hours equal one year's worth of work) are equivalent to one FTE.
2. The first column shows the "base" number of FTEs in 1993. The second column (1993) shows the actual number of FTEs for the year just completed when the president's budget was submitted. The third column (1994) shows the number of FTEs expected in the fiscal year underway when the president's budget was submitted to Congress. The fourth column (1995) was the number of FTEs expected as a result of the president's proposals.

Federal Government Financing and Debt. This table (table 27) shows how the president expected to finance the budget and the resulting levels of borrowing and debt. The following points should be noted.

1. The table was in billions of dollars. This means that $4,925.0 is $4.9 trillion.
2. The federal government borrows from both the public and from various government accounts. "Gross federal debt" is the sum of these two.

Table 26 FEDERAL EMPLOYMENT IN THE EXECUTIVE BRANCH
(Civilian employment as measured by full-time equivalents in thousands)

Agency	1993 Base	1993 Actual	Estimate		Change: 1993 base to 1995	
			1994	1995	FTE's	Percent
Cabinet agencies:						
Agriculture	114.6	113.4	110.2	108.5	–6.1	–5.3%
Commerce	36.7	36.1	35.8	35.8	–0.9	–2.6%
Defense—military functions	931.4	931.8	886.0	854.9	–76.5	–8.2%
Education	5.0	4.9	5.1	5.2	0.2	2.4%
Energy	20.6	20.3	20.4	20.6	....	....
Health and Human Services	130.0	129.0	127.7	127.2	–2.8	–2.2%
Housing and Urban Development	13.6	13.3	13.3	13.4	–0.2	–1.8%
Interior	77.9	76.7	76.0	74.6	–3.3	–4.3%
Justice	99.4	95.4	97.2	101.9	2.5	2.5%
Labor	19.9	19.6	19.4	19.5	–0.4	–2.3%
State	26.0	25.6	25.4	25.0	–1.0	–4.0%
Transportation	71.1	69.9	68.9	67.5	–3.6	–5.0%
Treasury	166.1	161.1	161.2	157.6	–8.5	–5.1%
Veterans Affairs	232.4	234.4	235.1	229.7	–2.7	–1.1%
Other agencies (excluding Postal Service):						
Agency For International Development	4.4	4.1	4.0	4.0	–0.4	–8.6%
Corps of Engineers	29.2	28.4	28.5	27.8	–1.4	–4.7%
Environmental Protection Agency	19.0	18.3	18.6	19.4	0.4	2.2%
Equal Employment Opportunity Commission	2.9	2.8	2.9	3.0	0.1	5.6%
Federal Emergency Management Agency	2.7	2.6	2.6	2.7	....	–1.1%
Federal Deposit Insurance Corporation and Resolution Trust Corporation	21.3	21.6	20.4	15.1	–6.2	–28.8%
General Services Administration	20.7	20.2	20.1	19.7	–1.0	–4.7%
National Aeronautics and Space Administration .	25.7	24.9	24.5	23.6	–2.1	–8.2%
National Archives and Records Administration ...	2.8	2.6	2.7	2.6	–0.2	–4.7%
National Labor Relations Board	2.1	2.1	2.1	2.1	....	–4.2%
National Science Foundation	1.3	1.2	1.2	1.3	....	–4.0%
Nuclear Regulatory Commission	3.4	3.4	3.3	3.2	–0.2	–5.5%
Office of Personnel Management	6.2	5.9	6.0	5.8	–0.4	–7.3%
Panama Canal Commission	8.7	8.5	8.6	8.8	0.1	0.7%
Peace Corps	1.3	1.2	1.2	1.2	–0.1	–1.0%
Railroad Retirement Board	1.9	1.8	1.8	1.8	–0.1	–4.7%
Securities and Exchange Commission	2.7	2.7	2.7	2.9	0.2	7.2%
Small Business Administration	4.0	3.9	3.8	3.8	–0.2	–4.4%
Smithsonian Institution	4.9	4.5	4.8	4.7	–0.2	–3.6%
Tennessee Valley Authority	19.1	17.3	17.3	16.6	–2.5	–13.2%
United States Information Agency	8.7	8.3	8.5	8.3	–0.4	–5.0%
All other small agencies	17.5	16.4	17.0	17.2	–0.3	–1.8%
Total, Executive Branch civilian employment	2,155.2	2,134.3	2,084.2	2,036.9	–118.3	....
FTE reduction from the base	....	–20.9	–71.0	–118.3	....	....
Percentage reduction from the base	....	–1.0%	–3.3%	–5.5%	....	....
Percentage reduction target/FTE reduction target	....	–1.0%	–2.5%	–4.0%	–100.0	....

Reprinted from Office of Management and Budget, *Budget of the United States Government, Fiscal Year 1995* (Washington, D.C.: U.S. Government Printing Office, 1994), p. 248.

3. Most federal debt is issued by the Treasury Department and is commonly referred to as "public debt." Several individual federal agencies also issue debt and this is appropriately known as "agency debt."

Outlays by Agency and Function. The next two tables (tables 28 and 29) showed the outlay impact of the administration's proposals.

Table 27 FEDERAL GOVERNMENT FINANCING AND DEBT (In billions of dollars) **1**

	1993 Actual	Estimate 1994	1995	1996	1997	1998	1999
FINANCING							
Surplus or deficit (−)	−254.7	−234.8	−165.1	−169.6	−186.4	−190.5	−181.1
(On-budget)	−300.0	−290.1	−225.0	−236.3	−265.5	−279.2	−278.6
(Off-budget)	45.3	55.3	59.9	66.7	79.2	88.7	97.6
Means of financing other than borrowing from the public:							
Change in:							
Treasury operating cash balance	6.3	12.5	—	—	—	—	—
Checks outstanding, etc.	0.4	−0.9	−0.4	—	—	—	—
Deposit fund balances	−0.4	−0.5	−1.7	—	—	—	—
Seigniorage on coins	0.4	0.6	0.6	0.6	0.6	0.6	0.6
Less: Net financing disbursements:							
Direct loan financing accounts	−3.8	−6.4	−10.1	−15.9	−17.9	−18.9	−19.0
Guaranteed loan financing accounts	4.6	4.2	3.0	2.5	2.3	1.4	0.4
Total, means of financing other than borrowing from the public	7.4	9.5	−8.6	−12.8	−15.0	−16.8	−18.0
Total, requirement for borrowing from the public	−247.3	−225.2	−173.7	−182.4	−201.4	−207.3	−199.1
Reclassification of debt	−1.3	—	—	—	—	—	—
Change in debt held by the public	248.5	225.2	173.7	182.4	201.4	207.3	199.1
DEBT, END OF YEAR							
Gross Federal debt:							
Debt issued by Treasury	4,326.5	4,652.1	4,936.0	5,243.0	5,577.2	5,929.4	6,281.4
Debt issued by other agencies	24.8	23.9	24.2	24.1	24.1	24.1	24.1
Total, gross Federal debt	4,351.2	4,676.0	4,960.1	5,267.1	5,601.3	5,953.5	6,305.4
Held by:							
Government accounts	1,104.0	1,203.6	1,314.0	1,438.5	1,571.3	1,716.3	1,869.1
The public	3,247.2	3,472.4	3,646.1	3,828.5	4,029.9	4,237.2	4,436.3
(Federal Reserve Banks)	325.7						
(Other)	2,921.5						
DEBT SUBJECT TO STATUTORY LIMITATION, END OF YEAR							
Debt issued by Treasury	4,326.5	4,652.1	4,936.0	5,243.0	5,577.2	5,929.4	6,281.4
Less: Treasury debt not subject to limitation	−15.6	−15.6	−15.6	−15.6	−15.6	−15.6	−15.6
Agency debt subject to limitation	0.2	0.1	0.1	0.1	0.1	0.1	0.1
Adjustment for discount and premium	4.5	4.5	4.5	4.5	4.5	4.5	4.5
Total, debt subject to statutory limitation	4,315.6	4,641.1	4,925.0	5,232.0	5,566.2	5,918.4	6,270.3

3

Reprinted from Office of Management and Budget, *Budget of the United States Government, Fiscal Year 1995* (Washington, D.C.: U.S. Government Printing Office, 1994), p. 249.

The following applies to both tables.

1. The tables were in billions of dollars.
2. The first column (1993) showed the actual outlays from the fiscal year that had just been completed when the budget was submitted to Congress. The second column (1994) showed the amount that was expected to be spent in the fiscal year underway when the budget was submitted. The third column (1995) was the president's proposal. The fifth through eighth columns were projections of the

Table 28 OUTLAYS BY AGENCY (In billions of dollars) **1**

Agency **2**	1993 Actual	Estimate					
		1994	1995	1996	1997	1998	1999
Cabinet Agencies:							
Agriculture	63.1	64.9	60.3	61.0	62.6	63.3	64.7
Commerce	2.8	3.2	3.6	4.3	4.6	4.9	5.5
Defense—Military	278.6	267.5	259.3	249.1	244.6	244.7	245.5
Education	30.3	28.7	29.7	28.3	30.3	30.7	31.2
Energy	16.9	17.2	15.7	16.7	16.7	16.6	17.2
Health and Human Services	581.1	631.3	672.1	723.0	768.1	799.9	835.3
On-budget	(282.8)	(316.6)	(341.6)	(373.2)	(402.8)	(414.8)	(429.4)
Off-budget	(298.3)	(314.7)	(330.5)	(349.8)	(365.3)	(385.2)	(405.9)
Housing and Urban Development	25.2	25.5	27.7	28.4	28.1	27.9	28.5
Interior	6.8	7.2	7.2	7.1	7.0	7.0	7.0
Justice	10.2	10.8	11.3	13.6	15.0	16.2	17.7
Labor	44.7	37.1	34.0	35.2	35.9	36.5	37.0
State	5.2	5.8	5.4	5.3	5.4	5.5	5.6
Transportation	34.5	36.7	37.3	38.5	38.8	39.0	39.2
Treasury	298.8	309.3	327.7	345.4	362.9	380.4	397.6
Veterans Affairs	35.5	37.9	38.1	37.4	39.7	40.2	41.8
Major Agencies:							
Corps of Engineers, Military Retirement and Other Defense	29.3	31.0	30.9	32.0	33.2	34.6	36.8
Environmental Protection Agency	5.9	6.5	6.7	6.9	7.2	7.5	7.7
Executive Office Of the President	0.2	0.2	0.2	0.2	0.2	0.2	0.2
Funds Appropriated to the President	11.2	11.4	11.1	11.4	11.1	11.3	11.3
General Services Administration	0.7	1.0	0.9	1.6	1.0	0.3	-0.2
The Judiciary	2.6	2.9	3.1	3.1	3.1	3.1	3.1
Legislative Branch	2.4	2.8	2.9	3.1	3.2	3.3	3.4
National Aeronautics and Space Administration	14.3	14.2	14.4	14.4	14.4	14.5	14.6
Office of Personnel Management	36.8	38.1	40.2	42.3	44.5	47.2	49.7
Small Business Administration	0.8	0.6	0.5	0.5	0.5	0.6	0.6
All Other Agencies	-10.0	15.7	9.2	5.7	10.4	11.5	12.8
On-budget	(-11.5)	(13.9)	(5.9)	(5.4)	(10.9)	(12.6)	(14.2)
Off-budget	(1.4)	(1.7)	(3.3)	(0.2)	(-0.5)	(-1.1)	(-1.5)
Undistributed Offsetting Receipts	-119.7	-123.7	-132.3	-134.2	-137.5	-145.7	-151.7
On-budget	(-86.5)	(-88.2)	(-93.9)	(-92.1)	(-91.1)	(-94.3)	(-94.7)
Off-budget	(-33.2)	(-35.5)	(-38.4)	(-42.1)	(-46.4)	(-51.4)	(-56.9)
Allowances			1.9	16.5	40.5	76.2	92.0
Total	1,408.2	1,483.8	1,518.9	1,596.9	1,691.4	1,777.4	1,854.0
On-budget	(1,141.6)	(1,203.0)	(1,223.6)	(1,288.9)	(1,373.1)	(1,444.8)	(1,506.5)
Off-budget	(266.6)	(280.9)	(295.4)	(308.0)	(318.3)	(332.7)	(347.6)

Reprinted from Office of Management and Budget, *Budget of the United States Government, Fiscal Year 1995* (Washington, D.C.: U.S. Government Printing Office, 1994), p. 250.

amounts that would be spent in those years assuming that the president's proposals were enacted.

Budget Authority by Agency and Function. The next two tables (tables 30 and 31) showed the budget authority impact of the administration's proposals. The following applies to both tables.

1. The tables were in billions of dollars.

Table 29 OUTLAYS BY FUNCTION (In billions of dollars) [1]

Function	1993 Actual	Estimate					
		1994	1995	1996	1997	1998	1999
National defense:							
Department of Defense—Military ..	278.6	267.4	259.2	249.1	244.6	244.7	245.5
Other	12.5	12.5	11.5	11.9	11.8	11.9	12.0
International affairs	16.8	19.0	17.8	17.9	17.7	18.0	18.2
General science, space, and technology	17.0	17.3	16.9	17.1	17.1	17.2	17.4
Energy	4.3	5.0	4.6	5.0	5.0	4.8	5.0
Natural resources and environment ..	20.2	22.3	21.8	22.1	22.0	21.4	20.8
Agriculture	20.4	16.9	12.8	12.7	13.1	13.5	13.9
Commerce and housing credit	-22.7	0.5	-5.5	-9.0	-5.7	-5.4	-3.9
On-budget	(-24.2)	(-1.2)	(-8.7)	(-9.2)	(-5.2)	(-4.3)	(-2.4)
Off-budget	(1.4)	(1.7)	(3.3)	(0.2)	(-0.5)	(-1.1)	(-1.5)
Transportation	35.0	37.6	38.4	39.5	39.9	40.3	40.4
Community and regional development	9.1	9.3	9.2	9.0	8.9	8.5	8.5
Education, training, employment, and social services	50.0	50.8	53.5	54.5	57.9	60.3	62.2
Health	99.4	112.3	123.1	149.6	180.0	221.1	235.9
Medicare	130.6	143.7	156.2	176.0	195.8	205.2	218.1
Income security	207.3	214.6	221.4	230.8	242.5	253.0	265.2
Social Security	304.6	320.5	337.2	356.8	372.7	393.1	414.3
On-budget	(6.2)	(5.8)	(6.6)	(7.0)	(7.4)	(7.9)	(8.4)
Off-budget	(298.3)	(314.7)	(330.5)	(349.8)	(365.3)	(385.2)	(405.9)
Veterans benefits and services	35.7	38.1	39.2	38.2	41.5	40.3	41.9
Administration of justice	15.0	16.5	17.3	19.6	21.0	22.2	23.7
General government	13.0	14.3	13.8	15.3	14.5	13.7	13.1
Net interest	198.8	203.4	212.8	224.2	234.0	244.6	254.4
On-budget	(225.6)	(232.5)	(244.5)	(259.1)	(272.8)	(287.8)	(302.4)
Off-budget	(-26.8)	(-29.1)	(-31.7)	(-34.9)	(-38.8)	(-43.2)	(-48.0)
Allowances	....	....	0.2	-1.9	-3.5	-9.5	-12.2
Undistributed offsetting receipts:							
Employer share, employee retirement (on-budget)	-28.2	-28.2	-28.5	-27.6	-27.5	-28.3	-28.8
Employer share, employee retirement (off-budget)	-6.4	-6.5	-6.8	-7.2	-7.6	-8.3	-8.9
Rents and royalties on the Outer Continental Shelf	-2.8	-2.7	-3.0	-2.7	-2.8	-2.8	-2.8
Other undistributed offsetting receipts	....	-0.5	-4.3	-4.2	-1.6	-2.0	....
Total, Undistributed offsetting receipts	-37.4	-37.9	-42.6	-41.7	-39.4	-41.4	-40.5
On-budget	(-31.0)	(-31.4)	(-35.8)	(-34.5)	(-31.8)	(-33.1)	(-31.6)
Off-budget	(-6.4)	(-6.5)	(-6.8)	(-7.2)	(-7.6)	(-8.3)	(-8.9)
Total	1,408.2	1,483.8	1,518.9	1,596.9	1,691.4	1,777.4	1,854.0
On-budget	(1,141.6)	(1,203.0)	(1,223.6)	(1,288.9)	(1,373.1)	(1,444.8)	(1,506.5)
Off-budget	(266.6)	(280.9)	(295.4)	(308.0)	(318.3)	(332.7)	(347.6)

Reprinted from Office of Management and Budget, *Budget of the United States Government, Fiscal Year 1995* (Washington, D.C.: U.S. Government Printing Office, 1994), p. 251.

2. The first column (1993) showed the actual outlays from the fiscal year that had just been completed when the budget was submitted to Congress. The second column (1994) showed the amount that was expected to be spent in the fiscal year underway when the budget was submitted. The third column (1995) was the president's proposal. The fourth through seventh columns were projections of

Table 30 BUDGET AUTHORITY BY AGENCY (In billions of dollars)

Agency	1993 Actual	Estimate					
		1994	1995	1996	1997	1998	1999
Cabinet Agencies:							
Agriculture	67.9	65.3	61.7	62.4	64.3	64.8	66.2
Commerce	3.2	3.6	4.2	4.5	4.8	5.0	6.0
Defense—Military	267.4	249.0	252.2	243.4	240.2	246.7	253.0
Education	31.5	28.8	31.7	29.1	30.9	31.7	32.3
Energy	17.7	16.8	15.9	16.7	16.9	16.9	17.5
Health and Human Services	586.7	643.8	667.0	724.2	772.5	804.2	840.7
On-budget	(286.6)	(327.6)	(334.9)	(374.0)	(403.3)	(415.3)	(430.8)
Off-budget	(300.1)	(316.2)	(332.0)	(350.4)	(369.2)	(388.9)	(409.8)
Housing and Urban Development ..	26.5	25.6	27.5	34.8	36.3	38.5	39.7
Interior	6.9	7.5	7.1	7.2	7.0	7.1	7.1
Justice	10.5	10.3	12.8	15.0	15.9	16.7	17.9
Labor	46.9	38.6	36.0	36.8	37.8	38.0	39.1
State	5.3	5.7	5.3	5.2	5.3	5.4	5.5
Transportation	40.0	37.7	40.8	39.3	40.6	38.8	38.8
Treasury	300.5	310.1	328.7	346.4	364.1	381.6	398.6
Veterans Affairs	36.0	36.5	37.8	38.7	39.8	40.1	41.6
Major Agencies:							
Corps of Engineers, Military Retirement and Other Defense	29.9	30.6	30.6	32.1	33.1	34.8	36.6
Environmental Protection Agency ..	6.7	6.4	6.9	7.2	7.5	7.7	8.0
Executive Office Of the President ..	0.2	0.2	0.2	0.2	0.2	0.2	0.2
Funds Appropriated to the President	24.8	11.0	11.3	9.7	9.4	9.4	9.4
General Services Administration ...	0.6	0.6	1.6	0.1	0.1	0.1	0.1
The Judiciary	2.6	2.8	3.2	3.2	3.2	3.2	3.2
Legislative Branch	2.6	2.7	2.9	3.1	3.2	3.3	3.4
National Aeronautics and Space Administration	14.3	14.5	14.3	14.4	14.5	14.6	14.6
Office of Personnel Management	39.3	40.2	42.1	44.1	46.9	49.4	51.8
Small Business Administration	1.2	0.7	0.8	0.8	0.8	0.8	0.9
All Other Agencies	24.1	39.5	23.7	22.1	19.6	20.8	19.5
On-budget	(21.8)	(35.2)	(18.4)	(20.1)	(19.3)	(19.2)	(19.5)
Off-budget	(2.2)	(4.3)	(5.3)	(2.1)	(0.3)	(1.6)	*
Undistributed Offsetting Receipts	-119.7	-123.7	-132.3	-134.2	-137.5	-145.7	-151.7
On-budget	(-86.5)	(-88.2)	(-93.9)	(-92.1)	(-91.1)	(-94.3)	(-94.7)
Off-budget	(-33.2)	(-35.5)	(-38.4)	(-42.1)	(-46.4)	(-51.4)	(-56.9)
Allowances	....	....	3.0	16.6	40.6	76.3	91.9
Total	1,473.6	1,504.7	1,537.0	1,623.5	1,718.1	1,810.3	1,892.2
On-budget	(1,204.4)	(1,219.8)	(1,238.0)	(1,313.1)	(1,395.0)	(1,471.3)	(1,539.2)
Off-budget	(269.1)	(284.9)	(298.9)	(310.4)	(323.1)	(339.1)	(352.9)

Reprinted from Office of Management and Budget, *Budget of the United States Government, Fiscal Year 1995* (Washington, D.C.: U.S. Government Printing Office, 1994), p. 252.

the amounts that would be spent in those years assuming that the president's proposals were enacted.

Summary of Receipts, Outlays, and Surpluses or Deficits. This table (an excerpt of which is shown in table 32) showed 210 years of budget surpluses and deficits going back to 1789 and ahead to 1999. The following should be noted.

Table 31 BUDGET AUTHORITY BY FUNCTION (In billions of dollars) **1**

Function **2**	1993 Actual	Estimate					
		1994	1995	1996	1997	1998	1999
National defense:							
Department of Defense—Military ..	267.2	249.0	252.2	243.4	240.2	246.7	253.0
Other	13.9	12.0	11.5	11.9	11.8	12.0	12.1
International affairs	32.3	18.8	18.8	17.0	17.0	17.0	17.2
General science, space, and technology	17.2	17.5	17.3	17.2	17.3	17.4	17.6
Energy	8.3	4.7	4.7	6.2	6.0	5.6	6.0
Natural resources and environment ..	21.6	22.2	21.6	22.2	21.9	21.9	21.4
Agriculture	19.1	16.1	13.0	12.0	12.6	12.6	13.0
Commerce and housing credit	9.9	28.2	11.3	8.1	5.4	5.9	5.0
On-budget	(7.7)	(23.9)	(5.9)	(6.0)	(5.1)	(4.4)	(5.0)
Off-budget	(2.2)	(4.3)	(5.3)	(2.1)	(0.3)	(1.6)	*
Transportation	40.4	38.9	41.8	40.4	41.7	40.0	40.0
Community and regional development	10.2	8.4	9.3	8.9	8.8	8.8	8.8
Education, training, employment, and social services	52.8	53.4	57.7	56.7	60.2	62.5	64.7
Health	108.6	116.1	118.4	151.6	181.9	222.2	237.0
Medicare	124.8	150.6	156.1	176.6	195.5	205.1	218.6
Income security	214.8	215.2	221.7	239.9	253.0	265.4	278.7
Social Security	306.3	322.0	338.7	357.4	376.6	396.8	418.2
On-budget	(6.2)	(5.8)	(6.6)	(7.0)	(7.4)	(7.9)	(8.4)
Off-budget	(300.1)	(316.2)	(332.0)	(350.4)	(369.2)	(388.9)	(409.8)
Veterans benefits and services	36.3	36.7	38.9	39.5	41.6	40.2	41.8
Administration of justice	15.2	15.9	19.0	21.1	22.0	22.7	24.0
General government	13.2	13.6	14.7	13.9	13.9	13.7	13.5
Net interest	198.8	203.4	212.8	224.2	234.0	244.6	254.4
On-budget	(225.6)	(232.5)	(244.5)	(259.1)	(272.8)	(287.8)	(302.4)
Off-budget	(−26.8)	(−29.1)	(−31.7)	(−34.9)	(−38.8)	(−43.2)	(−48.0)
Allowances	....	....	0.1	−3.0	−4.0	−9.6	−12.4
Undistributed offsetting receipts:							
Employer share, employee retirement (on-budget)	−28.2	−28.2	−28.5	−27.6	−27.5	−28.3	−28.8
Employer share, employee retirement (off-budget)	−6.4	−6.5	−6.8	−7.2	−7.6	−8.3	−8.9
Rents and royalties on the Outer Continental Shelf	−2.8	−2.7	−3.0	−2.7	−2.8	−2.8	−2.8
Other undistributed offsetting receipts	....	−0.5	−4.3	−4.2	−1.6	−2.0	....
Total, Undistributed offsetting receipts	−37.4	−37.9	−42.6	−41.7	−39.4	−41.4	−40.5
On-budget	(−31.0)	(−31.4)	(−35.8)	(−34.5)	(−31.8)	(−33.1)	(−31.6)
Off-budget	(−6.4)	(−6.5)	(−6.8)	(−7.2)	(−7.6)	(−8.3)	(−8.9)
Total	**1,473.6**	**1,504.7**	**1,537.0**	**1,623.5**	**1,718.1**	**1,810.3**	**1,892.2**
On-budget	(1,204.4)	(1,219.8)	(1,238.0)	(1,313.1)	(1,395.0)	(1,471.3)	(1,539.2)
Off-budget	(269.1)	(284.9)	(298.9)	(310.4)	(323.1)	(339.1)	(352.9)

Reprinted from Office of Management and Budget, *Budget of the United States Government, Fiscal Year 1995* (Washington, D.C.: U.S. Government Printing Office, 1994), p. 253.

1. The table was in millions of dollars. It had to be. In the early years of the United States the amounts were so small that they would have appeared as fractions if the table had been in billions.
2. The table shows the totals for the budget as a whole and divides that amount into on-budget and off-budget (see the glossary) spending and revenues.

Table 32 SUMMARY OF RECEIPTS, OUTLAYS, AND SURPLUSES OR DEFICITS(–): 1789–1999 (In millions of dollars)

Year	Total			On-Budget			Off-Budget		
	Receipts	Outlays	Surplus or Deficit (–)	Receipts	Outlays	Surplus or Deficit (–)	Receipts	Outlays	Surplus or Deficit (–)
1789–1849	1,160	1,090	70	1,160	1,090	70			
1850–1900	14,462	15,453	–991	14,462	15,453	–991			
1901	588	525	63	588	525	63			
1902	562	485	77	562	485	77			
1903	562	517	45	562	517	45			
1904	541	584	–43	541	584	–43			
1905	544	567	–23	544	567	–23			
1906	595	570	25	595	570	25			
1907	666	579	87	666	579	87			
1908	602	659	–57	602	659	–57			
1909	604	694	–89	604	694	–89			
1910	676	694	–18	676	694	–18			
1911	702	691	11	702	691	11			
1912	693	690	3	693	690	3			
1913	714	715	–*	714	715	–*			
1914	725	726	–*	725	726	–*			
1915	683	746	–63	683	746	–63			
1916	761	713	48	761	713	48			
1917	1,101	1,954	–853	1,101	1,954	–853			
1918	3,645	12,677	–9,032	3,645	12,677	–9,032			
1919	5,130	18,493	–13,363	5,130	18,493	–13,363			
1920	6,649	6,358	291	6,649	6,358	291			
1921	5,571	5,062	509	5,571	5,062	509			
1922	4,026	3,289	736	4,026	3,289	736			
1923	3,853	3,140	713	3,853	3,140	713			
1924	3,871	2,908	963	3,871	2,908	963			
1925	3,641	2,924	717	3,641	2,924	717			
1926	3,795	2,930	865	3,795	2,930	865			
1927	4,013	2,857	1,155	4,013	2,857	1,155			
1928	3,900	2,961	939	3,900	2,961	939			
1929	3,862	3,127	734	3,862	3,127	734			
1930	4,058	3,320	738	4,058	3,320	738			
1931	3,116	3,577	–462	3,116	3,577	–462			
1932	1,924	4,659	–2,735	1,924	4,659	–2,735			
1933	1,997	4,598	–2,602	1,997	4,598	–2,602			
1934	2,955	6,541	–3,586	2,955	6,541	–3,586			
1935	3,609	6,412	–2,803	3,609	6,412	–2,803			
1936	3,923	8,228	–4,304	3,923	8,228	–4,304			
1937	5,387	7,580	–2,193	5,122	7,582	–2,460	265	–2	267
1938	6,751	6,840	–89	6,364	6,850	–486	387	–10	397
1939	6,295	9,141	–2,846	5,792	9,154	–3,362	503	–13	516
1940	6,548	9,468	–2,920	5,998	9,482	–3,484	550	–14	564
1941	8,712	13,653	–4,941	8,024	13,618	–5,594	688	35	653
1942	14,634	35,137	–20,503	13,738	35,071	–21,333	896	66	830
1943	24,001	78,555	–54,554	22,871	78,466	–55,595	1,130	89	1,041
1944	43,747	91,304	–47,557	42,455	91,190	–48,735	1,292	114	1,178
1945	45,159	92,712	–47,553	43,849	92,569	–48,720	1,310	143	1,167
1946	39,296	55,232	–15,936	38,057	55,022	–16,964	1,238	210	1,028
1947	38,514	34,496	4,018	37,055	34,193	2,861	1,459	303	1,157
1948	41,560	29,764	11,796	39,944	29,396	10,548	1,616	368	1,248
1949	39,415	38,835	580	37,724	38,408	–684	1,690	427	1,263
1950	39,443	42,562	–3,119	37,336	42,038	–4,702	2,106	524	1,583
1951	51,616	45,514	6,102	48,496	44,237	4,259	3,120	1,277	1,843
1952	66,167	67,686	–1,519	62,573	65,956	–3,383	3,594	1,730	1,864
1953	69,608	76,101	–6,493	65,511	73,771	–8,259	4,097	2,330	1,766
1954	69,701	70,855	–1,154	65,112	67,943	–2,831	4,589	2,912	1,677

Reprinted from Office of Management and Budget, *Budget of the United States Government, Fiscal Year 1995* (Washington, D.C.: U.S. Government Printing Office, 1994), p. 254.

3. Off-budget spending did not start until fiscal 1937.
4. The totals for 1789–1849 and 1850 to 1900 have been combined into a single line. Note that for the 60-year period from 1789 to 1849 the United States had an aggregate $70 million *surplus*.

Chapter Ten

BUDGET OF THE UNITED STATES GOVERNMENT— ANALYTICAL PERSPECTIVES

This document of the Clinton fiscal 1995 budget included most of the material that in previous years could be found in the *Special Analyses*.

Analytical Perspectives was, in fact, a combination of things. It included the economics and revenue sections that in previous presidential administrations most often had been in the basic budget document. It also included the Budget Enforcement Act preview report and the current services estimates that have been in a variety of documents over the years. And it included the cross-cutting discussions of the president's budget proposal that had almost always been in *Special Analyses*. As a result, *Analytical Perspectives* was a hybrid document that was both old in the sense that the material had always been presented before and new because it had never before been combined in this way.

ECONOMIC AND ACCOUNTING ANALYSES

The first section included three chapters that both explained the president's economic forecast in detail and analyzed the budget from two largely technical accounting perspectives.

While interesting, the accounting discussions were clearly of secondary importance to the economic forecast, which was critical to understanding the president's proposal. Furthermore, the accounting analyses may or may not be a part of future presidential budgets while the economic forecast will always be included.

The first table (table 33) showed the short-range and long-range economic outlook. Several elements should be noted.

1. The table was in calendar years as opposed to fiscal years.

Table 33 ECONOMIC ASSUMPTIONS (calendar years; dollar amounts in billions)

	Actual 1992	1993	1994	1995	1996	1997	1998	1999
				Projections				
Gross Domestic Product (GDP):								
Levels, dollar amounts in billions:								
Current dollars	6,038	6,371	6,736	7,118	7,522	7,950	8,400	8,870
Constant (1987) dollars	4,986	5,126	5,284	5,433	5,579	5,725	5,873	6,021
Implicit price deflator (1987=100), annual average	121.1	124.3	127.5	131.0	134.8	138.9	143.0	147.3
Percent change, fourth quarter over fourth quarter:								
Current dollars	6.7	5.0	5.8	5.6	5.7	5.7	5.7	5.6
Constant (1987) dollars	3.9	2.3	3.0	2.7	2.7	2.6	2.6	2.5
Implicit price deflator (1987=100)	2.8	2.6	2.7	2.8	2.9	3.0	3.0	3.0
Percent change, year over year:								
Current dollars	5.5	5.5	5.7	5.7	5.7	5.7	5.7	5.6
Constant (1987) dollars	2.6	2.8	3.1	2.8	2.7	2.6	2.6	2.5
Implicit price deflator (1987=100)	2.9	2.6	2.6	2.8	2.9	3.0	3.0	3.0
Incomes, billions of current dollars:								
Personal income	5,145	5,385	5,691	6,016	6,365	6,746	7,148	7,551
Wages and salaries [2]	2,973	3,083	3,261	3,442	3,636	3,849	4,071	4,293
Corporate profits before tax	395	447	508	531	555	573	595	631
Consumer Price Index (all urban): [3]								
Level (1982–84=100), annual average	140.3	144.5	148.6	153.3	158.3	163.6	169.2	174.9
Percent change, fourth quarter over fourth quarter	3.1	2.8	3.0	3.2	3.3	3.4	3.4	3.4
Percent change, year over year	3.0	3.0	2.8	3.2	3.3	3.3	3.4	3.4
Unemployment rate, civilian, percent: [4]								
Fourth quarter level	7.3	6.7	6.4	6.0	5.8	5.6	5.5	5.5
Annual average	7.4	6.8	6.5	6.1	5.9	5.7	5.5	5.5
Federal pay raises, January, percent [5]	4.2	3.7	....	1.6	2.2	2.5	2.5	2.5
Interest rates, percent:								
91-day Treasury bills [6]	3.5	3.0	3.4	3.8	4.1	4.4	4.4	4.4
10-year Treasury notes	7.0	5.9	5.8	5.8	5.8	5.8	5.8	5.8

Reprinted from Office of Management and Budget, Analytical Perspectives, Budget of the United States Government, Fiscal Year 1995 (Washington, D.C.: U.S. Government Printing Office, 1994), p. 4.

2. Many of the figures were in percentages, not dollars. If a particular figure was in dollars, it was in billions.
3. Figures were shown in both current and constant dollars in many cases.
4. These were the actual figures for calendar year 1992 and projections for 1993–1999.

The second major table (table 34) showed the sensitivity of the budget to changes in the economic forecast. This table is important because, to the extent that the economy performs differently from what is assumed in the budget, the deficit will be higher or lower.

Several points about this table should be noted.

1. The table was in billions of dollars.
2. A positive number indicated that the deficit would increase. A negative number indicated that the deficit would be reduced.
3. Changes opposite from those shown in the table would have approximately the same impact on the deficit, but in the opposite direction. For example, a one percent higher real GDP growth in 1994 including lower unemployment would reduce the deficit by about $7.5 billion in 1994.

FEDERAL RECEIPTS AND COLLECTIONS

Besides providing the aggregate level of revenues, the second section in *Analytical Perspectives* divided the totals into their various sources, explained the expected impact of all the administration's revenue proposals, and gave special attention to user fees and tax expenditures.

The first chapter, *Federal Receipts*, included several tables that deserve special attention. The first (table 35) showed all federal receipts according to their source. The following should be noted.

1. The table was in billions of dollars.
2. The totals in the first column (1993) were the actual figures for the year just completed when the budget was submitted to Congress. Those in the second column (1994) were an estimate based on existing law as changed by any Clinton proposals that were included in the 1995 budget but which affected the current fiscal year. The third column (1995) included changes that had already

Table 34 SENSITIVITY OF THE BUDGET TO ECONOMIC ASSUMPTIONS (In billions of dollars) 1

Budget effect	1994	1995	1996	1997	1998	1999
Real Growth and Employment						
Effects of 1 percent lower real GDP growth in calendar year 1994 only, including higher unemployment:1						
Receipts	-6.6	-14.4	-16.8	-17.3	-18.0	-18.8
Outlays	1.0	5.0	6.5	8.1	9.9	11.6
Deficit increase (+)	7.5	19.4	23.3	25.4	27.9	30.3
Effects of a sustained 1 percent lower annual real GDP growth rate during 1994–1999, including higher unemployment:1						
Receipts	-6.6	-21.3	-39.0	-58.0	-78.5	-100.8
Outlays	1.0	6.9	14.1	21.9	34.0	45.3
Deficit increase (+)	7.5	28.2	53.1	80.0	112.5	146.2
Effects of a sustained 1 percent lower annual real GDP growth rate during 1994–1999, with no change in unemployment:						
Receipts	-6.6	-21.6	-40.1	-60.3	-82.4	-106.6
Outlays	0.1	0.8	2.4	5.3	9.4	14.9
Deficit increase (+)	6.7	22.4	42.5	65.5	91.7	121.5
Inflation and Interest Rates						
Effects of 1 percentage point higher rate of inflation and interest rates during calendar year 1994 only:						
Receipts	7.3	15.4	16.0	15.4	16.2	17.0
Outlays	5.7	13.3	10.9	9.4	9.2	9.4
Deficit increase (+)	-1.6	-2.0	-5.2	-6.0	-7.0	-7.6
Effects of a sustained 1 percentage point higher rate of inflation and interest rates during 1994–1999:						
Receipts	7.3	23.2	40.6	58.2	77.5	98.7
Outlays	5.8	19.1	30.6	42.4	55.5	75.0
Deficit increase (+)	-1.6	-4.1	-10.0	-15.8	-22.0	-23.6

Reprinted from Office of Management and Budget, Analytical Perspectives, Budget of the United States Government, Fiscal Year 1995 (Washington, D.C.: U.S. Government Printing Office, 1994), p. 8.

Table 35 RECEIPTS BY SOURCE—SUMMARY (In billions of dollars)

Source	1993 actual	Estimate					
		1994	1995	1996	1997	1998	1999
Individual income taxes	509.7	549.9	595.0	627.7	664.1	701.6	745.1
Corporation income taxes	117.5	130.7	140.4	145.8	149.8	152.5	157.2
Social insurance taxes and contributions	428.3	461.9	490.4	518.3	548.5	580.0	610.2
(On-budget)	(116.4)	(125.7)	(135.2)	(143.6)	(151.0)	(158.6)	(165.0)
(Off-budget)	(311.9)	(336.2)	(355.2)	(374.7)	(397.5)	(421.4)	(445.1)
Excise taxes	48.1	54.6	71.9	71.7	72.7	73.6	74.9
Estate and gift taxes	12.6	12.7	13.9	15.0	16.1	17.3	18.5
Customs duties	18.8	19.2	20.9	21.3	22.2	23.1	24.0
Miscellaneous receipts	18.6	20.0	21.3	27.6	31.6	38.7	43.1
Total receipts	1,153.5	1,249.1	1,353.8	1,427.3	1,505.1	1,586.9	1,672.9
(On-budget)	(841.6)	(912.9)	(998.6)	(1,052.6)	(1,107.6)	(1,165.5)	(1,227.8)
(Off-budget)	(311.9)	(336.2)	(355.2)	(374.7)	(397.5)	(421.4)	(445.1)

Reprinted from Office of Management and Budget, *Analytical Perspectives, Budget of the United States Government, Fiscal Year 1995* (Washington, D.C.: U.S. Government Printing Office, 1994), p. 35.

been enacted into law and the estimated impact of all new administration revenue proposals. The figures for the fourth through seventh columns (1996–1999) were estimates of the revenues from current tax laws plus the effects of the revenue changes in those years that the administration proposed in its fiscal 1995 budget and was assuming would be adopted.

The second table (table 36) showed the impact of recently enacted laws and the revenue proposals included in the administration's budget on total receipts. The following points should be noted.

1. The table was in billions of dollars.
2. The baseline, that is, the revenues expected to be collected under existing law and based on the economic forecast in the president's budget, was the starting point.
3. This showed the revenue impact of legislation enacted since January 1, 1993, but not the president's proposals. More detailed estimates for these same legislative initiatives were provided in the next table (table 37).
4. This was the revenue impact of the revenue proposals included in the president's 1995 budget.

As noted above, the third table (table 37) provided additional details on the estimates for enacted legislation shown in table 35. The following should be noted.

1. The table was in billions of dollars.
2. All of the columns showed estimates for either the year underway when the budget was submitted to Congress (1994) or the years afterward.

The fourth table (table 38) showed the revenue impact of all of the receipts proposals that were included in the budget. The following should be noted.

1. The table was in billions of dollars.
2. The totals in the first column (1994) showed the impact of the proposals included in the fiscal 1995 budget on the then current fiscal year. There was little impact because fiscal 1994 was already underway when the 1995 budget was submitted to Congress and was likely to be further along by the time the administration's proposal was enacted.

Table 36 CHANGES IN RECEIPTS (In billions of dollars) [1]

			Estimate			
	1994	1995	1996	1997	1998	1999
Receipts under tax rates and structure in effect January 1, 1993[1]	1,224.0	1,292.8	1,352.4	1,405.2	1,478.7	1,555.5
Enacted legislative changes:						
Omnibus Budget Reconciliation Act of 1993[2]	24.3	45.3	52.5	65.9	58.3	57.9
North America Free Trade Agreement Implementation Act[2]	-0.1	-0.1	-0.2	-0.1	1.2	-1.6
Social security (OASDI) taxable earnings base increases:						
$57,600 to $60,600 on Jan. 1, 1994	1.0	3.1	3.4	3.9	4.4	5.0
$60,600 to $62,100 on Jan. 1, 1995		0.5	1.5	1.8	2.0	2.2
$62,100 to $63,900 on Jan. 1, 1996			0.7	2.0	2.2	2.5
$63,900 to $66,600 on Jan. 1, 1997				1.0	3.1	3.4
$66,600 to $69,300 on Jan. 1, 1998					1.1	3.1
$69,300 to $72,300 on Jan. 1, 1999						1.2
Proposals[2]	-0.1	12.2	16.9	25.5	35.9	43.7
Total, receipts under existing and proposed legislation	1,249.1	1,353.8	1,427.3	1,505.1	1,586.9	1,672.9

Reprinted from Office of Management and Budget, *Analytical Perspectives, Budget of the United States Government, Fiscal Year 1995* (Washington, D.C.: U.S. Government Printing Office, 1994), p. 35.

Table 37 EFFECT OF MAJOR LEGISLATION ENACTED IN 1993 ON RECEIPTS (In billions of dollars)

	Estimate					
	1994	1995	1996	1997	1998	1999
Omnibus Budget Reconciliation Act of 1993						
Individual income taxes	9.8	24.5	26.1	32.1	26.0	27.3
Corporation income taxes	6.8	7.6	8.9	14.2	11.9	10.7
Social insurance taxes and contributions	2.0	6.6	7.1	8.8	9.8	9.2
Excise taxes	6.0	6.1	9.8	10.0	9.9	9.9
Estate and gift taxes	0.5	0.5	0.6	0.6	0.6	0.7
Customs duties						
Miscellaneous receipts	-0.9	.....	.....	0.1	0.1	.....
Total, Omnibus Budget Reconciliation Act of 1993[1]	24.3	45.3	52.5	65.9	58.3	57.9
North America Free Trade Agreement Implementation Act						
Individual income taxes	*	0.2	0.2	0.2	1.0	-0.5
Corporation income taxes	0.1	0.2	0.2	0.2	0.2	0.3
Social insurance taxes and contributions	*	0.1	0.2	0.2	0.9	-0.5
Excise taxes	*	0.1	*	0.1	*	0.2
Customs duties	-0.3	-0.6	-0.8	-0.9	-1.0	-1.1
Total, North America Free Trade Agreement Implementation Act[1]	-0.1	-0.1	-0.2	-0.1	1.2	-1.6
ADDENDUM						
Total effect on receipts by source:						
Individual income taxes	9.9	24.6	26.3	32.3	27.0	26.9
Corporation income taxes	6.9	7.8	9.1	14.5	12.2	11.0
Social insurance taxes and contributions	2.1	6.7	7.3	9.0	10.7	8.8
Excise taxes	6.0	6.2	9.9	10.1	9.9	10.1
Estate and gift taxes	0.5	0.5	0.6	0.6	0.6	0.7
Customs duties	-1.2	-0.6	-0.8	-0.9	-1.0	-1.1
Miscellaneous receipts	.....	.....	.....	0.1	0.1	.....
Total effect on receipts[1]	24.1	45.2	52.4	65.7	59.5	56.3

Reprinted from Office of Management and Budget, *Analytical Perspectives, Budget of the United States Government, Fiscal Year 1995* (Washington, D.C.: U.S. Government Printing Office, 1994), p. 40.

Table 38 EFFECT OF PROPOSALS ON RECEIPTS (In billions of dollars)

			Estimate			
	1994	1995	1996	1997	1998	1999
Health Security Act:						
Increase tax on tobacco products [1]		12.0	11.3	11.2	11.1	11.0
Levy assessment on corporate alliance employers [1]			3.8	5.0	5.1	5.1
Increase deduction for health insurance costs of the self-employed	-0.1	-0.5	-0.6	-0.9	-1.7	-2.5
Limit exclusion of employer-provided health coverage				5.3	8.1	8.7
Provide deduction for qualified long-term care services			-0.1	-0.2	-0.2	-0.2
Modify tax treatment of long-term care insurance premiums and benefits			-0.1	-0.2	-0.3	-0.4
Modify tax treatment of accelerated death benefits	-*		-*	-*	-*	-*
Provide tax credit for cost of personal assistance services			-*	-0.1	-0.1	-0.1
Provide tax credit for health service providers in shortage areas		-*	-*	-*	-*	-*
Increase expensing limit for medical equipment in shortage areas			-*	-*	-*	-*
Modify self-employment tax treatment of certain S corporation shareholders and partners			0.2	0.5	0.5	0.5
Modify penalty for failure to report payments to independent contractors		0.1	0.1	0.1	0.1	0.1
Modify tax treatment of health care organizations				0.1	0.2	0.2
Relate early retiree health premium discounts to income				*	*	0.1
Levy assessments on employers to pay for early retirees [1]					2.4	4.3
Modify employer contributions to post-retirement medical and life insurance reserves and retiree health accounts		*	*	*	*	0.1
Recapture medicare Part B subsidies			0.2	0.9	0.8	0.9
Extend medicare coverage to all State and local government employee [1]			1.6	1.6	1.5	1.5
Levy assessment on premiums for health coverage purchased through regional alliances [1]			0.5	1.6	4.3	5.5
Effect of employer mandate, cost containment, and subsidies on individual income and payroll taxes			0.1	0.9	4.4	9.3
Subtotal, Health Security Act [1]	**-0.1**	**11.6**	**16.9**	**25.6**	**36.2**	**44.0**
Other proposals:						
Modify Federal pay raise (receipt effect)		-0.1	-0.1	-0.2	-0.3	-0.4
Levy surcharge on civil judgements		*	*	*	*	*

Reprinted from Office of Management and Budget, *Analytical Perspectives, Budget of the United States Government, Fiscal Year 1995* (Washington, D.C.: U.S. Government Printing Office, 1994), p. 44.

The fifth table (table 39) provided additional details on the information that was shown in summary form in the first table (35) of this chapter. The following points are important to note.

1. Unlike the first table, this one was in millions of dollars.
2. Also unlike the first table, this one only provided estimates for three years—the actual amounts from the year just completed (1993), the projected receipts for the year underway when the budget was submitted (1994) assuming that the president's proposals were enacted, and the estimated revenues for the budget year (1995) assuming that the president's proposals were enacted.

The second chapter, *User Fees and Other Collections*, discussed revenues other than taxes.

User fees are the charges imposed by the government for various activities, such as visiting a national park, and for using certain ser-

Table 39 RECEIPTS BY SOURCE (In millions of dollars) **1**

Source	1993 actual	1994 estimate	1995 estimate
Individual income taxes (federal funds):			
Withheld	430,427	455,119	482,654
Other	154,800	174,824	201,816
Refunds	−75,546	−79,978	−87,351
Proposals		37	50
Health Security Act (proposal)		−101	−2,122
Total net individual income taxes	**509,680**	**549,901**	**595,048**
Corporation income taxes:			
Federal funds:			
Gross collections	130,917	145,566	157,150
Refunds	−14,027	−15,529	−16,834
Proposals			−4
Health Security Act (proposal)		−1	−604
Total Federal funds net corporation income taxes	116,891	130,035	139,708
Trust funds:			
Gross collections (Hazardous substance superfund)	629	684	729
Total Trust funds net corporation income taxes	629	684	729
Total net corporation income taxes	**117,520**	**130,719**	**140,437**

Reprinted from Office of Management and Budget, *Analytical Perspectives, Budget of the United States Government, Fiscal Year 1995* (Washington, D.C.: U.S. Government Printing Office, 1994), p. 45.

vices, such as a corporation having the Food and Drug Administration review a new product application. They are different from taxes in the sense that the fee can be avoided if the activity is not undertaken or the service not used. User fees are recorded in the budget as federal receipts.

Offsetting collections are revenues that result from a business-like transaction between the federal government and the public. These collections frequently are not listed in the budget as receipts but as "negative outlays," that is, they reduce the level of spending for a particular program rather than increase the overall amount of receipts in the budget as a whole. They are deducted from spending when total outlays are calculated.

For most readers, table 40 (an excerpt of which is displayed) was most important. It showed a five-year projection of the impact of the administration's user fees and offsetting collections proposals. The following points should be noted.

1. The table was in millions of dollars.
2. The table is usually divided between those proposals that are recorded as negative outlays and those that are listed as revenue increases. However, all of the Clinton Administration's fiscal 1995 proposals had an outlay impact only.
3. The table was also divided into those proposals affecting discretionary and mandatory programs.

The third chapter in this section dealt with tax expenditures. Tax expenditures are provisions of the tax code that encourage individuals or corporations to do or not do something by granting them a decrease in their taxes. They are another way in which the federal government tries to accomplish its goals and, therefore, are an alternative to spending, credit, and regulation.

The narrative and tables in this section were presented in a relatively straightforward and nonpartisan manner, making them easy to read and use. Table 41 (an excerpt of which is shown) was the basic table from this chapter. The following points should be noted.

1. The table was in millions of dollars.
2. The tax expenditures were displayed by function.
3. Even though the numbers were displayed as being positive, they show the expected revenue loss from each provision.

Table 40 PROPOSED USER FEES AND OTHER COLLECTIONS (In millions of dollars)

		Estimate			
	1995	1996	1997	1998	1999
Outlay offsets: 2					
Discretionary: 3					
Agriculture:					
Meat/poultry plant overtime inspection fee (FSIS)	-103	-103	-103	-103	-103
Catastrophic Crop Insurance fee for administrative activities (FSA)	-40	-40	-40	-40	-40
Commodity standards and overtime inspection fees (AMS)	-6	-6	-6	-6	-6
Licensing fees (PSA)	-9	-12	-12	-12	-12
Standardization fee (FGIS)	-5	-5	-5	-5	-5
Guaranteed loan fee (FmHA)	-13	-13	-13	-13	-13
Commerce:					
Fisheries management program fees [1]	-82	-82	-82	-82	-82
Marine sanctuary fee	-3	-3	-3	-3	-3
Aeronautical chart fee	-3	-3	-3	-3	-3
Health and Human Services:					
Food and Drug Administration	-338	-350	-368	-378	-389
Interior:					
National Park Service entrance and recreation fees	-27	-33	-33	-37	-33
Justice:					
Bankruptcy reorganization petition fee	-5	-5	-5	-5	-5
Pre-merger notification filing fee	-13	-13	-13	-13	-13
Transportation:					
FAA certification and surveillance of foreign repair stations	-2	-2	-2	-2	-2
Treasury:					
Definitive marketable securities fee	-1	-1	-1	-1	-1
Treasury direct account fee	-2	-2	-2	-2	-2
Customs merchandise processing fee	-94	-94	-94	-94	-94
IRS installment agreements	-54	-54	-54	-54	-54
IRS tax return copy fee	-5	-5	-5	-5	-5
IRS refund indicator fee	-87	-87	-87	-87	-87
Environmental Protection Agency:					
Pesticide registration fee	-15	-15	-15	....	....

Table 40 PROPOSED USER FEES AND OTHER COLLECTIONS (In millions of dollars) (continued)

Federal Trade Commission:					
Pre-merger notification filing fee	-13	-13	-13	-13	-13
Securities and Exchange Commission:					
Fee increases [1]	-378	-356	-366	-372	-377
Small Business Administration:					
Service fees	-26	-27	-28	-29	-30
Corps of Engineers:					
Wetland permit fees	-6	-12	-12	-12	-12
Subtotal, discretionary	-1,329	-1,336	-1,363	-1,371	-1,384
Mandatory: 3					
Interior:					
Hardrock royalty [2]	....	-16	-112	-110	-108
Fee collection support, National Park System	-5	-8	-10	-12	-13
National Park Renewal Fund	....	-12	-25	-34	-42
Justice:					
Surcharge on civil judgments [1]	-39	-39	-39	-39	-39
Transportation:					
Tonnage duty fees	-100	-100	-100	-100	-100
Extend rail safety	....	-39	-40	-42	-43
Treasury:					
Federal firearms dealer license fee [1]	-25	-25	-23	-23	-23
Alcohol labeling program fee [1]	-5	-5	-5	-5	-5
Explosives license and permit fees [1]	-3	-3	-3	-3	-3
Firearms importer permits [1]	-1	-1	-1	-1	-1
Alcohol and tobacco permit applications fee [1]	-6	-6	-6	-6	-6
Environmental Protection Agency:					
Reregistration of pesticides fee	-5	-5	-5	-19	-19
Subtotal, mandatory	-189	-259	-371	-395	-403
Total user fees and other collections	-1,518	-1,595	-1,734	-1,765	-1,787

Reprinted from Office of Management and Budget, Analytical Perspectives, Budget of the United States Government, Fiscal Year 1995 (Washington, D.C.: U.S. Government Printing Office, 1994), p. 48.

Table 41 TOTAL REVENUE LOSS ESTIMATES FOR TAX EXPENDITURES IN THE INCOME TAX (In millions of dollars)

	Total Revenue Loss						
	1993	1994	1995	1996	1997	1998	1999
National defense:							
Exclusion of benefits and allowances to armed forces personnel	2,115	2,060	2,030	2,020	2,015	2,030	2,055
International affairs:							
Exclusion of income earned abroad by United States citizens	510	860	895	945	1,000	1,055	1,115
Exclusion of income of foreign sales corporations	1,200	1,300	1,400	1,500	1,600	1,700	1,800
Inventory property sales source rules exception	1,100	1,200	1,300	1,400	1,500	1,600	1,700
Interest allocation rules exception for certain financial operations	100	95	95	95	95	95	95
Deferral of income from controlled foreign corporations (normal tax method)	1,600	1,600	1,700	1,800	2,000	2,200	2,400
General science, space, and technology:							
Expensing of research and experimentation expenditures (normal tax method)	2,060	2,230	2,390	2,560	2,740	2,930	3,130
Credit for increasing research activities	1,240	1,395	1,270	740	315	135	45
Suspension of the allocation of research and experimentation expenditures	0	270	270	0	0	0	0
Energy:							
Expensing of exploration and development costs:							
Oil and gas	185	145	140	100	60	55	95
Other fuels	20	20	20	20	20	25	25
Excess of percentage over cost depletion:							
Oil and gas	995	1,010	1,035	1,055	1,065	1,090	1,105
Other fuels	100	100	100	100	105	105	105
Alternative fuel production credit	760	900	970	1,000	990	940	880
Exception from passive loss limitation for working interests in oil and gas properties	50	50	50	50	50	50	50
Capital gains treatment of royalties on coal	10	15	15	15	15	15	15
Exclusion of interest on State and local IDBs for energy facilities	165	175	175	175	175	175	165
New technology credit	55	60	65	70	75	80	85
Alcohol fuel credit [1]	15	15	35	45	50	50	50
Tax credit and deduction for clean-fuel burning vehicles and properties	15	50	65	65	65	75	80
Exclusion from income of conservation subsidies provided by public utilities	50	100	145	175	190	190	190

Reprinted from Office of Management and Budget, *Analytical Perspectives, Budget of the United States Government, Fiscal Year 1995* (Washington, D.C.: U.S. Government Printing Office, 1994), p. 54.

Table 42 (an excerpt of which is displayed) showed the "outlay equivalent" of the revenue losses associated with the tax expenditures. Outlay equivalents are the amount that the federal government would have to spend to accomplish the same policy with the revenue loss. For example, the outlay equivalent of the $2,060 million tax expenditure for the exclusion of benefits and allowances to armed services personnel in 1994 shown on table 40 was estimated to be $2,395 million. The narrative included in this section explained why the outlay amounts are not generally equal to the revenue losses.

FEDERAL SPENDING

This section included six chapters. The first, *Federal Spending by Function, Subfunction, and Major Program*, was clearly the most important and is found somewhere in every president's budget. Until the fiscal 1990 budget, this chapter included a lengthy narrative description of the president's proposals, as well as a variety of tables. The Bush fiscal 1991 and 1992 budgets changed this substantially by eliminating the narrative and leaving it up to the reader to analyze the information presented. The Clinton 1995 budget continued the Bush practice.

There were two basic tables, one for budget authority (see table 43) and one for outlays. The following points should be noted.

1. Because individual programs were shown, the tables had to be in millions of dollars.
2. The first column (1993) was the actual amount of either budget authority or outlays for the fiscal year that had just been completed when the budget was submitted. The second column (1994) was the current estimate for the fiscal year that was underway when the budget was submitted to Congress. The third column (1995) was the president's proposal for the budget year.
3. The last four columns (1996–1999) showed a projection of the level requested for fiscal 1995. They were not, however, binding commitments by the White House for those years.

The next five chapters included information that in previous budgets would have been included in a separate document titled *Special*

Table 42 OUTLAY EQUIVALENT ESTIMATES FOR TAX EXPENDITURES IN THE INCOME TAX (In millions of dollars)

	Outlay Equivalents						
	1993	1994	1995	1996	1997	1998	1999
National defense:							
Exclusion of benefits and allowances to armed forces personnel	2,465	2,395	2,365	2,350	2,355	2,375	2,395
International affairs:							
Exclusion of income earned abroad by United States citizens	675	1,135	1,185	1,255	1,325	1,400	1,480
Exclusion of income of foreign sales corporations	1,845	2,000	2,155	2,310	2,460	2,615	2,770
Inventory property sales source rules exception	1,690	1,845	2,000	2,155	2,310	2,460	2,615
Interest allocation rules exception for certain financial operations	150	140	140	140	140	140	140
Deferral of income from controlled foreign corporations (normal tax method)	1,600	1,600	1,700	1,800	2,000	2,200	2,400
General science, space, and technology:							
Expensing of research and experimentation expenditures (normal tax method)	2,060	2,230	2,390	2,560	2,740	2,930	3,130
Credit for increasing research activities	1,900	2,150	1,950	1,145	485	205	65
Suspension of the allocation of research and experimentation expenditures	0	385	385	—	—	—	—
Energy:							
Expensing of exploration and development costs:							
Oil and gas	185	145	140	100	60	55	95
Other fuels	20	20	20	20	20	25	25
Excess of percentage over cost depletion:							
Oil and gas	1,400	1,425	1,455	1,480	1,505	1,535	1,560
Other fuels	140	140	140	140	150	150	150
Alternative fuel production credit	1,070	1,260	1,370	1,400	1,390	1,330	1,240
Exception from passive loss limitation for working interests in oil and gas properties	50	50	50	50	50	50	50
Capital gains treatment of royalties on coal	15	20	20	20	20	20	20
Exclusion of interest on State and local IDBs for energy facilities	235	245	250	255	250	245	240
New technology credit	85	90	95	100	105	110	115
Alcohol fuel credit [1]	15	15	35	45	50	50	50
Tax credit and deduction for clean-fuel burning vehicles and properties	20	65	90	90	95	105	110
Exclusion from income of conservation subsidies provided by public utilities	70	140	205	245	265	265	265

Reprinted from Office of Management and Budget, Analytical Perspectives, Budget of the United States Government, Fiscal Year 1995 (Washington, D.C.: U.S. Government Printing Office, 1994), p. 62.

Table 43 BUDGET AUTHORITY BY FUNCTION AND PROGRAM—(In millions of dollars)

Major missions and programs	1993 actual	1994	1995	Estimate 1996	1997	1998	1999
650 Social Security:							
651 Social security:							
Old-age and survivors insurance (OASI):							
Existing Law	271,282	283,845	296,715	311,587	326,733	342,636	359,534
Proposed legislation not subject to PAYGO			-17	-13	-8	-8	-8
Subtotal, Old-age and survivors insurance (OASI)	271,282	283,845	296,698	311,574	326,725	342,628	359,526
Disability insurance (DI):							
Existing Law	35,060	38,135	42,003	45,887	49,940	54,216	58,725
Proposed legislation not subject to PAYGO			-25	-19	-13	-13	-13
Subtotal, Disability insurance (DI)	35,060	38,135	41,978	45,868	49,927	54,203	58,712
Social security interfunds	-4	-16	-16	-16	-16	-16	-16
Total, Social Security	306,338	321,964	338,660	357,426	376,636	396,815	418,221
On-budget	(6,248)	(5,790)	(6,639)	(7,004)	(7,447)	(7,910)	(8,404)
Off-budget	(300,090)	(316,174)	(332,021)	(350,422)	(369,189)	(388,905)	(409,817)
700 Veterans benefits and services:							
701 Income security for veterans:							
Compensation:							
Existing Law	13,429	14,014	14,173	14,172	14,163	14,134	14,132
Proposed legislation not subject to PAYGO			347	790	1,266	1,753	2,264
Proposed legislation subject to PAYGO			*	*	*	*	*
Subtotal, Compensation	13,429	14,014	14,520	14,961	15,429	15,888	16,396
Pensions	3,477	3,398	3,344	3,314	3,304	3,296	3,768
Burial benefits and miscellaneous assistance	99	108	111	114	118	121	124

Reprinted from Office of Management and Budget, Analytical Perspectives, Budget of the United States Government, Fiscal Year 1995 (Washington, D.C.: U.S. Government Printing Office, 1994), p. 90.

Analyses. This document provided a variety of crosscutting looks at the impact of the administration's proposals.

The Clinton fiscal 1995 budget included the following analyses.

☐ Federal Investment Outlays and Capital Budgeting
☐ Research and Development Expenditures
☐ Underwriting Federal Credit and Insurance
☐ Aid to State and Local Governments
☐ Federal Employment

In addition, a separate section later in the document titled *Other Technical Presentations* included six other analyses.

☐ Trust Funds and Federal Funds
☐ National Income and Product Accounts
☐ Comparison of Actual to Estimated Totals for 1993
☐ Relationship of Budget Authority to Outlays
☐ Off-Budget Federal Entities
☐ Crosscutting Categories

Virtually all of the tables in these chapters were easy to read and use. In addition, the chapters included explanations that were very helpful.

Because of the growing importance of the programs it describes, one of the chapters, *Trust Funds and Federal Funds*, deserves particular attention.

Federal trust funds are special programs that are financed primarily by earmarked receipts. The largest and best known trust funds are Social Security, Medicare, unemployment, airports and airways, and highways.

Federal funds are all programs other than trust funds.

There were two major tables in this chapter. The first (table 44) showed the receipts, outlays, and surplus or deficit by "fund group," that is, categorized by either trust or federal fund. The following points should be noted.

1. The table was in billions of dollars.
2. Both trust funds and federal funds were shown.

The other table (table 45) showed the expected receipts, spending, and surplus or deficit of each of the major trust funds. The following should be noted.

Table 44 RECEIPTS, OUTLAYS, AND SURPLUS OR DEFICIT BY FUND GROUP (In billions of dollars)

	1993 actual	1994	1995	1996	1997	1998	1999
		Estimate					
Receipts:							
Federal funds cash income:							
From the public	717.7	777.9	859.4	901.1	947.1	998.5	1,051.8
From trust funds	3.9	3.9	4.1	4.2	4.3	4.4	4.5
Total, Federal funds cash income	721.6	781.8	863.4	905.3	951.4	1,002.9	1,056.3
Trust funds cash income:							
From the public	482.9	522.3	554.4	587.6	620.6	653.5	686.4
From Federal funds:							
Interest	82.3	85.8	88.9	92.5	98.1	104.3	111.1
Other	136.3	121.5	120.5	145.6	160.4	168.7	179.2
Total, trust funds cash income	701.5	729.6	763.8	825.7	879.1	926.6	976.7
Offsetting receipts	-269.6	-262.4	-273.4	-303.7	-325.4	-342.6	-360.1
Total, unified budget receipts	1,153.5	1,249.1	1,353.8	1,427.3	1,505.1	1,586.9	1,672.9
Outlays:							
Federal funds cash outgo	1,076.3	1,116.2	1,131.1	1,194.0	1,267.9	1,336.8	1,389.4
Trust funds cash outgo	601.5	630.0	661.2	706.5	748.9	783.2	824.7
Offsetting receipts	-269.6	-262.4	-273.4	-303.7	-325.4	-342.6	-360.1
Total, unified budget outlays	1,408.2	1,483.8	1,518.9	1,596.9	1,691.4	1,777.4	1,854.0
Surplus or deficit (-):							
Federal funds	-354.7	-334.4	-267.7	-288.8	-316.5	-333.8	-333.1
Trust funds	100.0	99.6	102.6	119.2	130.1	143.4	152.0
Total, unified surplus/deficit (-)	-254.7	-234.8	-165.1	-169.6	-186.4	-190.5	-181.1

Reprinted from Office of Management and Budget, *Analytical Perspectives, Budget of the United States Government, Fiscal Year 1995* (Washington, D.C.: U.S. Government Printing Office, 1994), p. 246.

Table 45 INCOME, OUTGO, AND BALANCES OF MAJOR TRUST FUNDS (In billions of dollars) **1**

| | 1993 actual | Estimate | | | | | |
		1994	1995	1996	1997	1998	1999
Federal old-age, survivors and disability insurance trust funds							
Balance, start of year	327.1	373.9	430.9	494.0	561.0	639.7	727.3
Income:							
Governmental receipts	311.9	336.2	355.2	374.7	397.5	421.4	445.1
Proprietary receipts	....	....	....	....	....	....	....
Receipts from Federal funds:							
Interest	26.8	29.1	31.7	34.9	38.8	43.2	48.0
Other	12.7	12.3	13.4	14.2	15.1	16.2	17.3
Receipts from Trust funds	....	....	....	....	....	....	....
Subtotal, income	351.4	377.5	400.3	423.8	451.4	480.7	510.4
Outgo:							
To the public	300.8	316.5	333.1	352.7	368.5	388.8	410.0
Payments to Other funds	3.8	3.9	4.0	4.2	4.2	4.3	4.4
Subtotal, outgo	304.6	320.5	337.2	356.9	372.7	393.1	414.4
Change in fund balance:							
Surplus or deficit (-):							
Excluding interest	20.0	28.0	31.4	32.0	39.9	44.5	48.1
Interest	26.8	29.1	31.7	34.9	38.8	43.2	48.0
Subtotal, surplus or deficit (-)	46.8	57.1	63.1	67.0	78.6	87.7	96.1
Adjustments:							
Transfers/lapses (net)	....	....	....	....	....	....	....
Other adjustments	....	....	....	....	....	....	....
Total, change in fund balance	46.8	57.1	63.1	67.0	78.6	87.7	96.1

2 (Governmental receipts / Receipts from Federal funds)

Reprinted from Office of Management and Budget, Analytical Perspectives, Budget of the United States Government, Fiscal Year 1995 (Washington, D.C.: U.S. Government Printing Office, 1994), p. 251.

1. The table was in billions of dollars.
2. "Governmental receipts" are primarily taxes. "Proprietary receipts" are derived from business-like transactions between the federal government and the public. "Interfund receipts" are receipts by one fund or payments from a program in the federal funds group.

FEDERAL BORROWING AND DEBT

This section included one chapter, which dealt with the impact of the Clinton Administration's proposals on the federal deficit and national debt.

The tables in this chapter were relatively easy to read and use. However, as table 46 shows, several things should be kept in mind.

1. The table was in billions of dollars. This means that $4,676.0 billion is $4.7 trillion.
2. The federal government borrows from the public and from various government accounts. "Gross federal debt" is the sum of these two.
3. Most federal debt is issued by the Treasury and is commonly referred to as "public debt." Several individual federal agencies also issue debt and this is known appropriately as "agency debt."

BUDGET ENFORCEMENT ACT PREVIEW REPORT

This section included the report required by the Budget Enforcement Act along with other materials. As explained in chapters 2 and 6 of *The Guide to the Federal Budget*, BEA requires that the Office of Management and Budget send to Congress a sequester "preview" report on or before the day that the president's budget is submitted.

As is the case with the other two sequester reports that BEA requires—the update report in August and the final report 15 days after Congress adjourns for the year—the preview report must include revised estimates of the discretionary spending cap and a pay-as-you-go status report based on mandatory spending and entitlement legislation enacted the previous session of Congress. Through fiscal 1995, a projection of the deficit for the budget year compared with the maximum deficit amount was also required.

Table 46 FEDERAL GOVERNMENT FINANCING AND DEBT (In billions of dollars)

	1993 actual	Estimate					
		1994	1995	1996	1997	1998	1999
FINANCING							
Surplus or deficit (−)	−254.7	−234.8	−165.1	−169.6	−186.4	−190.5	−181.1
(On-budget)	−300.0	−290.1	−225.0	−236.3	−265.5	−279.2	−278.6
(Off-budget)	45.3	55.3	59.9	66.7	79.2	88.7	97.6
Means of financing other than borrowing from the public:							
Change in:[2]							
Treasury operating cash balance	6.3	12.5	—	—	—	—	—
Checks outstanding, etc.[3]	0.4	−0.9	−0.4	—	—	—	—
Deposit fund balances	−0.4	−0.5	−1.7	—	—	—	—
Seigniorage on coins	0.4	0.6	0.6	0.6	0.6	0.6	0.6
Less: Net financing disbursements:							
Direct loan financing accounts	−3.8	−6.4	−10.1	−15.9	−17.9	−18.9	−19.0
Guaranteed loan financing accounts	4.6	4.2	3.0	2.5	2.3	1.4	0.4
Total, means of financing other than borrowing from the public	7.4	9.5	−8.6	−12.8	−15.0	−16.8	−18.0
Total, requirement for borrowing from the public	−247.3	−225.2	−173.7	−182.4	−201.4	−207.3	−199.1
Reclassification of debt[4]	−1.3	—	—	—	—	—	—
Change in debt held by the public	248.5	225.2	173.7	182.4	201.4	207.3	199.1
DEBT, END OF YEAR[1]							
Gross Federal debt:							
Debt issued by Treasury	4,326.5	4,652.1	4,936.0	5,243.0	5,577.2	5,929.4	6,281.4
Debt issued by other agencies	24.8	23.9	24.2	24.1	24.1	24.1	24.1
Total, gross Federal debt	4,351.2	4,676.0	4,960.1	5,267.1	5,601.3	5,953.5	6,305.4
Held by:							
Government accounts	1,104.0	1,203.6	1,314.0	1,438.5	1,571.3	1,716.3	1,869.1

Reprinted from Office of Management and Budget, *Analytical Perspectives, Budget of the United States Government, Fiscal Year 1995* (Washington, D.C.: U.S. Government Printing Office, 1994), p. 187.

In addition, OMB must explain any differences between its estimates and those provided by the Congressional Budget Office in its sequestration report, which is required to be submitted to Congress at least five days before the president's budget is released.

The fiscal 1995 report included four key tables.

The first table dealt with the discretionary spending limits between fiscal 1991 and 1995. When using table 47, the following should be noted.

1. The table was in millions of dollars.
2. Both budget authority and outlays were shown.
3. The first column was the first year that BEA was in effect.
4. This line shows the revised limit based on all of the adjustments that were either required or allowed to be made by BEA.

The second table (table 48) showed the discretionary spending limits between 1994 and 1998 and how they would be affected by the proposals in the Clinton fiscal 1995 budget. The following points should be noted.

1. The table was in billions of dollars.
2. Both budget authority and outlays were shown.
3. The figures for the president's proposals for 1996–1999 were only estimates based on the fiscal 1995 request.

The third table (table 49) displayed the pay-as-you-go impact of the proposals enacted as of December 31, 1993. The following points should be noted.

1. The table was in million of dollars.
2. Only outlays were shown because that is what affects the deficit.

The fourth table in this section (table 50) showed the revised BEA maximum deficit amounts compared with the deficit in the president's budget. The following points should be noted.

1. The table was in billions of dollars.
2. Only outlays were shown because that is what affects the deficit.

The next two chapters in this section provided updated estimates for two budget procedures that were established by executive orders issued by President Clinton in 1993.

Table 47 SUMMARY OF CHANGES TO DISCRETIONARY SPENDING LIMITS, 1991–1995 (In millions of dollars)

		1991	1992	1993	1994	1995
TOTAL DISCRETIONARY						
Statutory Caps as Set in OBRA 1990	BA	491.7	503.4	511.5	510.8	517.7
	OL	514.4	524.9	534.0	534.8	540.8
Adjustments for Allowances	BA		3.6	2.9	2.9	
	OL	2.6	3.1	2.7	3.4	1.3
Adjustments for IRS Funding, IMF, and Debt Forgiveness	BA	0.2	0.2	12.5	0.2	0.2
	OL	0.3	0.3	0.3	0.4	
Adjustments for Changes in Inflation	BA		-0.5	-5.1	-9.5	-11.8
	OL		-0.3	-2.5	-5.8	-8.8
Adjustments for Redefinition of Concepts (credit reform, etc.), and credit reestimates	BA		7.7	8.7	8.6	9.3
	OL		1.1	2.9	2.8	3.4
Adjustments for Emergency Requirements[1]	BA	0.9	8.3	4.6	0.4	
	OL	1.1	1.8	5.4	4.3	1.6
Subtotal, Adjustments Excluding Desert Shield/Desert Storm	BA	1.1	19.3	23.6	2.6	-2.5
	OL	3.9	5.9	8.8	5.1	-2.2
Adjustments for Desert Shield/Desert Storm	BA	44.2	14.0	0.6	*	*
	OL	33.3	14.9	7.5	2.8	1.0
Preview Report Discretionary Spending Limits	BA	537.1	536.6	535.7	513.4	515.2
	OL	551.6	545.7	550.3	542.7	539.6

Reprinted from Office of Management and Budget, Analytical Perspectives, Budget of the United States Government, Fiscal Year 1995 (Washington, D.C.: U.S. Government Printing Office, 1994), p. 197.

Table 48 DISCRETIONARY SPENDING LIMITS, 1994–1998 (In billions of dollars)

		1994	1995	1996	1997	1998
Total discretionary spending limits, December 10, 1993 Final Sequester Report	BA	513,177	517,398	519,142	528,079	530,639
	OL	542,606	540,498	547,733	547,502	547,875
Adjustments:						
1993 Inflation	BA		-2,023			
	OL		-849			
Reestimates of credit reform subsidies	BA		57	58	59	61
	OL		16	38	44	50
Statutory and other shifts between categories	BA		-254	-569	-583	-608
	OL		-110	-638	-844	-871
Emergency appropriations (release of contingencies)	BA	186				
	OL	102	75	5	1	1
Reestimates of emergency flood spending	BA					
	OL		6	180	176	
Subtotal, adjustments for the Preview Report	BA	186	-2,220	-511	-524	-547
	OL	102	-862	-415	-623	-820
Preview Report discretionary limits	BA	513,363	515,178	518,631	527,555	530,092
	OL	542,708	539,636	547,318	546,879	547,055
Further adjustments authorized under the Budget Enforcement Act:						
IRS funding	BA		188			
	OL		184			
Special allowances	BA		2,880			
	OL		1,438	753	396	134
Proposed emergency supplemental appropriations	BA	1,942				
	OL	1,124	642	96	30	17
Estimated discretionary spending limits including IRS, special allowances, and emergencies	BA	515,305	518,246	518,631	527,555	530,092
	OL	543,832	541,900	548,167	547,305	547,206

Reprinted from Office of Management and Budget, Analytical Perspectives, Budget of the United States Government, Fiscal Year 1995 (Washington, D.C.: U.S. Government Printing Office, 1994), p. 199.

Table 49 PAY-AS-YOU-GO LEGISLATION ENACTED AS OF DECEMBER 31, 1993
(In millions of dollars)

	Change in the Baseline deficit				
	1994	1995	1996	1997	1998
Revenue impact of enacted legislation	−1,265	−1,194	221	166	−629
Outlay impact of enacted legislation	1,270	225	−671	−635	−485
Total impact of enacted legislation	4	−969	−450	−469	−1,114
MEMORANDUM					
Deficit impact of OBRA 1993: [1]					
Revenue impact	−27,419	−46,948	−54,333	−62,836	−58,559
Outlay impact	−19,333	−35,765	−46,221	−66,062	−87,287
Total impact of OBRA 1993—Public Law 103–66	−46,752	−82,713	−100,554	−128,898	−145,846

Reprinted from Office of Management and Budget, *Analytical Perspectives, Budget of the United States Government, Fiscal Year 1995* (Washington, D.C.: U.S. Government Printing Office, 1994), p. 200.

Review of Direct Spending and Receipts dealt with the mandatory spending targets established in Executive Order 12857 (see chapter 2) issued by President Clinton in August 1993. That order requires that the targets be adjusted for a variety of circumstances, such as increases in the number of people who are eligible to receive benefits under current law. The tables in this chapter, which are presented in a straightforward manner and are easy to read and use, provide the details on these adjustments.

Deficit Reduction Fund dealt with Executive Order 12858, which was also issued by President Clinton in August 1993. This order requires that amounts equal to the spending cuts and revenue increases resulting from the Omnibus Budget Reconciliation Act of 1993 be credited to a fund. This one-page chapter provided the status of that fund.

Current Services. According to the Clinton fiscal 1995 budget, "the current services baseline is designed to show what receipts, outlays, deficits, and budget authority would be if no changes are made to laws already enacted."

This chapter included a number of tables. Some showed the economic or programmatic assumptions on which the estimates were based and are largely self-explanatory. Others showed the differences between what the president had proposed and what would be spent or collected if current law were continued without change. Any proposal that deviated from the current services level for an activity showed an increase or decrease from existing policy.

Table 50 MAXIMUM DEFICIT AMOUNTS (In billions of dollars) **1**

	1995
Maximum deficit amount before adjustments	287.2
Change in deposit insurance	−10.4
Other adjustments for up-to-date economic and technical assumptions ...	−37.5
Current maximum deficit amount	239.2
Current estimated deficit	238.2
Excess deficit	−1.0
MEMORANDUM	
Current maximum deficit amount	239.2
End-of-session cap adjustment [1]	2.3
Related debt service	0.1
Subtotal	2.4
End-of-session maximum deficit amount	241.5

Reprinted from Office of Management and Budget, *Analytical Perspectives, Budget of the United States Government, Fiscal Year 1995* (Washington, D.C.: U.S. Government Printing Office, 1994), p. 201.

Table 51, which displayed the president's receipts proposals by source, is typical of what was shown. The following should be noted.

1. The table was in billions of dollars.
2. The first column (1993 actual) showed the actual amount of revenue collected by the federal government from each of the noted sources.
3. The remaining columns (1994–1999) showed the current services baseline level of revenues, that is, the amount that would be collected if current law was not changed.

The final major section[1] was a series of very useful tables showing *Federal Programs by Agency and Account*. These tables showed all the programs administered by each department and agency regardless of their function. Note the following points in table 52.

1. The table was in millions of dollars.
2. Budget authority and outlays were both listed.
3. Activities within the same department or agency are often distributed among several different functions. In this table some programs

Table 51 BASELINE RECEIPTS BY SOURCE (In billions of dollars)

	1993 actual	1994	1995	1996	1997	1998	1999
				Estimates			
Individual income taxes	509.7	550.0	597.1	631.0	664.4	699.1	739.7
Corporation income taxes	117.5	130.7	141.0	146.4	150.3	152.9	157.5
Social insurance taxes and contributions	428.3	461.9	492.1	518.7	546.4	576.4	605.1
On-budget	116.4	125.7	135.6	142.3	149.1	156.4	162.5
Off-budget	311.9	336.2	356.6	376.4	397.3	420.0	442.6
Excise taxes	48.1	54.6	55.8	56.6	57.8	58.8	60.2
Other	50.0	52.0	55.6	57.8	60.8	63.9	66.7
Total	1,153.5	1,249.1	1,341.6	1,410.4	1,479.6	1,551.0	1,629.2
On-budget	(841.6)	(913.0)	(985.1)	(1,034.1)	(1,082.3)	(1,131.1)	(1,186.6)
Off-budget	(311.9)	(336.2)	(356.6)	(376.4)	(397.3)	(420.0)	(442.6)

Reprinted from Office of Management and Budget, Analytical Perspectives, Budget of the United States Government, Fiscal Year 1995 (Washington, D.C.: U.S. Government Printing Office, 1994), p. 218.

Table 52 DEPARTMENT OF HOUSING AND URBAN DEVELOPMENT
(In millions of dollars) **1**

Account		1993 actual	1994 estimate	1995 estimate

Housing Programs
Federal funds

General and Special Funds:

Housing programs annual contributions for assisted housing:

Appropriation, current	604 BA	8,597	9,313	9,469
Appropriation, permanent	BA **2**	100	....	....
Outlays	O	14,484	13,975	13,995
Outlays for grants to State and local governments	O	(8,899)	(8,107)	(7,881)
Appropriation, current	BA		A – 46	
Outlays	O		A – 3	A – 5
Appropriation, current	BA		H – 180	
Outlays	O		H – 5	H – 30
Outlays for grants to State and local governments	O			H (– 13)
Total Housing programs annual contributions for assisted housing	BA	8,697	9,087	9,469
	O	14,484	13,967	13,959

Other assisted housing programs (Community development): **3**

(Reappropriation)	(451) BA	3	....	....
(Outlays)	O	1	1	....
(Outlays for grants to State and local governments)	O	(1)	(1)	....
(Housing assistance): **3**				
(Appropriation, current)	(604) BA	....	– 72	– 281
(Outlays)	O	796	816	806
Total Other assisted housing programs	BA	3	– 72	– 281
	O	797	817	806

Reprinted from Office of Management and Budget, *Analytical Perspectives, Budget of the United States Government, Fiscal Year 1995* (Washington, D.C.: U.S. Government Printing Office, 1994), p. 355.

of the Department of Housing and Urban Development were in subfunction 451 (a subfunction of function 450: Community and Regional Development) and some were in subfunction 604 (Income Security).

Note

1. Another section followed this one in the fiscal 1995 budget—Budget System and Concepts and Glossary. It did not, however, provide any specific information on the Clinton budget proposal but was instead a general overview of the federal budget process.

Chapter Eleven

BUDGET OF THE UNITED STATES GOVERNMENT, APPENDIX

This document of the Clinton fiscal 1995 budget provided the most details on the president's proposals.

Federal Programs by Function and Subfunction. Until the fiscal 1990 budget, this part of the budget included a lengthy narrative description of the president's proposals, as well as a variety of tables. The Bush fiscal 1991 and 1992 budgets changed this substantially by eliminating the narrative entirely and leaving it up to the reader to know what each program was intended to do. In a return to past practice, the Clinton fiscal 1995 budget included narratives for most programs.

DETAILED BUDGET ESTIMATES

This section included the same material that prior to the Bush fiscal 1991 budget was displayed in the Budget of the United States Government, Appendix.

This was the most detailed of all the sections in the Clinton budget. For each department and agency, the appendix included, by appropriations account, the following:

1. The proposed text of appropriations language;
2. A detailed expenditure and financing schedule;
3. New legislative proposals, if any;
4. An explanation of the work to be performed and the funds needed; and
5. A schedule of permanent positions.

It also included proposed general provisions applicable to the appropriations of entire agencies or groups of agencies; supplemental

DRUG ENFORCEMENT ADMINISTRATION

Federal Funds

General and special funds:

SALARIES AND EXPENSES

For necessary expenses of the Drug Enforcement Administration, including not to exceed $70,000 to meet unforeseen emergencies of a confidential character, to be expended under the direction of, and to be accounted for solely under the certificate of, the Attorney General; expenses for conducting drug education and training programs, including travel and related expenses for participants in such programs and the distribution of items of token value that promote the goals of such programs; purchase of not to exceed [1,117] *1,115* passenger motor vehicles [of which 1,117 are] for replacement only for police-type use without regard to the general purchase price limitation for the current fiscal year; and acquisition, lease, maintenance, and operation of aircraft; [$722,000,000] *$723,714,000,* of which not to exceed $1,800,000 for research shall remain available until expended, and of which not to exceed $4,000,000 for purchase of evidence and payments for information, not to exceed $4,000,000 for contracting for ADP and telecommunications equipment, and not to exceed $2,000,000 for technical and laboratory equipment shall remain available until September 30, [1995] *1996,* and of which not to exceed [$45,000] *$50,000* shall be available for official reception and representation expenses. *(Reorganization Plan No. 2 of 1973; Reorganization Plan No. 1 of 1968; 21 U.S.C. 801–966 as amended; 40 U.S.C. 304; Department of Justice and Related Agencies Appropriations Act, 1994.)*

Reprinted from Office of Management and Budget, Budget of the United States Government Appendix, Fiscal Year 1995 (Washington, D.C.: U.S. Government Printing Office, 1994), p. 594.

and rescission proposals; advance appropriations, advance funding, and forward funding; and budget estimates for government-sponsored enterprises (GSEs) and the Board of Governors of the Federal Reserve Board.

Each appropriation account in every department and agency was explained with the following four elements:

1. Proposed Text of Appropriations Language

The appropriations language proposed for the coming fiscal year was listed under its account title, for example, "Salaries and Expenses" of the Drug Enforcement Administration in the paragraph shown above. The items enclosed with the bold-type brackets "[ ]" were proposed for deletion from the then current-year (1995) appropriation. The material in italic type was proposed substitute or additional language. At the end of the paragraph, printed in italic type in parentheses, were citations to any relevant authorizing legislation and to the appropriations act from which the basic text of the proposed language was taken.

2. Program and Financing Schedule

Table 53 was the basic table. Note the following points in the example shown from the Drug Enforcement Administration.

1. Unlike most other tables in the budget, this one was in thousands of dollars.
2. Everything in this section was in terms of budget authority. The final figure, circled in the third column, was the total budget authority requested.
3. The first column (1993 actual) contained the actual figures for the fiscal year just completed. The second column (1994) contained the most recent estimate of the spending that was expected to occur in the then current fiscal year. The third column (1995) was the president's proposal for the coming fiscal year.
4. This section referred to outlays.

3. Narrative Statement of Program and Performance

Narrative statements, such as the excerpt on page 153 from the Drug Enforcement Administration, presented the objectives of the program and purpose of the appropriation.

4. Object Classification Schedules

The "object classes," such as the one shown in table 54 from the Drug Enforcement Administration, indicated the nature of the things proposed for purchase. Note the following points.

1. The table was in thousands of dollars.
2. The first column (1993 actual) contained the actual figures for the fiscal year that had just been completed. The second column (1994) contained the most recent estimate of the spending expected in the then current fiscal year. The third column (1995) was the president's proposal for the coming fiscal year.

Table 53 PROGRAM AND FINANCING (In thousands of dollars) **1**

Identification code 15–1100–0–1–751	1993 actual	1994 est.	1995 est.
Program by activities:			
Direct program:			
00.01 Enforcement	424,640	415,079	413,380
00.02 Investigative support	254,916	243,079	232,189
00.04 Program direction	78,174	85,192	78,145
00.91 Total direct program	757,730	743,350	723,714
01.01 Reimbursable program	189,562	187,010	187,010
10.00 Total obligations	947,292	930,360	910,724
Financing:			
17.00 Recovery of prior year obligations	−1,473		
21.40 Unobligated balance available, start of year: Treasury balance	−24,059	−10,112	−4,000
24.40 Unobligated balance available, end of year: Treasury balance	10,112	4,000	4,000
25.00 Unobligated balance expiring	43		
39.00 **Budget authority (gross)**	**931,915**	**924,248**	**910,724**
Budget authority:			
Current:			
40.00 Appropriation	718,684	722,000	723,714
41.00 Transferred to other accounts	−6,520		
42.00 Transferred from other accounts	18,194	15,238	
43.00 **Appropriation (total)**	**730,358**	**737,238**	**723,714**
50.00 **Reappropriation**	**6,520**		
Permanent:			
60.25 **Appropriation (special fund, indefinite)**	**5,475**		
68.00 Spending authority from offsetting collections	189,562	187,010	187,010
Relation of obligations to outlays:			
71.00 Total obligations	947,292	930,360	910,724
72.40 Obligated balance, start of year: Treasury balance	143,653	81,043	203,098
74.40 Obligated balance, end of year: Treasury balance	−81,043	−203,098	−261,641
77.00 Adjustments in expired accounts	−35,979		
78.00 Adjustments in unexpired accounts	−1,473		
87.00 Outlays (gross)	972,450	808,305	852,181
Adjustments to gross budget authority and outlays:			
Offsetting collections from:			
Federal funds:			
88.00 Federal funds	−87,153	−84,858	−87,639
88.00 Federal funds (Drug Enforcement)	−99,348	−99,152	−96,371
88.40 Non-Federal sources	−3,061	−3,000	−3,000
88.90 **Total, offsetting collections**	**−189,562**	**−187,010**	**−187,010**
89.00 **Budget authority (net)**	**742,353**	**737,238**	**723,714**
90.00 **Outlays (net)**	**782,888**	**621,295**	**665,171**

3 (marker beside identification code row)

2 (markers beside rows 39.00, 43.00, and 89.00)

4 (bracket marker beside rows 71.00–87.00)

Note.—Includes $117 thousand in budget authority in 1995 for Mail Operations transferred from Salaries and Expenses, General Administration.

Reprinted from Office of Management and Budget, *Budget of the United States Government Appendix, Fiscal Year 1995* (Washington, D.C.: U.S. Government Printing Office, 1994), p. 594.

The 1995 request for the Drug Enforcement Administration (DEA) provides sufficient resources to permit that the number of agents in 1995 remain at 1994 levels. The mission of the DEA is to control abuse of narcotics and dangerous drugs by restricting the aggregate supply of those drugs. At the Federal level, DEA is the lead drug law enforcement agency. DEA accomplishes its objectives through coordination with State, local, and other Federal officials in drug enforcement activities, development and maintenance of drug intelligence systems, regulation of legitimate controlled substances activities, and enforcement coordination and intelligence-gathering activities with foreign government agencies.

Cooperation among Federal law enforcement agencies is extensive, especially within the 13 organized crime drug enforcement task forces (OCDETF). DEA's involvement is integral to this nationwide coordinated enforcement strategy. With the OCDETF program and the expansion of other agency cooperative efforts, overall drug enforcement capabilities have been significantly strengthened in recent years.

Reprinted from Office of Management and Budget, *Budget of the United States Government Appendix, Fiscal Year 1995* (Washington, D.C.: U.S. Government Printing Office, 1994), p. 594.

3. The total for 1995 is the same as the total for 1995 in line 10.00 of table 53.

A personnel summary for the account, such as the one displayed in table 55 for the United States Secret Service, usually followed the object classification schedule. Note that the table was in actual numbers.

Table 54   OBJECT CLASSIFICATION (In thousands of dollars) **1**

Identification code 15–1100–0–1–751	1993 actual	1994 est.	1995 est.	**2**
Direct obligations:				
Personnel compensation:				
11.1 Full-time permanent	261,327	257,446	261,695	
11.3 Other than full-time permanent	2,517	2,108	2,028	
11.5 Other personnel compensation	47,677	43,891	41,721	
11.8 Special personal services payments	337	....	....	
11.9 Total personnel compensation	311,858	303,445	305,444	
12.1 Civilian personnel benefits	89,598	99,929	95,285	
13.0 Benefits for former personnel	66	19	19	
21.0 Travel and transportation of persons	25,452	30,469	29,029	
22.0 Transportation of things	2,677	2,808	3,146	
23.1 Rental payments to GSA	55,300	72,448	68,327	
23.2 Rental payments to others	14,617	5,930	6,607	
23.3 Communications, utilities, and miscellaneous charges	41,781	60,861	61,661	
24.0 Printing and reproduction	1,311	1,719	1,684	
25.1 Consulting services	7,840	30,566	26,829	
25.2 Other services	123,465	81,859	86,135	
26.0 Supplies and materials	27,449	20,957	20,563	
31.0 Equipment	42,169	23,985	18,670	
32.0 Land and structures	13,768	8,193	154	
41.0 Grants, subsidies, and contributions	49	....	....	
42.0 Insurance claims and indemnities	330	162	161	
99.0 Subtotal, direct obligations	757,730	743,350	723,714	
99.0 Reimbursable obligations	189,562	187,010	187,010	
99.9 Total obligations	947,292	930,360	910,724	**3**

Reprinted from Office of Management and Budget, *Budget of the United States Government Appendix, Fiscal Year 1995* (Washington, D.C.: U.S. Government Printing Office, 1994), p. 595.

Table 55   U.S. SECRET SERVICE PERSONNEL SUMMARY

Identification code 20–1408–0–1–751	1993 actual	1994 est.	1995 est.
Total compensable workyears:			
1001 Full-time equivalent employment	4,567	4,659	4,588
1005 Full-time equivalent of overtime and holiday hours	1,128	1,075	1,079

Reprinted from Office of Management and Budget, *Budget of the United States Government Appendix, Fiscal Year 1995* (Washington, D.C.: U.S. Government Printing Office, 1994), p. 743.

Chapter Twelve

BUDGET OF THE UNITED STATES GOVERNMENT—HISTORICAL TABLES

After years of being available only in photocopy form to budget insiders, *Historical Tables* was published for the first time as a separate document in 1985. Prior to leaving office in January 1993, President Bush submitted to Congress a final budget document, *Budget Baselines, Historical Data and Alternatives for the Future*, that included all of the material that had previously been in the separate document.

In the fiscal 1995 Clinton budget, the tables in this document displayed information over a considerably longer period than the other documents of the budget—in some cases going back more than 50 years. Although the federal budget has greatly changed during this period, the figures in these tables were adjusted so that accurate comparisons could be made.

The tables were arranged into common themes. For example, part seven had five tables dealing with government receipts:

Table 2.1—Receipts by Source: 1934–1999
Table 2.2—Percentage Composition of Receipts by Source: 1934–1999
Table 2.3—Receipts by Source as Percentages of GDP: 1934–1999
Table 2.4—Composition of Social Insurance Taxes and Contributions of Excise Taxes: 1940–1999
Table 2.5—Composition of "Other Receipts": 1940–1999

Although the information in these tables was considerably drier and less interesting to read than the material presented in other parts of the budget, it was free from partisan interpretation. As a result, it was extremely useful.

Fifteen themes were included in the Clinton fiscal 1995 *Historical Tables*, as follows:

1. Overview of Federal Government Finances;

2. Composition of Federal Government Receipts;
3. Federal Government Outlays by Function;
4. Federal Government Outlays by Agency;
5. Budget Authority (On- and Off-Budget);
6. Composition of Federal Government Outlays;
7. Federal Debt;
8. Outlays by Budget Enforcement Act Categories;
9. Federal Government Outlays for Major Physical Capital Investment;
10. Federal Government Outlays for the Conduct of Research and Development and for the Conduct of Education and Training;
11. Federal Government Payments for Individuals;
12. Federal Grants to State and Local Governments;
13. Social Security and Medicare;
14. Federal Sector Transactions in the National Income and Product Accounts; and
15. Total (Federal and State, and Local) Government Finances.

The tables for each of these sections varied considerably, although many were similar to those found in other parts of the budget. All were comparatively easy to read and use.

CONCURRENT RESOLUTION ON THE BUDGET, FISCAL YEARS 1994-1998

103D CONGRESS 1st Session	HOUSE OF REPRESENTATIVES	REPORT 103–48

CONCURRENT RESOLUTION SETTING FORTH THE CONGRESSIONAL BUDGET FOR THE UNITED STATES GOVERNMENT FOR THE FISCAL YEARS 1994, 1995, 1996, 1997, and 1998

MARCH 31, 1993.—ORDERED TO BE PRINTED

Mr. SABO, from the committee of conference, submitted the following

CONFERENCE REPORT

[To accompany H. Con. Res. 64]

The committee of conference on the disagreeing votes of the two Houses on the amendment of the Senate to the concurrent resolution (H. Con. Res. 64), setting forth the congressional budget for the United States Government for the fiscal years 1994, 1995, 1996, 1997, and 1998, having met, after full and free conference, have agreed to recommend and do recommend to their respective Houses as follows:

That the House recede from its disagreement to the amendment of the Senate to the text of the resolution and agree to the same with an amendment as follows:

In lieu of the matter proposed to be inserted by the Senate amendment, insert the following:

SECTION 1. CONCURRENT RESOLUTION ON THE BUDGET FOR FISCAL YEAR 1994.

(a) *DECLARATION.—The Congress determines and declares that this resolution is the concurrent resolution on the budget for fiscal year 1994, including the appropriate budgetary levels for fiscal years 1995, 1996, 1997, and 1998, as required by section 301 of the Congressional Budget Act of 1974 (as amended by the Budget Enforcement Act of 1990).*

(b) *TABLE OF CONTENTS.—The table of contents for this concurrent resolution is as follows:*

Sec. 1. Concurrent resolution on the budget for fiscal year 1994.
Sec. 2. Recommended levels and amounts.
Sec. 3. Debt increase as a measure of deficit.
Sec. 4. Display of Federal retirement trust fund balances.

SEC. 2. RECOMMENDED LEVELS AND AMOUNTS.

The following budgetary levels are appropriate for the fiscal years 1994, 1995, 1996, 1997, and 1998:

(1) FEDERAL REVENUES.—*(A) For purposes of comparison with the maximum deficit amount under sections 601(a)(1) and 606 of the Congressional Budget Act of 1974 and for purposes of the enforcement of this resolution—*

(i) *The recommended levels of Federal revenues are as follows:*

Fiscal year 1994: $905,500,000,000.
Fiscal year 1995: $973,800,000,000.
Fiscal year 1996: $1,037,600,000,000.
Fiscal year 1997: $1,093,300,000,000.
Fiscal year 1998: $1,143,200,000,000.

(ii) *The amounts by which the aggregate levels of Federal revenues should be increased are as follows:*

Fiscal year 1994: $27,400,000,000.
Fiscal year 1995: $40,400,000,000.
Fiscal year 1996: $58,000,000,000.
Fiscal year 1997: $73,600,000,000.
Fiscal year 1998: $73,200,000,000.

(iii) *The amounts for Federal Insurance Contributions Act revenues for hospital insurance within the recommended levels of Federal revenues are as follows:*

Fiscal year 1994: $90,200,000,000.
Fiscal year 1995: $98,800,000,000.
Fiscal year 1996: $104,200,000,000.
Fiscal year 1997: $109,100,000,000.
Fiscal year 1998: $114,000,000,000.

(B) *For purposes of section 710 of the Social Security Act (excluding the receipts and disbursements of the Hospital Insurance Trust Fund)—*

(i) *The recommended levels of Federal revenues are as follows:*

Fiscal year 1994: $812,400,000,000.
Fiscal year 1995: $858,900,000,000.
Fiscal year 1996: $926,500,000,000.
Fiscal year 1997: $976,500,000,000.
Fiscal year 1998: $1,020,700,000,000.

(ii) *The amounts by which the aggregate levels of Federal revenues should be increased are as follows:*

Fiscal year 1994: $21,800,000,000.
Fiscal year 1995: $28,300,000,000.
Fiscal year 1996: $44,700,000,000.
Fiscal year 1997: $59,100,000,000.
Fiscal year 1998: $57,600,000,000.

(2) NEW BUDGET AUTHORITY.—(A) For purposes of comparison with the maximum deficit amount under sections 601(a)(1) and 606 of the Congressional Budget Act of 1974 and for purposes of the enforcement of this resolution, the appropriate levels of total new budget authority are as follows:

Fiscal year 1994: $1,223,400,000,000.
Fiscal year 1995: $1,289,600,000,000.
Fiscal year 1996: $1,347,500,000,000.
Fiscal year 1997: $1,409,900,000,000.
Fiscal year 1998: $1,474,500,000,000.

(B) For purposes of section 710 of the Social Security Act (excluding the receipts and disbursements of the Hospital Insurance Trust Fund), the appropriate levels of total new budget authority are as follows:

Fiscal year 1994: $1,136,400,000,000.
Fiscal year 1995: $1,192,100,000,000.
Fiscal year 1996: $1,239,100,000,000.
Fiscal year 1997: $1,290,300,000,000.
Fiscal year 1998: $1,341,800,000,000.

(3) BUDGET OUTLAYS.—(A) For purposes of comparison with the maximum deficit amount under sections 601(a)(1) and 606 of the Congressional Budget Act of 1974 and for purposes of the enforcement of this resolution, the appropriate levels of total budget outlays are as follows:

Fiscal year 1994: $1,218,300,000,000.
Fiscal year 1995: $1,280,600,000,000.
Fiscal year 1996: $1,323,200,000,000.
Fiscal year 1997: $1,371,300,000,000.
Fiscal year 1998: $1,435,900,000,000.

(B) For purposes of section 710 of the Social Security Act (excluding the receipts and disbursements of the Hospital Insurance Trust Fund), the appropriate levels of total budget outlays are as follows:

Fiscal year 1994: $1,133,000,000,000.
Fiscal year 1995: $1,184,500,000,000.
Fiscal year 1996: $1,216,100,000,000.
Fiscal year 1997: $1,252,300,000,000.
Fiscal year 1998: $1,303,600,000,000.

(4) DEFICITS.—(A) For purposes of comparison with the maximum deficit amount under sections 601(a)(1) and 606 of the Congressional Budget Act of 1974 and for purposes of the enforcement of this resolution, the amounts of the deficits are as follows:

Fiscal year 1994: $312,800,000,000.
Fiscal year 1995: $306,800,000,000.
Fiscal year 1996: $285,600,000,000.
Fiscal year 1997: $278,000,000,000.
Fiscal year 1998: $292,700,000,000.

(B) For purposes of section 710 of the Social Security Act (excluding the receipts and disbursements of the Hospital Insurance Trust Fund), the amounts of the deficits are as follows:

Fiscal year 1994: $320,600,000,000.
Fiscal year 1995: $315,600,000,000.
Fiscal year 1996: $299,600,000,000.

Fiscal year 1997: $275,800,000,000.
Fiscal year 1998: $282,900,000,000.
    (5) PUBLIC DEBT.—*The appropriate levels of the public debt are as follows:*
Fiscal year 1994: $4,731,900,000,000.
Fiscal year 1995: $5,097,900,000,000.
Fiscal year 1996: $5,453,700,000,000.
Fiscal year 1997: $5,812,700,000,000.
Fiscal year 1998: $6,182,400,000,000.
    (6) DIRECT LOAN OBLIGATIONS.—*The appropriate levels of total new direct loan obligations are as follows:*
Fiscal year 1994: $11,600,000,000.
Fiscal year 1995: $14,500,000,000.
Fiscal year 1996: $21,600,000,000.
Fiscal year 1997: $31,900,000,000.
Fiscal year 1998: $38,100,000,000.
    (7) PRIMARY LOAN GUARANTEE COMMITMENTS.—*The appropriate levels of new primary loan guarantee commitments are as follows:*
Fiscal year 1994: $149,700,000,000.
Fiscal year 1995: $146,900,000,000.
Fiscal year 1996: $144,200,000,000.
Fiscal year 1997: $138,800,000,000.
Fiscal year 1998: $136,100,000,000.

SEC. 3. DEBT INCREASE AS A MEASURE OF DEFICIT.
    The amounts of the increase in the public debt subject to limitation are as follows:
Fiscal year 1994: $372,300,000,000.
Fiscal year 1995: $366,000,000,000.
Fiscal year 1996: $355,800,000,000.
Fiscal year 1997: $359,100,000,000.
Fiscal year 1998: $369,700,000,000.

SEC. 4. DISPLAY OF FEDERAL RETIREMENT TRUST FUND BALANCES.
    The balances of the Federal retirement trust funds are as follows:
Fiscal year 1994: $1,056,500,000,000.
Fiscal year 1995: $1,171,600,000,000.
Fiscal year 1996: $1,294,700,000,000.
Fiscal year 1997: $1,420,200,000,000.
Fiscal year 1998: $1,544,600,000,000.

SEC. 5. SOCIAL SECURITY.
    (a) SOCIAL SECURITY REVENUES.—*For purposes of Senate enforcement under sections 302 and 311 of the Congressional Budget Act of 1974, the amounts of revenues of the Federal Old-Age and Survivors Insurance Trust Fund and the Federal Disability Insurance Trust Fund are as follows:*
Fiscal year 1994: $336,289,000,000.
Fiscal year 1995: $356,423,000,000.
Fiscal year 1996: $375,708,000,000.
Fiscal year 1997: $393,038,000,000.
Fiscal year 1998: $410,528,000,000.
    (b) SOCIAL SECURITY OUTLAYS.—*For purposes of Senate enforcement under sections 302 and 311 of the Congressional Budget*

Act of 1974, the amounts of outlays of the Federal Old-Age and Survivors Insurance Trust Fund and the Federal Disability Insurance Trust Fund are as follows:
  Fiscal year 1994: $274,813,000,000.
  Fiscal year 1995: $286,457,000,000.
  Fiscal year 1996: $297,401,000,000.
  Fiscal year 1997: $308,456,000,000.
  Fiscal year 1998: $319,408,000,000.

SEC. 6. MAJOR FUNCTIONAL CATEGORIES.

The Congress determines and declares that the appropriate levels of new budget authority, budget outlays, new direct loan obligations, new primary loan guarantee commitments, and new secondary loan guarantee commitments for fiscal years 1994 through 1998 for each major functional category are:
  (1) National Defense (050):
    Fiscal year 1994:
      (A) New budget authority, $263,400,000,000.
      (B) Outlays, $277,000,000,000.
      (C) New direct loan obligations, $0.
      (D) New primary loan guarantee commitments, $500,000,000.
    Fiscal year 1995:
      (A) New budget authority, $262,400,000,000.
      (B) Outlays, $272,100,000,000.
      (C) New direct loan obligations, $0.
      (D) New primary loan guarantee commitments, $500,000,000.
    Fiscal year 1996:
      (A) New budget authority, $253,600,000,000.
      (B) Outlays, $264,700,000,000.
      (C) New direct loan obligations, $0.
      (D) New primary loan guarantee commitments, $500,000,000.
    Fiscal year 1997:
      (A) New budget authority, $248,100,000,000.
      (B) Outlays, $248,900,000,000.
      (C) New direct loan obligations, $0.
      (D) New primary loan guarantee commitments, $500,000,000.
    Fiscal year 1998:
      (A) New budget authority, $253,900,000,000.
      (B) Outlays, $252,400,000,000.
      (C) New direct loan obligations, $0.
      (D) New primary loan guarantee commitments, $500,000,000.
  (2) International Affairs (150):
    Fiscal year 1994:
      (A) New budget authority, $19,700,000,000.
      (B) Outlays, $18,900,000,000.
      (C) New direct loan obligations, $2,700,000,000.
      (D) New primary loan guarantee commitments, $16,900,000,000.
    Fiscal year 1995:
      (A) New budget authority, $18,900,000,000.

(B) *Outlays, $18,300,000,000.*
(C) *New direct loan obligations, $2,800,000,000.*
(D) *New primary loan guarantee commitments, $17,300,000,000.*
Fiscal year 1996:
  (A) *New budget authority, $17,900,000,000.*
  (B) *Outlays, $17,500,000,000.*
  (C) *New direct loan obligations, $2,800,000,000.*
  (D) *New primary loan guarantee commitments, $17,800,000,000.*
Fiscal year 1997:
  (A) *New budget authority, $17,700,000,000.*
  (B) *Outlays, $17,100,000,000.*
  (C) *New direct loan obligations, $2,800,000,000.*
  (D) *New primary loan guarantee commitments, $18,200,000,000.*
Fiscal year 1998:
  (A) *New budget authority, $17,500,000,000.*
  (B) *Outlays, $17,000,000,000.*
  (C) *New direct loan obligations, $2,900,000,000.*
  (D) *New primary loan guarantee commitments, $18,700,000,000.*
(3) *General Science, Space, and Technology (250):*
Fiscal year 1994:
  (A) *New budget authority, $18,100,000,000.*
  (B) *Outlays, $17,600,000,000.*
  (C) *New direct loan obligations, $0.*
  (D) *New primary loan guarantee commitments, $0.*
Fiscal year 1995:
  (A) *New budget authority, $19,300,000,000.*
  (B) *Outlays, $18,600,000,000.*
  (C) *New direct loan obligations, $0.*
  (D) *New primary loan guarantee commitments, $0.*
Fiscal year 1996:
  (A) *New budget authority, $20,100,000,000.*
  (B) *Outlays, $19,600,000,000.*
  (C) *New direct loan obligations, $0.*
  (D) *New primary loan guarantee commitments, $0.*
Fiscal year 1997:
  (A) *New budget authority, $20,800,000,000.*
  (B) *Outlays, $20,400,000,000.*
  (C) *New direct loan obligations, $0.*
  (D) *New primary loan guarantee commitments, $0.*
Fiscal year 1998:
  (A) *New budget authority, $21,300,000,000.*
  (B) *Outlays, $21,100,000,000.*
  (C) *New direct loan obligations, $0.*
  (D) *New primary loan guarantee commitments, $0.*
(4) *Energy (270):*
Fiscal year 1994:
  (A) *New budget authority, $4,800,000,000.*
  (B) *Outlays, $3,800,000,000.*
  (C) *New direct loan obligations, $1,800,000,000.*
  (D) *New primary loan guarantee commitments, $0.*

Fiscal year 1995:
   (A) New budget authority, $5,900,000,000.
   (B) Outlays, $4,100,000,000.
   (C) New direct loan obligations, $1,800,000,000.
   (D) New primary loan guarantee commitments, $0.
Fiscal year 1996:
   (A) New budget authority, $5,100,000,000.
   (B) Outlays, $4,000,000,000.
   (C) New direct loan obligations, $1,800,000,000.
   (D) New primary loan guarantee commitments, $0.
Fiscal year 1997:
   (A) New budget authority, $5,200,000,000.
   (B) Outlays, $4,200,000,000.
   (C) New direct loan obligations, $1,800,000,000.
   (D) New primary loan guarantee commitments, $0.
Fiscal year 1998:
   (A) New budget authority, $5,400,000,000.
   (B) Outlays, $4,100,000,000.
   (C) New direct loan obligations, $1,800,000,000.
   (D) New primary loan guarantee commitments, $0.
(5) Natural Resources and Environment (300):
  Fiscal year 1994:
   (A) New budget authority, $20,600,000,000.
   (B) Outlays, $20,800,000,000.
   (C) New direct loan obligations, $100,000,000.
   (D) New primary loan guarantee commitments, $0.
  Fiscal year 1995:
   (A) New budget authority, $22,600,000,000.
   (B) Outlays, $20,800,000,000.
   (C) New direct loan obligations, $100,000,000.
   (D) New primary loan guarantee commitments, $0.
  Fiscal year 1996:
   (A) New budget authority, $22,300,000,000.
   (B) Outlays, $21,500,000,000.
   (C) New direct loan obligations, $100,000,000.
   (D) New primary loan guarantee commitments, $0.
  Fiscal year 1997:
   (A) New budget authority, $22,500,000,000.
   (B) Outlays, $21,900,000,000.
   (C) New direct loan obligations, $100,000,000.
   (D) New primary loan guarantee commitments, $0.
  Fiscal year 1998:
   (A) New budget authority, $22,500,000,000.
   (B) Outlays, $21,900,000,000.
   (C) New direct loan obligations, $100,000,000.
   (D) New primary loan guarantee commitments, $0.
(6) Agriculture (350):
  Fiscal year 1994:
   (A) New budget authority, $15,200,000,000.
   (B) Outlays, $14,400,000,000.
   (C) New direct loan obligations, $600,000,000.
   (D) New primary loan guarantee commitments, $7,000,000,000.
  Fiscal year 1995:

(A) New budget authority, $13,800,000,000.
(B) Outlays, $12,400,000,000.
(C) New direct loan obligations, $600,000,000.
(D) New primary loan guarantee commitments, $7,000,000,000.
Fiscal year 1996:
    (A) New budget authority, $12,900,000,000.
    (B) Outlays, $10,900,000,000.
    (C) New direct loan obligations, $600,000,000.
    (D) New primary loan guarantee commitments, $7,000,000,000.
Fiscal year 1997:
    (A) New budget authority, $12,600,000,000.
    (B) Outlays, $10,700,000,000.
    (C) New direct loan obligations, $700,000,000.
    (D) New primary loan guarantee commitments, $7,100,000,000.
Fiscal year 1998:
    (A) New budget authority, $12,600,000,000.
    (B) Outlays, $10,900,000,000.
    (C) New direct loan obligations, $700,000,000.
    (D) New primary loan guarantee commitments, $7,100,000,000.
  (7) Commerce and Housing Credit (370):
Fiscal year 1994:
    (A) New budget authority, $16,900,000,000.
    (B) Outlays, $8,600,000,000.
    (C) New direct loan obligations, $2,700,000,000.
    (D) New primary loan guarantee commitments, $78,100,000,000.
Fiscal year 1995:
    (A) New budget authority, $16,900,000,000.
    (B) Outlays, $13,100,000,000.
    (C) New direct loan obligations, $2,700,000,000.
    (D) New primary loan guarantee commitments, $80,100,000,000.
Fiscal year 1996:
    (A) New budget authority, $13,700,000,000.
    (B) Outlays, $3,400,000,000.
    (C) New direct loan obligations, $2,800,000,000.
    (D) New primary loan guarantee commitments, $82,100,000,000.
Fiscal year 1997:
    (A) New budget authority, $9,600,000,000.
    (B) Outlays, −$10,500,000,000.
    (C) New direct loan obligations, $2,100,000,000.
    (D) New primary loan guarantee commitments, $84,100,000,000.
Fiscal year 1998:
    (A) New budget authority, $10,400,000,000.
    (B) Outlays, −$7,100,000,000.
    (C) New direct loan obligations, $2,900,000,000.
    (D) New primary loan guarantee commitments, $86,300,000,000.

(8) Transportation (400):
  Fiscal year 1994:
    (A) New budget authority, $40,600,000,000.
    (B) Outlays, $36,500,000,000.
    (C) New direct loan obligations, $100,000,000.
    (D) New primary loan guarantee commitments, $0.
  Fiscal year 1995:
    (A) New budget authority, $41,000,000,000.
    (B) Outlays, $37,500,000,000.
    (C) New direct loan obligations, $100,000,000.
    (D) New primary loan guarantee commitments, $0.
  Fiscal year 1996:
    (A) New budget authority, $42,200,000,000.
    (B) Outlays, $39,200,000,000.
    (C) New direct loan obligations, $100,000,000.
    (D) New primary loan guarantee commitments, $0.
  Fiscal year 1997:
    (A) New budget authority, $43,700,000,000.
    (B) Outlays, $40,700,000,000.
    (C) New direct loan obligations, $100,000,000.
    (D) New primary loan guarantee commitments, $0.
  Fiscal year 1998:
    (A) New budget authority, $44,900,000,000.
    (B) Outlays, $42,000,000,000.
    (C) New direct loan obligations, $100,000,000.
    (D) New primary loan guarantee commitments, $0.
(9) Community and Regional Development (450):
  Fiscal year 1994:
    (A) New budget authority, $9,000,000,000.
    (B) Outlays, $8,800,000,000.
    (C) New direct loan obligations, $2,100,000,000.
    (D) New primary loan guarantee commitments, $2,400,000,000.
  Fiscal year 1995:
    (A) New budget authority, $8,600,000,000.
    (B) Outlays, $8,300,000,000.
    (C) New direct loan obligations, $2,100,000,000.
    (D) New primary loan guarantee commitments, $2,500,000,000.
  Fiscal year 1996:
    (A) New budget authority, $8,800,000,000.
    (B) Outlays, $8,100,000,000.
    (C) New direct loan obligations, $2,200,000,000.
    (D) New primary loan guarantee commitments, $2,500,000,000.
  Fiscal year 1997:
    (A) New budget authority, $8,900,000,000.
    (B) Outlays, $8,300,000,000.
    (C) New direct loan obligations, $2,300,000,000.
    (D) New primary loan guarantee commitments, $2,600,000,000.
  Fiscal year 1998:
    (A) New budget authority, $9,200,000,000.
    (B) Outlays, $8,600,000,000.

(C) New direct loan obligations, $2,300,000,000.

(D) New primary loan guarantee commitments, $2,600,000,000.

(10) Education, Training, Employment, and Social Services (500):

Fiscal year 1994:

(A) New budget authority, $55,800,000,000.

(B) Outlays, $52,100,000,000.

(C) New direct loan obligations, $400,000,000.

(D) New primary loan guarantee commitments, $20,700,000,000.

Fiscal year 1995:

(A) New budget authority, $59,200,000,000.

(B) Outlays, $54,800,000,000.

(C) New direct loan obligations, $3,300,000,000.

(D) New primary loan guarantee commitments, $19,600,000,000.

Fiscal year 1996:

(A) New budget authority, $62,800,000,000.

(B) Outlays, $54,900,000,000.

(C) New direct loan obligations, $10,100,000,000.

(D) New primary loan guarantee commitments, $13,700,000,000.

Fiscal year 1997:

(A) New budget authority, $65,100,000,000.

(B) Outlays, $62,100,000,000.

(C) New direct loan obligations, $20,100,000,000.

(D) New primary loan guarantee commitments, $5,000,000,000.

Fiscal year 1998:

(A) New budget authority, $67,400,000,000.

(B) Outlays, $64,800,000,000.

(C) New direct loan obligations, $26,200,000,000.

(D) New primary loan guarantee commitments, $0.

(11) Health (550):

Fiscal year 1994:

(A) New budget authority, $119,000,000,000.

(B) Outlays, $118,100,000,000.

(C) New direct loan obligations, $0.

(D) New primary loan guarantee commitments, $400,000,000.

Fiscal year 1995:

(A) New budget authority, $133,100,000,000.

(B) Outlays, $131,700,000,000.

(C) New direct loan obligations, $0.

(D) New primary loan guarantee commitments, $400,000,000.

Fiscal year 1996:

(A) New budget authority, $148,200,000,000.

(B) Outlays, $146,800,000,000.

(C) New direct loan obligations, $0.

(D) New primary loan guarantee commitments, $500,000,000.

Fiscal year 1997:

    (A) New budget authority, $163,700,000,000.
    (B) Outlays, $162,100,000,000.
    (C) New direct loan obligations, $0.
    (D) New primary loan guarantee commitments, $500,000,000.
    Fiscal year 1998:
      (A) New budget authority, $180,600,000,000.
      (B) Outlays, $178,800,000,000.
      (C) New direct loan obligations, $0.
      (D) New primary loan guarantee commitments, $500,000,000.
(12) Medicare (570):
    Fiscal year 1994:
      (A) New budget authority, $151,200,000,000.
      (B) Outlays, $149,800,000,000.
      (C) New direct loan obligations, $0.
      (D) New primary loan guarantee commitments, $0.
    Fiscal year 1995:
      (A) New budget authority, $171,600,000,000.
      (B) Outlays, $167,300,000,000.
      (C) New direct loan obligations, $0.
      (D) New primary loan guarantee commitments, $0.
    Fiscal year 1996:
      (A) New budget authority, $184,200,000,000.
      (B) Outlays, $183,000,000,000.
      (C) New direct loan obligations, $0.
      (D) New primary loan guarantee commitments, $0.
    Fiscal year 1997:
      (A) New budget authority, $201,600,000,000.
      (B) Outlays, $201,000,000,000.
      (C) New direct loan obligations, $0.
      (D) New primary loan guarantee commitments, $0.
    Fiscal year 1998:
      (A) New budget authority, $221,500,000,000.
      (B) Outlays, $221,100,000,000.
      (C) New direct loan obligations, $0.
      (D) New primary loan guarantee commitments, $0.
(13) For purposes of section 710 of the Social Security Act, Federal Supplementary Medical Insurance Trust Fund:
    Fiscal year 1994:
      (A) New budget authority, $51,200,000,000.
      (B) Outlays, $51,500,000,000.
      (C) New direct loan obligations, $0.
      (D) New primary loan guarantee commitments, $0.
    Fiscal year 1995:
      (A) New budget authority, $61,300,000,000.
      (B) Outlays, $58,400,000,000.
      (C) New direct loan obligations, $0.
      (D) New primary loan guarantee commitments, $0.
    Fiscal year 1996:
      (A) New budget authority, $63,700,000,000.
      (B) Outlays, $63,800,000,000.
      (C) New direct loan obligations, $0.
      (D) New primary loan guarantee commitments, $0.

Fiscal year 1997:
    (A) New budget authority, $71,200,000,000.
    (B) Outlays, $71,200,000,000.
    (C) New direct loan obligations, $0.
    (D) New primary loan guarantee commitments, $0.
Fiscal year 1998:
    (A) New budget authority, $80,000,000,000.
    (B) Outlays, $80,000,000,000.
    (C) New direct loan obligations, $0.
    (D) New primary loan guarantee commitments, $0.
(14) Income Security (600):
Fiscal year 1994:
    (A) New budget authority, $211,100,000,000.
    (B) Outlays, $210,800,000,000.
    (C) New direct loan obligations, $0.
    (D) New primary loan guarantee commitments, $0.
Fiscal year 1995:
    (A) New budget authority, $222,800,000,000.
    (B) Outlays, $223,400,000,000.
    (C) New direct loan obligations, $0.
    (D) New primary loan guarantee commitments, $0.
Fiscal year 1996:
    (A) New budget authority, $237,800,000,000.
    (B) Outlays, $232,200,000,000.
    (C) New direct loan obligations, $0.
    (D) New primary loan guarantee commitments, $0.
Fiscal year 1997:
    (A) New budget authority, $252,200,000,000.
    (B) Outlays, $243,000,000,000.
    (C) New direct loan obligations, $0.
    (D) New primary loan guarantee commitments, $0.
Fiscal year 1998:
    (A) New budget authority, $253,400,000,000.
    (B) Outlays, $252,300,000,000.
    (C) New direct loan obligations, $0.
    (D) New primary loan guarantee commitments, $0.
(15) Social Security (650):
Fiscal year 1994:
    (A) New budget authority, $6,100,000,000.
    (B) Outlays, $8,900,000,000.
    (C) New direct loan obligations, $0.
    (D) New primary loan guarantee commitments, $0.
Fiscal year 1995:
    (A) New budget authority, $6,700,000,000.
    (B) Outlays, $9,600,000,000.
    (C) New direct loan obligations, $0.
    (D) New primary loan guarantee commitments, $0.
Fiscal year 1996:
    (A) New budget authority, $7,300,000,000.
    (B) Outlays, $10,300,000,000.
    (C) New direct loan obligations, $0.
    (D) New primary loan guarantee commitments, $0.
Fiscal year 1997:
    (A) New budget authority, $7,900,000,000.

(B) Outlays, $11,000,000,000.
(C) New direct loan obligations, $0.
(D) New primary loan guarantee commitments, $0.
Fiscal year 1998:
    (A) New budget authority, $8,600,000,000.
    (B) Outlays, $11,700,000,000.
    (C) New direct loan obligations, $0.
    (D) New primary loan guarantee commitments, $0.
(16) Veterans Benefits and Services (700):
Fiscal year 1994:
    (A) New budget authority, $34,700,000,000.
    (B) Outlays, $36,300,000,000.
    (C) New direct loan obligations, $1,100,000,000.
    (D) New primary loan guarantee commitments, $23,700,000,000.
Fiscal year 1995:
    (A) New budget authority, $35,400,000,000.
    (B) Outlays, $35,500,000,000.
    (C) New direct loan obligations, $1,000,000,000.
    (D) New primary loan guarantee commitments, $19,500,000,000.
Fiscal year 1996:
    (A) New budget authority, $36,000,000,000.
    (B) Outlays, $34,600,000,000.
    (C) New direct loan obligations, $1,100,000,000.
    (D) New primary loan guarantee commitments, $20,100,000,000.
Fiscal year 1997:
    (A) New budget authority, $36,200,000,000.
    (B) Outlays, $36,400,000,000.
    (C) New direct loan obligations, $1,100,000,000.
    (D) New primary loan guarantee commitments, $20,800,000,000.
Fiscal year 1998:
    (A) New budget authority, $36,800,000,000.
    (B) Outlays, $36,900,000,000.
    (C) New direct loan obligations, $1,100,000,000.
    (D) New primary loan guarantee commitments, $20,400,000,000.
(17) Administration of Justice (750):
Fiscal year 1994:
    (A) New budget authority, $15,000,000,000.
    (B) Outlays, $15,300,000,000.
    (C) New direct loan obligations, $0.
    (D) New primary loan guarantee commitments, $0.
Fiscal year 1995:
    (A) New budget authority, $15,300,000,000.
    (B) Outlays, $15,600,000,000.
    (C) New direct loan obligations, $0.
    (D) New primary loan guarantee commitments, $0.
Fiscal year 1996:
    (A) New budget authority, $15,700,000,000.
    (B) Outlays, $15,900,000,000.
    (C) New direct loan obligations, $0.

       (D) New primary loan guarantee commitments, $0.
Fiscal year 1997:
       (A) New budget authority, $16,100,000,000.
       (B) Outlays, $16,100,000,000.
       (C) New direct loan obligations, $0.
       (D) New primary loan guarantee commitments, $0.
Fiscal year 1998:
       (A) New budget authority, $16,700,000,000.
       (B) Outlays, $16,500,000,000.
       (C) New direct loan obligations, $0.
       (D) New primary loan guarantee commitments, $0.
(18) General Government (800):
Fiscal year 1994:
       (A) New budget authority, $13,000,000,000.
       (B) Outlays, $13,100,000,000.
       (C) New direct loan obligations, $0.
       (D) New primary loan guarantee commitments, $0.
Fiscal year 1995:
       (A) New budget authority, $12,800,000,000.
       (B) Outlays, $14,200,000,000.
       (C) New direct loan obligations, $0.
       (D) New primary loan guarantee commitments, $0.
Fiscal year 1996:
       (A) New budget authority, $13,200,000,000.
       (B) Outlays, $13,900,000,000.
       (C) New direct loan obligations, $0.
       (D) New primary loan guarantee commitments, $0.
Fiscal year 1997:
       (A) New budget authority, $13,300,000,000.
       (B) Outlays, $13,800,000,000.
       (C) New direct loan obligations, $0.
       (D) New primary loan guarantee commitments, $0.
Fiscal year 1998:
       (A) New budget authority, $13,500,000,000.
       (B) Outlays, $13,900,000,000.
       (C) New direct loan obligations, $0.
       (D) New primary loan guarantee commitments, $0.
(19) Net Interest (900):
Fiscal year 1994:
       (A) New budget authority, $239,900,000,000.
       (B) Outlays, $239,900,000,000.
       (C) New direct loan obligations, $0.
       (D) New primary loan guarantee commitments, $0.
Fiscal year 1995:
       (A) New budget authority, $260,800,000,000.
       (B) Outlays, $260,800,000,000.
       (C) New direct loan obligations, $0.
       (D) New primary loan guarantee commitments, $0.
Fiscal year 1996:
       (A) New budget authority, $280,100,000,000.
       (B) Outlays, $280,100,000,000.
       (C) New direct loan obligations, $0.
       (D) New primary loan guarantee commitments, $0.
Fiscal year 1997:

(A) New budget authority, $297,700,000,000.
(B) Outlays, $297,700,000,000.
(C) New direct loan obligations, $0.
(D) New primary loan guarantee commitments, $0.
Fiscal year 1998:
    (A) New budget authority, $315,300,000,000.
    (B) Outlays, $315,300,000,000.
    (C) New direct loan obligations, $0.
    (D) New primary loan guarantee commitments, $0.
  (20) For purposes of section 710 of the Social Security Act,
Net Interest (900):
Fiscal year 1994:
    (A) New budget authority, $250,400,000,000.
    (B) Outlays, $250,400,000,000.
    (C) New direct loan obligations, $0.
    (D) New primary loan guarantee commitments, $0.
Fiscal year 1995:
    (A) New budget authority, $271,100,000,000.
    (B) Outlays, $271,000,000,000.
    (C) New direct loan obligations, $0.
    (D) New primary loan guarantee commitments, $0.
Fiscal year 1996:
    (A) New budget authority, $289,700,000,000.
    (B) Outlays, $289,700,000,000.
    (C) New direct loan obligations, $0.
    (D) New primary loan guarantee commitments, $0.
Fiscal year 1997:
    (A) New budget authority, $305,900,000,000.
    (B) Outlays, $305,900,000,000.
    (C) New direct loan obligations, $0.
    (D) New primary loan guarantee commitments, $0.
Fiscal year 1998:
    (A) New budget authority, $321,400,000,000.
    (B) Outlays, $321,400,000,000.
    (C) New direct loan obligations, $0.
    (D) New primary loan guarantee commitments, $0.
  (21) The corresponding levels of gross interest on the public
debt are as follows:
Fiscal year 1994: $307,443,000,000.
Fiscal year 1995: $327,744,000,000.
Fiscal year 1996: $347,046,,000,000.
Fiscal year 1997: $364,334,000,000.
Fiscal year 1998: $381,401,000,000.
  (22) Allowances (920):
Fiscal year 1994:
    (A) New budget authority, $0.
    (B) Outlays, $0.
    (C) New direct loan obligations, $0.
    (D) New primary loan guarantee commitments, $0.
Fiscal year 1995:
    (A) New budget authority, − $6,000,000.000.
    (B) Outlays, − $4,200,000,000.
    (C) New direct loan obligations, $0.
    (D) New primary loan guarantee commitments, $0.

Fiscal year 1996:
   (A) New budget authority, − $2,700,000,000.
   (B) Outlays, − $4,000,000,000.
   (C) New direct loan obligations, $0.
   (D) New primary loan guarantee commitments, $0.
Fiscal year 1997:
   (A) New budget authority, − $0,700,000,000.
   (B) Outlays, − $0,300,000,000.
   (C) New direct loan obligations, $0.
   (D) New primary loan guarantee commitments, $0.
Fiscal year 1998:
   (A) New budget authority, − $9,900,000,000.
   (B) Outlays, − $13,200,000,000.
   (C) New direct loan obligations, $0.
   (D) New primary loan guarantee commitments, $0.
(23) Undistributed Offsetting Receipts (950):
Fiscal year 1994:
   (A) New budget authority, − $30,700,000,000.
   (B) Outlays, − $32,400,000,000.
   (C) New direct loan obligations, $0.
   (D) New primary loan guarantee commitments, $0.
Fiscal year 1995:
   (A) New budget authority, − $31,500,000,000.
   (B) Outlays, − $33,300,000,000.
   (C) New direct loan obligations, $0.
   (D) New primary loan guarantee commitments, $0.
Fiscal year 1996:
   (A) New budget authority, − $31,700,000,000.
   (B) Outlays, − $33,400,000,000.
   (C) New direct loan obligations, $0.
   (D) New primary loan guarantee commitments, $0.
Fiscal year 1997:
   (A) New budget authority, − $32,300,000,000.
   (B) Outlays, − $33,300,000,000.
   (C) New direct loan obligations, $0.
   (D) New primary loan guarantee commitments, $0.
Fiscal year 1998:
   (A) New budget authority, − $32,100,000,000.
   (B) Outlays, − $33,100,000,000.
   (C) New direct loan obligations, $0.
   (D) New primary loan guarantee commitments, $0.
(24) For purposes of section 710 of the Social Security Act,
Undistributed Offsetting Receipts (950):
Fiscal year 1994:
   (A) New budget authority, − $28,200,000,000.
   (B) Outlays, − $29,900,000,000.
   (C) New direct loan obligations, $0.
   (D) New primary loan guarantee commitments, $0.
Fiscal year 1995:
   (A) New budget authority, − $29,000,000,000.
   (B) Outlays, − $30,800,000,000.
   (C) New direct loan obligations, $0.
   (D) New primary loan guarantee commitments, $0.
Fiscal year 1996:

    (A) *New budget authority,* −*$29,200,000,000.*
    (B) *Outlays,* −*$30,900,000,000.*
    (C) *New direct loan obligations, $0.*
    (D) *New primary loan guarantee commitments, $0.*
Fiscal year 1997:
    (A) *New budget authority,* −*$29,700,000,000.*
    (B) *Outlays,* −*$30,700,000,000.*
    (C) *New direct loan obligations, $0.*
    (D) *New primary loan guarantee commitments, $0.*
Fiscal year 1998:
    (A) *New budget authority,* −*$29,400,000,000.*
    (B) *Outlays,* −*$30,400,000,000.*
    (C) *New direct loan obligations, $0.*
    (D) *New primary loan guarantee commitments, $0.*

SEC. 7. RECONCILIATION.

    (a) COMMITTEES ON WAYS AND MEANS AND FINANCE.—*Not later than April 2, 1993, the House Committee on Ways and Means and the Senate Committee on Finance shall submit to their respective Houses reconciliation legislation containing recommendations to change laws to increase the statutory limit on the public debt to not more than $4,370,000,000,000.*

    (b) SENATE COMMITTEES.—*Not later than June 18, 1993, the committees named in this subsection shall submit their recommendations to the Committee on the Budget of the Senate. After receiving those recommendations, the Committee on the Budget shall report to the Senate a reconciliation bill carrying out all such recommendations without any substantive revision.*

    (1) COMMITTEE ON AGRICULTURE, NUTRITION, AND FORESTRY.—*The Senate Committee on Agriculture, Nutrition, and Forestry shall report changes in laws within its jurisdiction to reduce the deficit $118,000,000 in fiscal year 1994 and $3,170,000,000 for the period of fiscal years 1994 through 1998.*

    (2) COMMITTEE ON ARMED SERVICES.—*The Senate Committee on Armed Services shall report changes in laws within its jurisdiction to reduce the deficit $128,000,000 in fiscal year 1994 and $2,361,000,000 for the period of fiscal years 1994 through 1998.*

    (3) COMMITTEE ON BANKING, HOUSING, AND URBAN AFFAIRS.—*The Senate Committee on Banking, Housing, and Urban Affairs shall report changes in laws within its jurisdiction to reduce the deficit $401,000,000 in fiscal year 1994 and $3,131,000,000 for the period of fiscal years 1994 through 1998.*

    (4) COMMITTEE ON COMMERCE, SCIENCE, AND TRANSPORTATION.—*The Senate Committee on Commerce, Science, and Transportation shall report changes in laws within its jurisdiction to reduce the deficit $1,700,000,000 in fiscal year 1994 and $7,405,000,000 for the period of fiscal years 1994 through 1998.*

    (5) COMMITTEE ON ENERGY AND NATURAL RESOURCES.—*The Senate Committee on Energy and Natural Resources shall report changes in laws within its jurisdiction to reduce the deficit $118,000,000 in fiscal year 1994 and $737,000,000 for the period of fiscal years 1994 through 1998.*

    (6) COMMITTEE ON ENVIRONMENT AND PUBLIC WORKS.—*The Senate Committee on Environment and Public Works shall re-*

port changes in laws within its jurisdiction to reduce the deficit $13,000,000 in fiscal year 1994 and $1,254,000,000 for the period of fiscal years 1994 through 1998.

(7) COMMITTEE ON FINANCE.—(A) The Senate Committee on Finance shall report changes in laws within its jurisdiction that provide direct spending (as defined in section 250(c)(8) of the Balanced Budget and Emergency Deficit Control Act of 1985) to reduce outlays $2,346,000,000 in fiscal year 1994 and $35,157,000,000 for the period of fiscal years 1994 through 1998.

(B) The Senate Committee on Finance shall report changes in laws within its jurisdiction to increase revenues $27,293,000,000 in fiscal year 1994 and $272,105,000,000 for the period of fiscal years 1994 through 1998.

(C) The Senate Committee on Finance shall report changes in laws to increase the statutory limit on the public debt to not more than $4,900,000,000,000.

(8) The Senate Committee on Foreign Affairs shall report changes in laws within its jurisdiction to reduce the deficit $5,000,000 for the period of fiscal years 1994 through 1998.

(9) COMMITTEE ON GOVERNMENTAL AFFAIRS.—The Senate Committee on Governmental Affairs shall report changes in laws within its jurisdiction to reduce the deficit $77,000,000 in fiscal year 1994 and $10,638,000,000 for the period of fiscal years 1994 through 1998.

(10) COMMITTEE ON THE JUDICIARY.—The Senate Committee on the Judiciary shall report changes in laws within its jurisdiction to reduce the deficit $345,000,000 for the period of fiscal years 1994 through 1998.

(11) COMMITTEE ON LABOR AND HUMAN RESOURCES.—The Senate Committee on Labor and Human Resources shall report changes in laws within its jurisdiction to reduce the deficit $4,571,000,000 for the period of fiscal years 1994 through 1998.

(12) COMMITTEE ON VETERANS' AFFAIRS.—The Senate Committee on Veterans' Affairs shall report changes in laws within its jurisdiction to reduce the deficit $266,000,000 in fiscal year 1994 and $2,580,000,000 for the period of fiscal years 1994 through 1998.

(c) HOUSE COMMITTEES.—Not later than May 14, 1993, the committees named in this subsection shall submit their recommendations to the Committee on the Budget of the House of Representatives. After receiving those recommendations, the Committee on the Budget shall report to the House of Representatives a reconciliation bill carrying out all such recommendations without any substantive revision.

(1) COMMITTEE ON AGRICULTURE.—The Committee on Agriculture shall report changes in laws within its jurisdiction sufficient to reduce the deficit, as follows: $98,000,000 in fiscal year 1994, $119,000,000 in fiscal year 1995, $515,000,000 in fiscal year 1996, $1,041,000,000 in fiscal year 1997, and $1,177,000,000 in fiscal year 1998, and program changes in laws within its jurisdiction, sufficient to result in an increase of outlays as follows: $523,000,000 in fiscal year 1994, $1,524,000,000 in fiscal year 1995, $1,527,000,000 in fiscal year

1996, $1,533,000,000 in fiscal year 1997, and $1,551,000,000 in fiscal year 1998.

(2) COMMITTEE ON ARMED SERVICES.—The House Committee on Armed Services shall report changes in laws within its jurisdiction that provide direct spending sufficient to reduce outlays, as follows: $128,000,000 in fiscal year 1994, $292,000,000 in fiscal year 1995, $457,000,000 in fiscal year 1996, $643,000,000 in fiscal year 1997, and $841,000,000 in fiscal year 1998, and program changes in laws within its jurisdiction, sufficient to result in a reduction of outlays as follows: $2,012,000,000 in fiscal year 1994, $3,231,000,000 in fiscal year 1995, $4,117,000,000 in fiscal year 1996, $5,103,000,000 in fiscal year 1997, and $5,800,000,000 in fiscal year 1998.

(3) COMMITTEE ON BANKING, FINANCE AND URBAN AFFAIRS.—The House Committee on Banking, Finance and Urban Affairs shall report changes in laws within its jurisdiction that provide direct spending, sufficient to reduce outlays, as follows: $338,000,000 in fiscal year 1994, $346,000,000 in fiscal year 1995, $550,000,000 in fiscal year 1996, $769,000,000 in fiscal year 1997, and $789,000,000 in fiscal year 1998, program changes in laws within its jurisdiction, sufficient to result in an increase of outlays as follows: $5,000,000 in fiscal year 1994; and result in a reduction of outlays as follows: $18,000,000 in fiscal year 1995, $127,000,000 in fiscal year 1996, $227,000,000 in fiscal year 1997, and $260,000,000 in fiscal year 1998, and changes in laws within its jurisdiction to increase revenues, as follows: $63,000,000 in fiscal year 1994, $65,000,000 in fiscal year 1995, $68,000,000 in fiscal year 1996, $70,000,000 in fiscal year 1997, and $73,000,000 in fiscal year 1998.

(4) COMMITTEE ON EDUCATION AND LABOR.—The House Committee on Education and Labor shall report changes in laws within its jurisdiction that provide direct spending sufficient to increase outlays by $118,000,000 in fiscal year 1994, and to reduce outlays as follows: $72,000,000 in fiscal year 1995, $792,000,000 in fiscal year 1996, $2,173,000,000 in fiscal year 1997, and $2,898,000,000 in fiscal year 1998.

(5) COMMITTEE ON ENERGY AND COMMERCE.—The House Committee on Energy and Commerce shall report changes in laws within its jurisdiction that provide direct spending sufficient to reduce outlays, as follows: $4,342,000,000 in fiscal year 1994, $7,491,000,000 in fiscal year 1995, $13,422,000,000 in fiscal year 1996, $17,518,000,000 in fiscal year 1997, and $21,744,000,000 in fiscal year 1998.

(6) COMMITTEE ON FOREIGN AFFAIRS.—The House Committee on Foreign Affairs shall report changes in laws within its jurisdiction that provide direct spending sufficient to reduce outlays, as follows: $0 in fiscal year 1994, $1,000,000 in fiscal year 1995, $1,000,000 in fiscal year 1996, $1,000,000 in fiscal year 1997, and $2,000,000 in fiscal year 1998.

(7) COMMITTEE ON THE JUDICIARY.—The House Committee on the Judiciary shall report changes in laws within its jurisdiction that provide direct spending sufficient to reduce outlays, as follows: $0 in fiscal year 1994, $0 in fiscal year 1995,

$111,000,000 in fiscal year 1996, $115,000,000 in fiscal year 1997, and $119,000,000 in fiscal year 1998.

(8) COMMITTEE ON MERCHANT MARINE AND FISHERIES.— The House Committee on Merchant Marine and Fisheries shall report changes in laws within its jurisdiction that provide direct spending sufficient to reduce outlays, as follows: $0 in fiscal year 1994, $0 in fiscal year 1995, $67,000,000 in fiscal year 1996, $68,000,000 in fiscal year 1997, and $70,000,000 in fiscal year 1998.

(9) COMMITTEE ON NATURAL RESOURCES.—The House Committee on Natural Resources shall report changes in laws within its jurisdiction that provide direct spending sufficient to reduce outlays, as follows: $131,000,000 in fiscal year 1994, $157,000,000 in fiscal year 1995, $543,000,000 in fiscal year 1996, $569,000,000 in fiscal year 1997, and $591,000,000 in fiscal year 1998.

(10) COMMITTEE ON POST OFFICE AND CIVIL SERVICE.—The House Committee on Post Office and Civil Service shall report changes in laws within its jurisdiction that provide direct spending sufficient to reduce outlays, as follows: $77,000,000 in fiscal year 1994, $491,000,000 in fiscal year 1995, $2,669,000,000 in fiscal year 1996, $3,709,000,000 in fiscal year 1997, and $3,697,000,000 in fiscal year 1998, and program changes in laws within its jurisdiction, sufficient to result in a reduction of outlays as follows: $2,903,000,000 in fiscal year 1994, $4,660,000,000 in fiscal year 1995, $5,825,000,000 in fiscal year 1996, $7,169,000,000 in fiscal year 1997, and $8,164,000,000 in fiscal year 1998.

(11) COMMITTEE ON PUBLIC WORKS AND TRANSPORTATION.— The House Committee on Public Works and Transportation shall report changes in laws within its jurisdiction sufficient to reduce the deficit, as follows: $31,000,000 in fiscal year 1994, $49,000,000 in fiscal year 1995, $62,000,000 in fiscal year 1996, $76,000,000 in fiscal year 1997, and $78,000,000 in fiscal year 1998.

(12) COMMITTEE ON VETERANS' AFFAIRS.—The House Committee on Veterans' Affairs shall report changes in laws within its jurisdiction that provide direct spending sufficient to reduce outlays, as follows: $266,000,000 in fiscal year 1994, $364,000,000 in fiscal year 1995, $382,000,000 in fiscal year 1996, $405,000,000 in fiscal year 1997, and $1,163,000,000 in fiscal year 1998.

(13) COMMITTEE ON WAYS AND MEANS.—The House Committee on Ways and Means shall report changes in laws within its jurisdiction sufficient to reduce the deficit, as follows: by $29,441,000,000 in fiscal year 1994, by $41,415,000,000 in fiscal year 1995, by $61,912,000,000 in fiscal year 1996, by $81,794,000,000 in fiscal year 1997, and by $85,209,000,000 in fiscal year 1998, and changes in laws to increase the statutory limit on the public debt to not more than $4,900,000,000,000.

(14) DIRECT SPENDING.—For purposes of this subsection, the term "direct spending" means spending authority as defined in section 401(c)(2)(C) of the Congressional Budget Act of 1974

and new budget authority as defined in section 3(2) of the Congressional Budget Act of 1974.

SEC. 8. SALE OF GOVERNMENT ASSETS.

(a) SENSE OF THE CONGRESS.—*It is the sense of the Congress that—*

(1) *from time to time the United States Government should sell assets; and*

(2) *the amounts realized from such asset sales will not recur on an annual basis and do not reduce the demand for credit.*

(b) BUDGETARY TREATMENT.—*For purposes of points of order under this concurrent resolution and the Congressional Budget and Impoundment Control Act of 1974, the amounts realized from sales of assets (other than loan assets) shall not be scored with respect to the level of budget authority, outlays, or revenues.*

(c) DEFINITIONS.—*For purposes of this section—*

(1) *the term "sale of an asset" shall have the same meaning as under section 250(c)(21) of the Balanced Budget and Emergency Deficit Control Act of 1985 (as amended by the Budget Enforcement Act of 1990); and*

(2) *the term shall not include asset sales mandated by law before September 18, 1987, and routine, ongoing asset sales at levels consistent with agency operations in fiscal year 1986.*

SEC. 9. DEFICIT-NEUTRAL RESERVE FUND IN THE SENATE.

(a) INITIATIVES TO IMPROVE THE HEALTH AND NUTRITION OF CHILDREN AND TO PROVIDE FOR SERVICES TO SUPPORT AND PROTECT CHILDREN, AND TO IMPROVE THE WELL-BEING OF FAMILIES.—

(1) IN GENERAL.—*Budget authority and outlays may be allocated to a committee or committees for legislation that increases funding to improve the health and nutrition of children and to provide for services to support and protect children, and to improve the well-being and self-sufficiency of families and reduce dependency, including initiatives to expand childhood immunization and family preservation and support services, within a committee's jurisdiction if such a committee or the committee of conference on such legislation reports such legislation, if, to the extent that the costs of such legislation are not included in this concurrent resolution on the budget, the enactment of such legislation will not increase (by virtue of either contemporaneous or previously passed deficit reduction) the deficit in this resolution for—*

(A) *fiscal year 1994; and*

(B) *the period of fiscal years 1994 through 1998.*

(2) REVISED ALLOCATIONS.—*Upon the reporting of legislation pursuant to paragraph (1), and again upon the submission of a conference report on such legislation (if a conference report is submitted), the Chairman of the Committee on the Budget of the Senate may file with the Senate appropriately revised allocations under sections 302(a) and 602(a) of the Congressional Budget Act of 1974 and revised functional levels and aggregates to carry out this subsection. Such revised allocations, functional levels, and aggregates shall be considered for the purposes of the Congressional Budget Act of 1974 as allocations, functional*

*levels, and aggregates contained in this concurrent resolution
on the budget.*

*(3) REPORTING REVISED ALLOCATIONS.—The appropriate
committee may report appropriately revised allocations pursuant to sections 302(b) and 602(b) of the Congressional Budget
Act of 1974 to carry out this subsection.*

(b) ECONOMIC GROWTH INITIATIVES.—

*(1) IN GENERAL.—Budget authority and outlays may be al-
located to a committee or committees for legislation that increases funding for economic recovery or growth initiatives, including unemployment compensation, a dislocated worker program, job training, or other related programs within such a
committee's jurisdiction if such a committee or the committee of
conference on such legislation reports such legislation, if, to the
extent that the costs of such legislation are not included in this
concurrent resolution on the budget, the enactment of such legislation will not increase (by virtue of either contemporaneous
or previously passed deficit reduction) the deficit in this resolution for—*

(A) fiscal year 1994; and

(B) the period of fiscal years 1994 through 1998.

*(2) REVISED ALLOCATIONS.—Upon the reporting of legisla-
tion pursuant to paragraph (1), and again upon the submission
of a conference report on such legislation (if a conference report
is submitted), the Chairman of the Committee on the Budget of
the Senate may file with the Senate appropriately revised allocations under sections 302(a) and 602(a) of the Congressional
Budget Act of 1974 and revised functional levels and aggregates
to carry out this subsection. Such revised allocations, functional
levels, and aggregates shall be considered for the purposes of
the Congressional Budget Act of 1974 as allocations, functional
levels, and aggregates contained in this concurrent resolution
on the budget.*

*(3) REPORTING REVISED ALLOCATIONS.—The appropriate
committee may report appropriately revised allocations pursuant to section 302(b) and 602(b) of the Congressional Budget
Act of 1974 to carry out this subsection.*

*(c) CONTINUING IMPROVEMENTS IN ONGOING HEALTH CARE
PROGRAMS AND COMPREHENSIVE HEALTH CARE REFORM.—*

*(1) IN GENERAL.—Budget authority and outlays may be al-
located to a committee or committees for legislation that increases funding to make continuing improvements in ongoing
health care programs, to provide for comprehensive health care
reform, or to control health care costs within such a committee's
jurisdiction if such a committee or the committee of conference
on such legislation reports such legislation, if, to the extent that
the costs of such legislation are not included in this concurrent
resolution on the budget, the enactment of such legislation will
not increase (by virtue of either contemporaneous or previously
passed deficit reduction) the deficit in this resolution for—*

(A) fiscal year 1994; and

(B) the period of fiscal years 1994 through 1998.

*(2) REVISED ALLOCATIONS.—Upon the reporting of legisla-
tion pursuant to paragraph (1), and again upon the submission*

of a conference report on such legislation (if a conference report is submitted), the Chairman of the Committee on the Budget of the Senate may file with the Senate appropriately revised allocations under sections 302(a) and 602(a) of the Congressional Budget Act of 1974 and revised functional levels and aggregates to carry out this subsection. Such revised allocations, functional levels, and aggregates shall be considered for the purposes of the Congressional Budget Act of 1974 as allocations, functional levels, and aggregates contained in this concurrent resolution on the budget.

(3) REPORTING REVISED ALLOCATIONS.—The appropriate committee may report appropriately revised allocations pursuant to sections 302(b) and 602(b) of the Congressional Budget Act of 1974 to carry out this subsection.

(d) INITIATIVES TO IMPROVE EDUCATIONAL OPPORTUNITIES FOR INDIVIDUALS AT THE EARLY CHILDHOOD, ELEMENTARY, SECONDARY, OR HIGHER EDUCATION LEVELS, OR TO INVEST IN THE HEALTH OR EDUCATION OF AMERICA'S CHILDREN.—

(1) IN GENERAL.—Budget authority and outlays may be allocated to a committee or committees for direct spending legislation that increases funding to improve educational opportunities for individuals at the early childhood, elementary, secondary, or higher education levels, or to invest in the health or education of America's children within such a committee's jurisdiction if such a committee or the committee of conference on such legislation reports such legislation, if, to the extent that the costs of such legislation are not included in this concurrent resolution on the budget, the enactment of such legislation will not increase (by virtue of either contemporaneous or previously passed deficit reduction) the deficit in this resolution for—

(A) fiscal year 1994; and

(B) the period of fiscal years 1994 through 1998.

(2) REVISED ALLOCATIONS.—Upon the reporting of legislation pursuant to paragraph (1), and again upon the submission of a conference report on such legislation (if a conference report is submitted), the Chairman of the Committee on the Budget of the Senate may file with the Senate appropriately revised allocations under sections 302(a) and 602(a) of the Congressional Budget Act of 1974 and revised functional levels and aggregates to carry out this subsection. Such revised allocations, functional levels, and aggregates shall be considered for the purposes of the Congressional Budget Act of 1974 as allocations, functional levels, and aggregates contained in this concurrent resolution on the budget.

(3) REPORTING REVISED ALLOCATIONS.—The appropriate committee may report appropriately revised allocations pursuant to sections 302(b) and 602(b) of the Congressional Budget Act of 1974 to carry out this subsection.

(e) INITIATIVES TO PRESERVE AND REBUILD THE UNITED STATES MARITIME INDUSTRY.—

(1) IN GENERAL.—Budget authority and outlays may be allocated to a committee or committees for direct spending legislation that increases funding to preserve and rebuild the United States maritime industry within such a committee's jurisdiction

if such a committee or the committee of conference on such legislation reports such legislation, if, to the extent that the costs of such legislation are not included in this concurrent resolution on the budget, the enactment of such legislation will not increase (by virtue of either contemporaneous or previously passed deficit reduction) the deficit in this resolution for—

    (A) fiscal year 1994; and

    (B) the period of fiscal years 1994 through 1998.

    (2) REVISED ALLOCATIONS.—Upon the reporting of legislation pursuant to paragraph (1), and again upon the submission of a conference report on such legislation (if a conference report is submitted), the Chairman of the Committee on the Budget of the Senate may file with the Senate appropriately revised allocations under sections 302(a) and 602(a) of the Congressional Budget Act of 1974 and revised functional levels and aggregates to carry out this subsection. Such revised allocations, functional levels, and aggregates shall be considered for the purposes of the Congressional Budget Act of 1974 as allocations, functional levels, and aggregates contained in this concurrent resolution on the budget.

    (3) REPORTING REVISED ALLOCATIONS.—The appropriate committee may report appropriately revised allocations pursuant to sections 302(b) and 602(b) of the Congressional Budget Act of 1974 to carry out this subsection.

    (f) INITIATIVES TO REFORM THE FINANCING OF FEDERAL ELECTIONS.—

    (1) IN GENERAL.—Budget authority and outlays may be allocated to a committee or committees for direct spending legislation that increases funding to reform the financing of Federal elections within such a committee's jurisdiction if such a committee or the committee of conference on such legislation reports such legislation, if, to the extent that the costs of such legislation are not included in this concurrent resolution on the budget, the enactment of such legislation will not increase (by virtue of either contemporaneous or previously passed deficit reduction) the deficit in this resolution for—

    (A) fiscal year 1994; and

    (B) the period of fiscal years 1994 through 1998.

    (2) REVISED ALLOCATIONS.—Upon the reporting of legislation pursuant to paragraph (1), and again upon the submission of a conference report on such legislation (if a conference report is submitted), the Chairman of the Committee on the Budget of the Senate may file with the Senate appropriately revised allocations under sections 302(a) and 602(a) of the Congressional Budget Act of 1974 and revised functional levels and aggregates to carry out this subsection. Such revised allocations, functional levels, and aggregates shall be considered for the purposes of the Congressional Budget Act of 1974 as allocations, functional levels, and aggregates contained in this concurrent resolution on the budget.

    (3) REPORTING REVISED ALLOCATIONS.—The appropriate committee may report appropriately revised allocations pursuant to sections 302(b) and 602(b) of the Congressional Budget Act of 1974 to carry out this subsection.

(g) TRADE-RELATED LEGISLATION.—

(1) IN GENERAL.—Budget authority and outlays may be allocated to a committee or committees and the revenue aggregates may be reduced for legislation to implement the North American Free Trade Agreement and any other trade-related legislation within such a committee's jurisdiction if such a committee or the committee of conference on such legislation reports such legislation, if, to the extent that the costs of such legislation are not included in this concurrent resolution on the budget, the enactment of such legislation will not increase (by virtue of either contemporaneous or previously passed deficit reduction) the deficit in this resolution for—

(A) fiscal year 1994; and

(B) the period of fiscal years 1994 through 1998.

(2) REVISED ALLOCATIONS.—Upon the reporting of legislation pursuant to paragraph (1), and again upon the submission of a conference report on such legislation (if a conference report is submitted), the Chairman of the Committee on the Budget of the Senate may file with the Senate appropriately revised allocations under sections 302(a) and 602(a) of the Congressional Budget Act of 1974 and revised functional levels and aggregates to carry out this subsection. Such revised allocations, functional levels, and aggregates shall be considered for the purposes of the Congressional Budget Act of 1974 as allocations, functional levels, and aggregates contained in this concurrent resolution on the budget.

(3) REPORTING REVISED ALLOCATIONS.—The appropriate committee may report appropriately revised allocations pursuant to section 302(b) and 602(b) of the Congressional Budget Act of 1974 to carry out this subsection.

SEC. 10. SOCIAL SECURITY FIRE WALL POINT OF ORDER IN THE SENATE.

(a) ACCOUNTING TREATMENT.—Notwithstanding any other provision of this resolution, for the purpose of allocations and points of order under sections 302 and 311 of the Congressional Budget Act of 1974, the levels of social security outlays and revenues for this resolution shall be the current services levels.

(b) APPLICATION OF SECTION 301(i).—Notwithstanding any other rule of the Senate, in the Senate, the point of order established under section 301(i) of the Congressional Budget Act of 1974 shall apply to any concurrent resolution on the budget for any fiscal year (as reported and as amended), amendments thereto, or any conference report thereon.

SEC. 11. SENSE OF THE HOUSE REGARDING TAX REVENUES AND DEFICIT REDUCTION.

It is the sense of the House of Representatives that any legislation enacting tax increases called for in this budget resolution contain language providing that the net revenues generated by the legislation shall not be counted for the purpose of calculating the amount of any deficit increase called for in section 252(b) of the Balanced Budget and Emergency Deficit Control Act of 1985, as amended by the Omnibus Budget Reconciliation Act of 1990.

SEC. 12. ENFORCEMENT PROCEDURES.

    (a) PURPOSE.—The Senate declares that it is essential to—

    (1) ensure compliance with the deficit reduction goals embodied in this resolution;

    (2) extend the system of discretionary spending limits set forth in section 601 of the Congressional Budget Act of 1974;

    (3) extend the pay-as-you-go enforcement system;

    (4) prohibit the consideration of direct spending or receipts legislation that would decrease the pay-as-you-go surplus that the reconciliation bill pursuant to section 7 of this resolution will create under section 252 of the Balanced Budget and Emergency Deficit Control Act of 1985;

    (5) adopt as part of this concurrent resolution such of the enforcement procedures set forth in this subsection as this concurrent resolution may constitutionally include; and

    (6) enact, during this session of Congress, such of the enforcement procedures set forth in this subsection as only statute may constitutionally include.

    (b) DISCRETIONARY SPENDING LIMITS.—

    (1) DEFINITION.—As used in this section, for the discretionary category, the term "discretionary spending limit" means—

        (A) with respect to fiscal year 1996:

            $519,142,000,000 in new budget authority and $547,263,000,000 in outlays;

        (B) with respect to fiscal year 1997:

            $528,079,000,000 in new budget authority and $547,346,000,000 in outlays; and

        (C) with respect to fiscal year 1998:

            $530,639,000,000 in new budget authority and $547,870,000,000 in outlays;

as adjusted for changes in concepts and definitions, changes in inflation, and emergency appropriations.

    (2) POINT OF ORDER IN THE SENATE.—

        (A) Except as provided in subparagraph (B), it shall not be in order in the Senate to consider any concurrent resolution on the budget for fiscal year 1995, 1996, 1997, or 1998 (or amendment, motion, or conference report on such a resolution) that would exceed any of the discretionary spending limits in this section.

        (B) This subsection shall not apply if a declaration of war by the Congress is in effect or if a joint resolution pursuant to section 258 of the Balanced Budget and Emergency Deficit Control Act of 1985 has been enacted.

    (c) ENFORCING PAY-AS-YOU-GO.—At any time after the enactment of the reconciliation bill pursuant to section 7 of this resolution, it shall not be in order in the Senate to consider any bill, joint resolution, amendment, motion, or conference report, that would increase the deficit in this resolution for any fiscal year through fiscal year 1998 or would increase the deficit for any other fiscal year through fiscal year 2003, as measured by the sum of—

    (1) all applicable estimates of direct spending and receipts legislation applicable to that fiscal year, other than any amounts resulting from—

(A) *full funding of, and continuation of, the deposit insurance guarantee commitment in effect on the date of enactment of the Budget Enforcement Act of 1990; and*

(B) *emergency provisions as designated under section 252(e) of that Act; and*

(2) *the estimated amount of savings in direct spending programs applicable to that fiscal year resulting from the prior year's sequestration under that Act, if any (except for any amounts sequestered as a result of a net deficit increase in the fiscal year immediately preceding the prior fiscal year).*

(d) WAIVER.—*This section may be waived or suspended in the Senate only by the affirmative vote of three-fifths of the Members, duly chosen and sworn.*

(e) APPEALS.—*Appeals in the Senate from the decisions of the Chair relating to any provision of this section shall be limited to 1 hour, to be equally divided between, and controlled by, the appellant and the manager of the concurrent resolution, bill, or joint resolution, as the case may be. An affirmative vote of three-fifths of the Members of the Senate, duly chosen and sworn, shall be required in the Senate to sustain an appeal of the ruling of the Chair on a point of order raised under this section.*

(f) DETERMINATION OF BUDGET LEVELS.—*For purposes of this section, the levels of new budget authority, outlays, and receipts for a fiscal year shall be determined on the basis of estimates made by the Committee on the Budget of the Senate.*

(g) EXERCISE OF RULEMAKING POWERS.—*The Senate adopts the provisions of this section—*

(1) *as an exercise of the rulemaking power of the Senate, and as such they shall be considered as part of the rules of the Senate, and such rules shall supersede other rules only to the extent that they are inconsistent therewith; and*

(2) *with full recognition of the constitutional right of the Senate to change those rules (so far as they relate to the Senate) at any time, in the same manner, and to the same extent as in the case of any other rule of the Senate.*

SEC. 13. SENSE OF THE SENATE PROVISIONS.

The following subsections are set forth as the sense of the Senate:

(a) ASSUMPTIONS.—*The levels and amounts set forth in this resolution are based on the following assumptions:*

(1) REVENUES.—*(A) There shall not be an increase in inland barge fuel taxes beyond those increases already scheduled in current law.*

(B) *The Finance Committee will make every effort to find alternative sources of revenues before imposing new taxes on the benefits of Social Security beneficiaries with threshold incomes (for purposes of the taxation of Social Security benefits) of less than $32,000 for individuals and $40,000 for married couples filing joint returns.*

(C) *Consistent with the position of the Administration, the BTU tax will be imposed at the same rate on all fuels purchased by households for home heating purposes, and therefore the supplemental tax on oil will not be imposed on such fuels.*

(D) Any energy tax enacted during the One Hundred Third Congress should provide such relief to the agriculture industry as is necessary to ensure that the industry does not absorb a disproportionate impact of that tax.

(2) NATIONAL DEFENSE (FUNCTION 050).—(A) If the estimates for inflation for fiscal years 1994 through 1998 used in the President's fiscal year 1994 budget request and this concurrent resolution are too low, the amounts for budget authority and outlays for the National Defense (050) and other budget functions should be increased to offset the adverse effects of the higher inflation.

(B) If Congress does not enact legislation freezing Federal pay levels for fiscal year 1994 and reducing the rates of increase in Federal pay levels for fiscal years 1995 through 1997, as assumed for the President's fiscal year 1994 budget request and this concurrent resolution, there should be appropriate increases in the amounts of budget authority and outlays for the National Defense (050) and other budget functions in this concurrent resolution to allow the departments and agencies of the Federal Government to meet the resulting increases in costs for pay.

(C) Appropriations for fiscal year 1994 for the programs, projects, activities, and authorities under budget functional category 050 (National Defense) should be made at the levels of budget authority and outlays that are provided for in this concurrent resolution for such functional category for such fiscal year.

(D) If the appropriations for fiscal year 1994 for such programs, projects, activities, and authorities are less than the levels of budget authority and outlays that are provided for in this concurrent resolution for such functional category for such fiscal year, the savings resulting from the lesser levels of appropriations should be used only for reducing the deficit in the budget of the United States.

(E) The Congress should promptly reconsider the amounts determined and declared by the Congress in this resolution to be the appropriate levels of new budget authority, outlays, new direct loan obligations, and new primary loan guarantee commitments for fiscal years 1994 through 1998 for the National Defense (050) functional category, in the event of material change in situations affecting the security interests of the United States.

(3) GENERAL SCIENCE, SPACE, AND TECHNOLOGY (FUNCTION 250).—The budget authority and outlay figures for function 250 in this resolution do not assume any amounts for the National Aeronautics and Space Administration for any fiscal year from 1994 through 1998 in excess of the amounts proposed by the President for such fiscal year.

(4) NATURAL RESOURCES AND ENVIRONMENT (FUNCTION 300).—(A) Fees charged for domestic livestock grazing on lands under the jurisdiction of the Secretary of Agriculture and the Secretary of the Interior in western States should be set at an amount that permits the ranching industry to remain viable and reflects the economic realities of the in-

dustry, rather than at an amount that meets arbitrary revenue targets.

(B) Royalty fees charged for hardrock mining should be set at an amount that permits the mining industry to remain viable in the United States and reflects the economic realities of the industry, rather than at an amount that meets arbitrary revenue targets.

(5) EDUCATION, TRAINING, EMPLOYMENT, AND SOCIAL SERVICES (FUNCTION 500).—(A) The Head Start program will be funded at the level requested by the President for fiscal year 1998.

(B) The education reform and initiatives will be funded at the level requested by the President for fiscal year 1998.

(C) The defense conversion programs will be funded at the level requested by the President for fiscal year 1998.

(6) HEALTH (FUNCTION 550).—(A) The Committee on Labor and Human Resources will make every effort to embark upon a sustained investment strategy in health research and development over the next 5 years and support for the continuum of medical research should be a central feature in any plan to reform the United States health care system.

(B) The vast majority of rising mandatory program costs is due to increasing Federal health care costs, and these costs are assumed in the levels set forth in this resolution.

(C) Health care reform is essential to curb the escalating costs of health entitlement programs to reduce the deficit.

(D) The reduction in health costs in this budget resolution should be augmented by further savings in Federal health outlays as a part of comprehensive health care reform which will be reflected in future budget resolutions.

(E) Comprehensive health reform will result in long term savings both for the public and private sectors of the American economy, and reduce the deficit levels set forth in this resolution at an ever increasing pace.

(F) Health care reform legislation should receive priority attention by the United States Congress with a target date of enactment of such legislation being no later than September 30, 1993.

(7) INCOME SECURITY (FUNCTION 600).—The Women, Infants, and Children (WIC) program will be funded at the level requested by the President for fiscal year 1998.

(8) ADMINISTRATION OF JUSTICE (FUNCTION 750).—(A) The Community Policing ("Cops on the Beat") program will be funded at the level requested by the President for fiscal year 1998.

(B) Funds to reduce the availability and use of illegal drugs will be shifted over the next 5 years so that the allocation shall be equally distributed between the so-called "supply side" (interdiction, law enforcement, and international supply reduction efforts) and the so-called "demand side" *(education, rehabilitation, treatment, and research programs).*

(b) DEBT LIMIT IN RECONCILIATION.—(1) Any concurrent resolution on the budget that contains reconciliation directives shall include a directive with respect to the statutory limit on the public debt.

(2) Any change in the statutory limit on the public debt that is recommended pursuant to a reconciliation directive shall be included in the reconciliation legislation reported pursuant to section 310 of the Congressional Budget Act of 1974 for that fiscal year.

(3) Except as provided in paragraph (4), the Senate shall not consider any bill or joint resolution (or any amendment thereto or conference report thereon) that increases the statutory limit on the public debt during a fiscal year above the level set forth as appropriate for that fiscal year in the concurrent resolution on the budget for that fiscal year agreed to under section 301 of the Congressional Budget Act of 1974.

(4) The prohibition of paragraph (3) shall not apply to a reconciliation bill or reconciliation resolution reported pursuant to section 310(b) of the Congressional Budget Act of 1974 during any fiscal year (or any conference report thereon) that contains a provision that—

(A) increases the statutory limit on the public debt pursuant to a directive of the type described in section 310(a)(3) of that Act; and

(B) becomes effective on or after the first day of the following fiscal year.

(c) DEFICIT REDUCTION ACCOUNT.—It is assumed that the Committee on Finance of the Senate and the Committee on Ways and Means of the House of Representatives should report legislation to—

(1) establish a separate account in the Treasury into which all of the amounts by which the aggregate levels of Federal revenue should be increased would be deposited;

(2) ensure that any revenues deposited in such account would not be available for appropriation; and

(3) provide that any such revenues deposited in such account would be used to retire outstanding debt obligations of the United States Government.

(d) LINE-ITEM VETO AUTHORITY INCLUDING APPROPRIATIONS AND TAX EXPENDITURES.—The President should be granted line-item veto authority over items of appropriation and tax expenditures and that line-item veto authority should expire at the conclusion of the One Hundred Third Congress.

(e) USE OF SAVINGS FROM GOVERNMENT STREAMLINING.— Any amounts saved through the efforts of the National Performance Review Task Force headed by the Vice President and as a result of any other reorganization and streamlining of the Federal Government should be applied to offset the cost of any economic stimulus package enacted in fiscal year 1993, and any amounts saved in excess of those necessary to offset the cost of any such economic stimulus should be applied to reduce the Federal budget deficit and for no other purpose.

And the Senate agree to the same.

> MARTIN O. SABO,
> RICHARD GEPHARDT,
> DALE E. KILDEE,
> ANTHONY C. BEILENSON,
> HOWARD L. BERMAN,
> ROBERT E. WISE, Jr.,
> JOHN BRYANT,
> CHARLES W. STENHOLM,
> BARNEY FRANK,
> LOUISE SLAUGHTER,
> *Managers on the Part of the House.*

> JIM SASSER,
> FRITZ HOLLINGS,
> J. BENNETT JOHNSTON,
> *Managers on the Part of the Senate.*

VIEWS AND ESTIMATES REPORTS OF THE HOUSE COMMITTEES ON POST OFFICE AND CIVIL SERVICE AND WAYS AND MEANS

ONE HUNDRED THIRD CONGRESS

WILLIAM L. CLAY, MISSOURI, CHAIRMAN

PATRICIA SCHROEDER, Colorado
FRANK McCLOSKEY, Indiana
GARY L. ACKERMAN, New York
THOMAS C. SAWYER, Ohio
PAUL E. KANJORSKI, Pennsylvania
ELEANOR HOLMES NORTON, District of Columbia
BARBARA-ROSE COLLINS, Michigan
LESLIE L. BYRNE, Virginia
MELVIN L. WATT, North Carolina
ALBERT RUSSELL WYNN, Maryland
GREG LAUGHLIN, Texas
SANFORD D. BISHOP, JR., Georgia
SHERROD BROWN, Ohio
ALCEE L. HASTINGS, Florida

JOHN T. MYERS, Indiana
BENJAMIN A. GILMAN, New York
DON YOUNG, Alaska
DAN BURTON, Indiana
CONSTANCE A. MORELLA, Maryland
THOMAS J. RIDGE, Pennsylvania
THOMAS E. PETRI, Wisconsin
SHERWOOD L. BOEHLERT, New York
JIM SAXTON, New Jersey

House of Representatives

**Committee on Post Office
and Civil Service**

Washington, DC 20515–6243

TELEPHONE (202) 225–4054

February 25, 1994

The Honorable Martin Olav Sabo
Chairman
Committee on the Budget
H1-214 O'Neill House Office Building
Washington, D.C. 20515

Dear Mr. Chairman:

Pursuant to Section 301(d) of the Congressional Budget Act of 1974, there are transmitted herewith the views and recommendations of the Committee on Post Office and Civil Service, together with Supplemental Views, concerning the major policy issues in the President's fiscal year 1995 budget which fall under this Committee's jurisdiction.

These views and recommendations were circulated among all the Members of the Committee and were approved by a majority of those Members.

Sincerely,

William L. Clay

WILLIAM L. CLAY
Chairman

Committee on Post Office and Civil Service

Views and Recommendations

on Administration's FY 1995 Budget Proposals

General Overview

The budget proposed by President Clinton for fiscal year 1995 is less challenging overall to Federal employees and retirees than the proposal submitted for fiscal year 1994, which recommended substantial cuts in Federal employees' pay, retirement benefits, and health insurance benefits. In the area of Federal pay, however, the President has proposed underfunding Federal pay increases for fiscal year 1995. This threatens to severely undercut the goals of achieving pay comparability with the private sector and restoring regularity and order to the pay-setting process. The President also has proposed that agencies be charged the full cost of the Government's share of retirement benefits for employees covered by the Civil Service Retirement System (CSRS).

I.   FEDERAL EMPLOYEE PAY INCREASES

Administration Proposal: The President's budget proposes major changes in Federal employees' compensation. It proposes allocating $1.1 billion for civilian employee pay raises in 1995. This $1.1 billion would permit a national pay raise of 1.6 percent across the board for all civilian employees effective January 1, 1995. However, the Administration plans to consult with employee organizations and other interested parties on the best approach to distributing pay increases; i.e., a national pay raise, locality pay, or some combination of the two.

Committee Position: In late 1990, the Federal Employees Pay Comparability Act of 1990 (FEPCA) was enacted into law (Section 529 of Public Law 101-509). The primary purpose of FEPCA was to establish a system that would achieve pay comparability with the private sector and restore order and regularity to the pay-setting process. The average pay gap between public and private sector salaries was approximately 26 percent prior to the January 1994 adjustments.

Under current law, employees working in pay localities with a wage disparity of greater than 5 percent received an initial adjustment sufficient to reduce the disparity by 20 percent effective January 1994. Over the next eight fiscal years, the pay gap is to be closed an additional 10 percent each year until the pay disparity in each area has been closed by at least 95 percent.

Current law also provides that Federal employees are to receive annual pay increases based on the Employment Cost Index (ECI), which measures changes in salaries and wages of private sector employees. Current law requires that Federal employees receive adjustments based on the ECI minus 0.5 percent. FEPCA intended the ECI adjustment and locality pay adjustments to work in tandem to close the existing pay gaps for Federal sector jobs to within 95 percent of local private sector salaries.

The President's proposal to provide only $1.1 billion for civilian employee pay raises is significantly less than the $2.7 billion the Administration estimates would be necessary to cover both locality pay ($900,000,000) and the ECI adjustment of 2.6 percent ($1.8 billion) in fiscal year 1995 under current law. The projected funding levels for Federal employee pay contained in the President's budget indicate a planned continuation of such underfunding (see Budget of the United States Government: Analytical Perspectives, Fiscal Year 1995, "Table 1-1. Economic Assumptions," p. 4.).

FEPCA permits the President to establish an alternative level for the ECI adjustment (5 USC 5303(b)) and the locality pay adjustments (5 USC 5304a) when he determines it is appropriate "because of national emergency or serious economic conditions affecting the general welfare." To exercise his alternative pay authority with respect to the ECI adjustment, the President must submit a report to Congress by September 1 of the preceding calendar year describing the alternative plan and providing an assessment of the impact such plan will have on the Government's ability to recruit and retain well-qualified employees. Similarly, to exercise his alternative pay authority with respect to the locality pay adjustments, the President must submit a report to Congress at least one month before the adjustments would otherwise become payable describing the alternative plan and the reasons it is considered necessary. No change in law would be required for the President to modify the levels of the ECI and locality pay adjustments due in fiscal year 1995.

Last year, the President proposed eliminating the ECI adjustment for fiscal year 1994, reducing the adjustment by 1 percent in fiscal years 1995, 1996, and 1997, and delaying national implementation of locality pay until fiscal year 1995 under a "revised formula." The Committee rejected this approach and subsequently approved reconciliation legislation substantially adopting the President's proposal concerning the ECI adjustments, but keeping the implementation of locality pay on track for fiscal year 1994. In conference, however, the Committee's proposals were dropped from H.R. 2264, the Omnibus Budget Reconciliation Act of 1993. Subsequently, a provision was included in H.R. 2403, the Treasury, Postal Service, and General Government Appropriations Act, 1994, which eliminated the ECI adjustment for that year (Public Law 103-123).

The Committee believes that the President's FY 1995 proposal for Federal employee pay increases will further frustrate the goal of achieving pay comparability within the original nine-year timeframe established by FEPCA and will contribute to widening the current unacceptable pay gap.

II.   CIVIL SERVICE RETIREMENT

Administration Proposal: The President proposes to charge Federal agencies the full cost of the Government's share of retirement benefits for Federal employees covered by the Civil Service Retirement System (CSRS) and other, smaller, individual-agency systems. Currently, most Executive Branch employees contribute seven percent of their salary to the retirement fund and their agencies contribute an equal percentage, making the total contribution 14 percent (see 5 USC 8334(a)(1)). According to the Administration, the proposed increase in agency contributions would require raising the discretionary spending caps to accommodate this change.

Committee Position: The Committee has insufficient information upon which to judge the merits of the proposal at this time. More information is needed regarding the necessity for the proposed increased agency contribution, the amount of the increase, and the impact of the increase on the budgets of Federal agencies.

Although the President's budget states that this proposal will not affect the deficit, the Committee is concerned about the impact on the Postal Service which is an off-budget entity. Since 1971 the Postal Service has been reimbursing the CSRS for any unfunded liabilities for postal retirees. Since 1985 the Postal Service has been reimbursing the CSRS for COLA adjustments for Postal Service retirees. Pursuant to OBRA 1990 and 1993, the Postal Service is reimbursing CSRS for postal retiree COLAs between 1971 and 1985. The Committee does not have enough information to determine the extent of the impact of this proposal on the Postal Service. Moreover, in light of the Postal Service contributions to CSRS, over and above those of other government agencies, the Committee questions whether the application of this proposal to the Postal Service would be justified.

Supplemental Views

The Minority Members of the Committee on Post Office and
Civil Service find the Administration budget proposals a relief
from the previous year. Yet we note that these proposals appear
incomplete when compared with subsequent Administration
initiatives.

The Administration allocates $1.1 billion for pay increases,
but allows for Congressional discretion in determining the proper
allocation of any increase. Full funding of both locality pay
increases and the across-the-board adjustment would require the
Administration to ante up $2.7 billion. This $1.6 billion
shortfall contradicts the intention of the pay reform legislation
this Committee worked so hard to construct. In addition, the
Administration proposed last year to revamp the locality pay
formula. Its failure to include a revised formula in this budget
or to submit any legislation to the Congress indicates its lack
of resolve to correct problems that it perceives to exist.

These proposals also conspicuously remain silent on the
impact that reductions-in-force or the buyout legislation may
have on the budget process. We raise this issue because of the
torturous history the buyout legislation has had in this
Congress. The Minority faults the Administration for creating
the expectations of buyouts early in its tenure, thereby
artificially reducing retirement and attrition rates on the part
of federal employees hoping to cash in on government-financed
buyouts.

The Minority firmly supports efforts to avoid reductions-in-
force and pledges its continued assistance in working hand-in-
hand with our Majority counterparts to craft a legislative
measure which can enjoy broad bi-partisan support. We emphasize,
however, that in this instance the problem was self-created by
the Administration which in turn asked Congress to bail it out
from the predicament it had created.

This is the second year of the Administration's tenure and
the second time it has proposed less than full funding of
congressionally mandated pay raises. The Congressional Budget
Office reports that over the next five years combined locality
and annual pay adjustments would average slightly more than five
percent. The Administration has ignored the ramifications of
these projections in its budget proposals. CBO said that raises
of this size increase pressure to cut even more jobs in order to
fund such increases. The Minority is afraid that, once again,
Congress may be called on in an emergency like fashion to craft a
legislative solution for the Administration's shortsightedness.

We are encouraged by the Administration's kinder, gentler
tone this fiscal year when compared with the budget proposals for
Fiscal Year 1994. Committee Republicans firmly opposed President
Clinton's efforts to cut child-survivor benefits and retiree
health benefits, while proposing to freeze both national and
locality pay adjustments. Deficit reduction requires shared
sacrifice. This seems to be a lesson which this Administration is
finding hard to learn.

In summary, we stand with our Majority colleagues in
questioning the Administration's commitment towards
implementation of a prudent pay reform strategy. We share their
concerns regarding the lack of Administration-provided
information on which to enact any proposed increased agency
contributions for Civil Service Retirement System participants.
Moreover, the Minority questions Administration efforts to soft-
pedal the difficult choices it must make in the budget arena. We
encourage the Administration to exercise "truth-in-budgeting" and
submit its complete legislative agenda as it affects the budget
process, rather than depend on a piece meal approach whereby it

avoids the tough choices during the budget debate only to submit subsequent legislation which attempts the same goals.

Sherwood L. Boehlert	John T. Myers
Benjamin A. Gilman	Dan Burton
Thomas E. Petri	Don Young
Constance A. Morella	Thomas J. Ridge

COMMITTEE ON WAYS AND MEANS

U.S. HOUSE OF REPRESENTATIVES
WASHINGTON, DC 20515-6348

February 23, 1994

The Honorable Martin Olav Sabo
Chairman
Committee on the Budget
U.S. House of Representatives
H1-214 O'Neill House Office Building
Washington, D.C. 20515

Dear Mr. Chairman:

As required by section 301(d) of the Congressional Budget
Act of 1974, this letter transmits the views and estimates of the
Committee on Ways and Means on those aspects of the Federal
budget for fiscal year 1995 which fall within the Committee's
jurisdiction.

In his State of the Union message and his fiscal year 1995
budget, President Clinton proposed a continuation of the deficit
reduction effort begun with enactment last year of the Omnibus
Budget Reconciliation Act of 1993 (OBRA 1993). The
Administration's budget includes proposals for achieving the
required limits on discretionary spending as well as some
additional deficit-neutral spending. Administration officials
have stated that it will not be necessary for Congress to enact a
budget reconciliation bill again this year to achieve additional
savings.

However, the President has proposed a number of initiatives
which fall within the jurisdiction of the Committee on Ways and
Means. It is the longstanding tradition of this Committee to
approach new spending initiatives in a deficit-neutral manner.

    I.   <u>Administration Proposals with Budgetary Impact</u>.--
Briefly, the President's agenda includes:

        A.   <u>Health Care Reform</u>.-- Today, 14 percent of the U.S.
            gross domestic product (GDP) is spent on health care, a
            number that is expected to rise to 18 percent by the
            end of the decade. Yet, fifteen percent of all
            Americans do not have health insurance coverage. And
            many of those with insurance fear losing it -- if they
            change jobs or become sick. President Clinton's
            comprehensive proposal for reforming the nation's
            health care system, H.R. 3600, and several other bills
            are pending before Congress. The Committee plans to
            consider health reform this spring.

        B.   <u>GATT-Uruguay Round Implementing Legislation</u>.-- The
            Uruguay Round represents the largest, most
            comprehensive set of trade agreements since the
            inception of the General Agreement on Tariffs and Trade
            (GATT) in 1947. The Round will reduce tariffs,
            comprehensively cover trade in agriculture for the
            first time, phase out the current trade regime for
            textiles, provide new coverage of trade in services and
            intellectual property, and reduce other non-tariff
            barriers to trade.

President Clinton is expected to sign the Uruguay Round results on April 15 and submit legislation this year to implement the Round under the fast track procedures. The Committee plans to consider the implementing legislation this year.

C.   Welfare Reform.-- According to the Administration's fiscal year 1995 budget, the President will, in late spring, propose a comprehensive, deficit-neutral welfare reform plan. This proposal will be designed to promote parental responsibility, reward those who work, and reduce administrative complexity and bureaucracy. Our Subcommittee on Human Resources has already begun hearings in anticipation of possible action.

D.   A Workforce Security Initiative.-- More than two million Americans are permanently laid-off each year. Contraction of the defense industry, rapidly evolving technologies, and intensifying global competition continue to challenge the American worker. To address these developments, the Administration soon will propose a workforce security initiative. This plan would establish a re-employment system that includes a comprehensive worker adjustment program, a voluntary one-stop career center network, and a national labor market information system.

E.   Reform of the Pension Benefit Guaranty Corporation (PBGC).-- President Clinton has also proposed legislation to improve the funding of government-insured pension plans, limit growth in PBGC's exposure, and assist plan participants. The Committee expects to hold a hearing on this matter this spring and to work with the Committee on Education and Labor, which shares jurisdiction with us on this issue, on the reform measure.

II.   Public Debt Limit.-- The present statutory limit on the public debt is $4.9 trillion, a level that should be sufficient to accommodate Federal borrowing through late spring or early summer 1995, based on current estimates.

III.   Administrative Funding.-- The Committee remains concerned about the level of administrative funds available for programs that fall within the jurisdiction of the Committee on Ways and Means. In particular, we are concerned about administrative funding levels for the Internal Revenue Service, the Social Security program, the Medicare program, the unemployment compensation program, the Office of the U.S. Trade Representative, the U.S. Customs Service, and the Bureau of Alcohol, Tobacco and Firearms.

IV.   Additional Materials.-- In keeping with our tradition of assisting the Committee on the Budget in carrying out its responsibilities, I will forward at a later date our annual Committee print entitled "Background Materials and Data on Programs within the Jurisdiction of the Committee on Ways and Means -- 1994 Edition."

Finally, please note there may be additional deficit-neutral measures considered by the Committee during this year. I hope you find the views and recommendations of the Committee on Ways and Means useful. As always, I am available to answer any questions you or any other Members of your Committee may have on any aspect of this report.

With warm regards, I am

Sincerely yours,

Dan Rostenkowski
Chairman

BUDGET PROJECTIONS AND ECONOMIC ASSUMPTIONS

Effects on CBO Budget Projections of Selected Changes in Economic Assumptions (By fiscal year, in billions of dollars)

	1994	1995	1996	1997	1998	1999
Real Growth: Effect of 1-Percentage-Point Lower Annual Rate Beginning January 1994						
Change in Revenues	-8	-25	-46	-69	-93	-118
Change in Outlays						
Net interest (Debt service)	a	1	4	7	13	20
Other	1	2	4	6	9	11
Total	1	4	8	14	22	31
Change in Deficit	9	29	54	82	115	149
Unemployment: Effect of 1-Percentage-Point Higher Annual Rate Beginning January 1994						
Change in Revenues	-33	-49	-50	-52	-54	-57
Change in Outlays						
Net interest (Debt service)	1	3	7	10	14	18
Other	3	5	5	5	5	6
Total	4	8	12	15	20	24
Change in Deficit	37	57	62	67	74	81

**Inflation: Effect of 1-Percentage-Point
Higher Annual Rate Beginning January 1994**

Change in Revenues	7	20	35	51	68	87
Change in Outlays						
Net interest						
Higher rates	5	15	20	24	29	33
Debt service	a	a	a	a	a	a
Other	1	5	14	25	38	55
Total	5	20	34	49	66	88
Change in Deficit	-1	-1	-2	-2	-1	1

**Interest Rates: Effect of 1-Percentage-Point
Higher Annual Rates Beginning January 1994**

Change in Revenues	0	0	0	0	0	0
Change in Outlays						
Net interest						
Higher rates	5	15	20	24	29	33
Debt service	a	1	2	4	6	8
Other	a	1	1	1	1	a
Total	5	16	23	29	35	42
Change in Deficit	5	16	23	29	35	42

Source: Congressional Budget Office, *The Economic and Budget Outlook, Fiscal Years 1994–1998* (Washington, D.C.: U.S. Government Printing Office, 1993), p. 110.

FUNCTIONAL CATEGORIES OF THE FEDERAL BUDGET

Both the president's budget and congressional budget resolutions are required to list programs by "functional categories." These functions classify government activities by their primary purpose, regardless of which agency administers them. As a result, the programs of one department may be spread over several budget functions. (See chapter one.)

BUDGET FUNCTIONS

Number	Title
050	National Defense
150	International Affairs
250	General Science, Space, and Technology
270	Energy
300	Natural Resources and Environment
350	Agriculture
370	Commerce and Housing Credit
400	Transportation
450	Community and Regional Development
500	Education, Training, Employment, and Social Services
550	Health
570	Medicare
600	Income Security
650	Social Security[1]
700	Veterans Benefits and Services
750	Administration of Justice
800	General Government
900	Net Interest
920	Allowances
950	Undistributed Offsetting Receipts

Function 050: National Defense

Funds in this function develop, maintain, and equip the military forces of the United States and finance defense-related activities of the Department of Energy. Major areas of funding include pay and benefits to active military and civilian personnel; military retired pay; procurement of weapons systems and supporting equipment including research, development, test and evaluation; military construction, including family housing; and operations and maintenance of the defense establishment. Funding is also provided for the development and procurement of nuclear weapons and naval reactors.

Major Federal Programs

   Atomic energy defense activities
   Defense-related activities
   Department of Defense—military

Major Federal Departments and Agencies

   Department of Energy (nuclear weapons and naval reactors)
   Department of Defense
   Federal Emergency Management Agency
   Selective Service System

Function 150: International Affairs

Funds in this function finance the foreign affairs establishment, including embassies and other diplomatic missions abroad; loans and technical assistance activities in the less developed countries; security supporting assistance and military assistance to foreign governments; foreign military sales made through the trust fund; U.S. contributions to international financial institutions; and Export-Import Bank activities.

Major Federal Programs

   Export promotion
   Food for peace
   Foreign affairs
   Foreign aid
   Foreign military sales
   Security assistance
   U.S. contributions to international financial institutions

Major Federal Departments and Agencies

Agency for International Development
Department of Agriculture
Department of Defense
Department of State
Department of the Treasury
Export-Import Bank of the United States
International Communications Agency

Function 250: General Science, Space, and Technology

This function includes space research and technology, general science, and basic research not covered in other functions. It represents a substantial portion of total federal research and development outlays and includes the basic science and research programs of the National Science Foundation, the high-energy and nuclear physics programs of the Energy Department, a small Smithsonian Institution program, and the nonaeronautical programs of the National Aeronautics and Space Administration.

Major Federal Programs

General science and basic research
Space research, technology, and applications

Major Federal Departments

Department of Energy
National Aeronautics and Space Administration
National Science Foundation

Function 270: Energy

This function includes nearly all federal civilian energy and energy-related programs. Nuclear energy defense activities are funded in the National Defense (050) function.

Major Federal Programs

Energy conservation
Energy information, policy, and regulation
Energy research, development, and demonstration
Energy supply
Nuclear regulation

Strategic petroleum reserve
Synthetic fuels
Tennessee Valley Authority power

Major Federal Departments and Agencies

Department of Energy
Nuclear Regulatory Commission
Rural Electrification Administration
Tennessee Valley Authority

Function 300: Natural Resources and Environment

Programs in this function are designed primarily to develop, manage, and maintain the nation's natural resources and environment. This includes the nation's water, mineral, timber, wildlife, fish, and other resources; the management of the national parks, forests, refuges, and other public lands; and the protection of the environment.

Major Federal Programs

Development, regulation, and conservation of minerals
Implementation of national environmental programs
Management and acquisition of national parks
Management and preservation of public lands
Natural resources management, development, and conservation
Sewage treatment plant construction grant programs
Water resources programs

Major Federal Departments and Agencies

Army Corps of Engineers
Department of Agriculture
Department of Commerce
Department of Interior
Environmental Protection Agency

Function 350: Agriculture

Programs in this function are designed to assist food purchasers, provide market information and services, and support food research. Farmers are assisted through deficiency payments, disaster payments, product purchases, insurance, nonresource loans, and regular loans. Market information and services include Department of Agriculture administration, animal disease prevention, distribution of market information, and numerous regulatory activities. Research provides for the direct support of federal biological research facilities, grants for state-supported facilities, and economic analysis.

Major Federal Programs

Consumer protection, marketing, and regulatory programs
Economic information
Extension programs
Farm loans
Federal crop insurance
Price support and related programs
Research programs

Major Federal Departments and Agencies

Commodity Credit Corporation
Department of Agriculture
Farmers Home Administration (FmHA)

Function 370: Commerce and Housing Credit

This function includes many of the federal programs that provide aid to businesses. It also provides assistance through the government's unsubsidized housing programs.

Major Federal Programs

Mortgage insurance programs
Payments to the U.S. Postal Service
Rural housing programs
Secondary-market support for insured mortgages
Section 202 elderly and handicapped housing
Small business loan and guarantee assistance
Thrift and deposit insurance

Major Federal Departments and Agencies

Farmers Home Administration (FmHA)
Federal Deposit and Insurance Corporation
Federal Housing Administration
Government National Mortgage Association (GNMA)
International Trade Administration
Resolution Trust Corporation

Securities and Exchange Commission
Small Business Administration
U.S. Postal Service

Function 400: Transportation

This function funds transportation activities, including ground (highway, railroads, and mass transportation), air, and water transportation programs. It also includes major grants-in-aid programs to support state and local activities.

Major Federal Programs

Airways and airports
Coast Guard
Highway construction and safety
Maritime subsidies
Mass transit
Railroad assistance

Major Federal Departments and Agencies

Department of Commerce
Department of Transportation
Interstate Commerce Commission
National Aeronautics and Space Administration

Function 450: Community and Regional Development

This function funds a wide variety of urban and rural development grants and disaster and emergency aid programs.

Major Federal Programs

Appalachian Regional Commission and other regional aid programs
Community development block grants
Disaster relief
Economic development assistance
Flood insurance
Native American programs
Rehabilitation loans
Rural development assistance
Small Business Administration disaster loan programs

Major Federal Departments and Agencies

Bureau of Indian Affairs
Department of Housing and Urban Development
Economic Development Administration
Farmers Home Loan Administration
Small Business Administration

Function 500: Education, Training, Employment, and Social Services

This function includes programs designed to promote the extension of knowledge and skills and to help individuals become self-supporting. This includes child development; elementary, secondary, vocational, and higher education; employment and training and public service employment; and grants to states for general and social services. Funds in this function may be made available as income support such as cash payments (scholarships, loans, and stipends, etc.) to enable individuals to participate in education or training programs; grants to states, local governments, Indian tribes, or public and private institutions to operate local educational, employment, training, or social service programs; and direct research and departmental management expenditures.

Major Federal Programs

Child Care
Community services block grants
Financial assistance for elementary and secondary education
Grants to states for social and child welfare services
Handicapped education
Higher education student assistance
Human development services
Impact Aid
Job Training Partnership Act
National Service Corps
Occupational, vocational, and adult education

Major Federal Departments and Agencies

Action
Bureau of Indian Affairs
Corporation for National & Community Service
Department of Education
Department of Health and Human Services

Department of Labor
Office of Personnel Management

Function 550: Health

The major purpose of this function is to promote physical and mental health. Programs include financing of medical care for aged, poor, and disabled persons; providing health care for certain groups such as Native Americans and merchant seamen; and grants to states, localities, and community groups to support health services programs. This function also includes research into the causes and cures of diseases; promotion of consumer and occupational health and safety; training and health care facilities; and food, drug, and other product safety and inspection programs. This function does not include Medicare, which is listed in its own function (570).

Major Federal Programs

Alcoholism, drug abuse, and mental health research, training, and services
Community health centers
Disease prevention and control
Health resources development
Immunizations
Maternal and child health
Migrant health centers
Medicaid

Major Federal Departments and Agencies

Department of Agriculture
Department of Health and Human Services
Department of Labor
National Institutes of Health
Office of Personnel Management

Function 570: Medicare

This function includes funding for the Medicare programs—Part A Hospital Insurance (HI) and Part B Supplementary Medical Insurance (SMI)—as well as the costs of administering these programs.

Major Federal Program

Medicare

Major Federal Department

Department of Health and Human Services

Function 600: Income Security

Programs in this function provide cash and in-kind benefits to individuals who need permanent or temporary income assistance. More than half of the estimated outlays go to retirees through such programs as federal civilian and military retirement and railroad retirement. In-kind assistance includes food stamps and other food programs as well as subsidized housing. Special benefits for the physically challenged and unemployment benefits are also included in this function.

Major Federal Programs

Aid to Families with Dependent Children
Child nutrition
Federal employee retirement and disability
Food stamps
Housing assistance
Low Income Energy Assistance
Railroad retirement
Refugee assistance
Special benefits for disabled coal miners
Supplemental Security Income
Trade Adjustment Assistance
Unemployment compensation
Women, Infants, and Children supplemental feeding program (WIC)

Major Federal Departments and Agencies

Department of Agriculture
Department of Health and Human Services
Department of Housing and Urban Development
Department of Labor
Department of State
Office of Personnel Management
Railroad Retirement Board

Function 650: Social Security[1]

This function includes funding for the Old Age, Survivors, and Disability Insurance (OASDI) programs including program administration.

Major Federal Program

Old Age, Survivors, and Disability Insurance

Major Federal Department

Social Security Administration

Function 700: Veterans Benefits and Services

Programs in this function are administered by the Department of Veterans Affairs to support former members of the armed services, their survivors, and their dependents. More than half of the outlays are for income security programs: compensation, pensions, and life insurance. Nearly one-third is for medical care. The remaining programs fund education, training, rehabilitation, housing, and other benefits.

Major Federal Programs

Veterans disability compensation
Veterans education and training (GI bill)
Veterans guaranteed housing loans
Veterans hospital and medical care
Veterans life insurance
Veterans pensions

Major Federal Department

Department of Veterans Affairs

Function 750: Administration of Justice

This function includes all major federal law enforcement activities. The largest programs are the operations of the Federal Bureau of Investigation, the U.S. Customs Service, and the Immigration and Naturalization Service. Other programs fund other federal law enforcement including many anti-drug efforts, correctional activities, the judiciary, and prosecutions from the savings and loan crisis.

Major Federal Programs

Anti-drug activities
Courts
Customs
Immigration and naturalization

Financial Institutions Reform, Recovery, and Enforcement Act
Judiciary
Juvenile delinquency prevention
Law enforcement assistance
Legal services
Prisons

Major Federal Departments and Agencies

Civil Rights Commission
Department of Justice
Department of the Treasury
Drug Enforcement Administration
Federal Bureau of Investigation
Legal Services Corporation

Function 800: General Government

This function includes the overhead costs of the legislative branch and executive office of the president, payments to the District of Columbia, and portions of certain taxes and other charges shared with state and local governments.

Major Federal Programs

District of Columbia federal payment
Federal buildings fund
Income tax administration
Legislative branch activities
Payments in lieu of taxes to state and local governments

Major Federal Departments and Agencies

Congress and its agencies
Department of the Treasury
Department of the Interior
Executive Office of the President
General Services Administration
Internal Revenue Service
Office of Personnel Management

Function 900: Net Interest

This function includes payments made by the government for interest on the national debt and for other reasons (income tax refunds, for example), and certain offsetting receipts (interest earned by federal trust funds, for example).

Major Federal Programs

Interest on the national debt
Interest on income tax refunds
Interest received by certain federal trust funds

Major Federal Department

Department of the Treasury

Function 920: Allowances

Allowances include estimates for civilian agency pay increases and contingencies to cover anticipated expenses not included in the account of a particular executive agency.

Major Federal Programs

Contingencies for unexpected requirements
Pay raise for federal civilian employees

Function 950: Undistributed Offsetting Receipts

Undistributed offsetting receipts are miscellaneous receipts of the federal government that are deducted from the budget authority and outlays of the government as a whole rather than from individual departments or agencies or from particular programs. The major items in this function are the employer share of employee retirement funds, rents and royalties from oil leases in the Outer Continental Shelf, and receipts from the sale of federal assets.

Note

1. Social Security was taken "off-budget" and removed from the deficit calculation in the Omnibus Budget Reconciliation Act of 1990 (P.L. 101-508). Some tables displaying the federal budget by function may still include the social security function, however, especially if the table shows the "consolidated" budget.

PRESIDENT CLINTON'S FISCAL 1994 RESCISSION MESSAGE

TO THE CONGRESS OF THE UNITED STATES:

In accordance with the Congressional Budget and Impoundment Control Act of 1974, I herewith report 37 proposed rescissions of budget authority, totaling $1.9 billion.

These proposed rescissions affect programs of the Departments of Agriculture, Commerce, Defense, Energy, Housing and Urban Development, Interior, State, and Transportation, International Security Assistance programs, and programs of the Agency for International Development, the Army Corps of Engineers, the General Services Administration, the Small Business Administration, the State Justice Institute, and the United States Information Agency. The details of these proposed rescissions are set forth in the attached letter from the Director of the Office of Management and Budget and in the accompanying report.

Concurrent with these proposals, I am transmitting to the Congress FY 1994 supplemental appropriations language requests that would remove a variety of restrictions that impede effective functioning of the government, including certain proposals outlined in the recommendations of the National Performance Review.

Together, the supplemental language requests and the rescission proposals would result in a total budget authority reduction of $2.0 billion. My Administration is committed to working closely with the Congress to produce legislation that will achieve this level of savings.

THE WHITE HOUSE,
November 1, 1993

GLOSSARY

Account According to the Budget Enforcement Act, an item for which appropriations are made in any appropriation act. For items that are not provided in an appropriation act, an account is an item for which there is a designated budget account identification number in the president's budget.

Advance appropriation Budget authority provided in an appropriation act which is first available in a fiscal year beyond the fiscal year for which the appropriation act is enacted.

Advance funding Budget authority provided in an appropriation act that allows funds to be spent during this fiscal year even though the appropriation actually is for the next fiscal year. Advance funding generally is used to avoid requests for supplemental appropriations for entitlement programs late in a fiscal year when the appropriations for the current fiscal year are insufficient.

Aggregates The totals relating to the whole budget rather than a particular function, program, or line item. The budget aggregates are budget authority, outlays, revenues, deficit/surplus, and the level of public debt.

Allowance As used by Congress in a budget resolution, an allowance is a special functional classification designed to include an amount to cover possible requirements, such as a pay raise for federal employees. (See appendix D.)

Appropriation An act of Congress that provides the legal authority for federal agencies to incur obligations and make payments from the Treasury for specified purposes. An appropriation is the most common means of providing budget authority and usually follows the passage of an authorization. The three major types of appropriations are regular, supplemental, and continuing (see chapter 1).

These definitions have been adapted, in part, from U.S. General Accounting Office, *A Glossary of Terms Used in the Federal Budget Process*, Exposure Draft, Report No. PAD-GAO/AFMD-2.1.1 (Washington, D.C.: Government Printing Office, January 1993).

Authorization An act of Congress that establishes or continues the operation of a federal program or agency either for a specified period of time or indefinitely; specifies its general goals and conduct; and often sets a ceiling on the amount of budget authority that can be provided in an annual appropriation. An authorization for an agency or program usually is required before an appropriation for that same agency or program can be passed (see chapter 1).

Authorization committee A standing committee of the House or Senate with legislative jurisdiction over the subject matter of those laws that establish or continue the operation of federal programs or agencies. Authorization committees also have jurisdiction where "backdoor" spending authority is provided in substantive legislation.

Backdoor authority or **backdoor spending** Budget authority provided without the passage of an appropriation. The most common forms of backdoor authority are borrowing authority, contract authority, and entitlement authority.

Balanced budget When annual revenues equal annual outlays, measured by fiscal years. (See chapter 1.)

Balanced Budget and Emergency Deficit Control Act of 1985 The law (P.L. 99-177) that created the budget process commonly known as Gramm-Rudman-Hollings (GRH) from the names of its three principal sponsors—Senators Phil Gramm (R-TX), Warren Rudman (R-NH), and Ernest Hollings (D-SC).

Balanced Budget and Emergency Deficit Control Reaffirmation Act of 1987 An amendment to the Balanced Budget and Emergency Deficit Control Act of 1985 adopted in Public Law 100-119 that revised the Gramm-Rudman-Hollings budget process. The revised process continued to be known by that name.

Baseline A projection of the federal revenues, spending, deficit or surplus, and public debt that will occur under certain specified assumptions, usually if there is no change in existing laws. A baseline is not a forecast of a future budget, only a benchmark against which proposed changes in taxes or spending can be measured. The Budget Enforcement Act of 1990 defined its baseline as "a projection of current-year levels of new budget authority, outlays, receipts, and the surplus or deficit into the budget year and the outyears based on laws enacted. . ." (see chapter 1).

BEA See *Budget Enforcement Act of 1990.*

Biennial Budget A budget covering two fiscal years.

Block grant See *grant.*

Borrowing authority A form of budget authority that permits a federal agency (other than the Treasury and Federal Financing Bank) to borrow funds from the public or another federal fund or account and to incur obligations and make payments for specified purposes out of that borrowed money. Borrowing authority differs from an appropriation, which permits a federal agency to incur obligations and make payments directly from the Treasury. Borrowing authority is a type of backdoor spending.

Breach The amount by which new budget authority or outlays within a category of discretionary spending established by the Budget Enforcement Act of 1990 is above that category's limit (see *Category*).

Budget authority The authority granted to a federal agency to enter into commitments that result in immediate or future outlays. Budget authority is not necessarily the amount of money an agency or department actually will spend during a fiscal year but merely the upper limit on the amount of new spending commitments it can make. The four basic types of budget authority are appropriations, borrowing authority, contract authority, and the authority to obligate and expend the proceeds of offsetting receipts and collections. "One-year" budget authority must be obligated by the department or agency that received it only during a specific fiscal year. "Multi-year" authority must be obligated for a specified period in excess of one year. "No-year" authority remains available for obligation for an indefinite period. (See chapter 1.)

Budget Enforcement Act of 1990 Technically an amendment to the Balanced Budget and Emergency Deficit Control Act of 1985 (as amended by the Balanced Budget and Emergency Deficit Control Reaffirmation Act of 1987) that was adopted in Public Law 101-508. This revision to the federal budget process was so substantial that the "Budget Enforcement Act" (BEA) rather than Gramm-Rudman-Hollings has become the name most often used.

Budgetary resources The forms of spending authority given to a department or agency to incur obligations. These include new budget authority, unobligated balances, direct spending authority, and obligation limitations.

Budget Year The fiscal year that starts on October 1 of the calendar year in which the current session of Congress begins. In effect, the budget year is the budget that Congress is currently working on. For example, the 104th Congress will convene in January 1995 and will debate the fiscal 1996 budget. Fiscal 1996 begins on October 1, 1995, so the budget year is 1996 (see current year and outyear).

Capital Budget A budget that separates capital and operating expenses.

Categorical grant See *grant*.

Category For fiscal 1991–1993, all discretionary spending was divided into three categories—defense, international, and domestic. For fiscal 1994–1998, the three categories were combined into a single category that includes all discretionary spending. The Budget Enforcement Act of 1990 designated the category for every discretionary program for 1991–1993. The category for a new discretionary program is determined by the Office of Management and Budget in consultation with the House and Senate Appropriations and Budget Committees.

Concurrent resolution on the budget Legislation passed by Congress that establishes, reaffirms, or revises the congressional budget for a fiscal year. The congressional budget resolution is expected to pass by April 15. This resolution establishes binding figures for the aggregate levels of budget authority, outlays, revenues, and deficit or surplus, the appropriate level of the public debt, and an estimate of the budget authority and outlays for each of the budget functions. If needed, subsequent budget resolutions for a fiscal year may be adopted at any time after the passage of the April 15 resolution. A budget resolution does not require the president's signature to become effective. A budget resolution may contain "reconciliation" instructions to congressional committees (see chapter 4).

Congressional budget The budget passed by Congress in a concurrent resolution on the budget.

Congressional Budget Act of 1974 The law (P.L. 93-344) that established the congressional budget process, the House and Senate Budget Committees, and the Congressional Budget Office (see chapter 2).

Constant dollars The dollar value of goods and services adjusted for inflation. Constant dollars are determined by dividing current dollars by a price index, a process generally known as "deflating." The resulting dollar value is what would exist if prices had remained at the same level as in the period chosen for comparison.

Continuing Resolution Legislation that may be enacted to provide budget authority for a department or agency or a specific program when Congress and the president have not completed action on the regular appropriation for that department, agency, or program by the start of the fiscal year. The continuing resolution thus allows the department, agency, or program to continue operating (see chapter 5).

Contract authority A type of budget authority that permits a federal agency to incur obligations before appropriations have been passed.

Contract authority must be funded subsequently by an appropriation so that the commitments entered into can be paid.

Controllability The ability of Congress and the president to increase or decrease spending for a particular program in a fiscal year. "Relatively uncontrollable" refers to spending that will occur without any new action by Congress and the president and usually refers to spending that results from mandatory programs such as entitlements, permanent appropriations, and commitments now coming due from budget authority enacted in previous years. "Relatively controllable" refers to spending that will occur only if an appropriation is enacted (see chapter 1).

Credit reform The revised method of accounting for federal credit programs as created by the Federal Credit Reform Act of 1990, which added title V to the Congressional Budget Act of 1990.

Crosswalk A procedure for translating budget information from one form to another—for example, from a budget resolution to an authorization or appropriations bill.

Current dollars The dollar value of a good or service in terms of the prices prevailing at the time the good was sold or service rendered. This is the opposite of constant dollars.

Current level The amounts of new budget authority, outlays, and revenues required by existing law to be spent.

Current services An estimate of the budget authority and outlays that would be needed in the next fiscal year to continue federal programs at their current levels. These estimates reflect the anticipated costs of continuing programs at their present spending levels without any policy changes, that is, ignoring all new presidential and congressional initiatives that have not been enacted into law (see *current level* and *baseline*).

Current year The current fiscal year. Technically, current year refers to the fiscal year that immediately precedes the budget year. For example, the 104th Congress will convene in January 1995 and will be debating the fiscal 1996 budget, so the budget year is 1996. That means that the current year is 1995.

Deferral An action by the president that temporarily withholds or delays the obligation or expenditure of budget authority. A deferral must be reported by the president to Congress and the comptroller general in a deferral message. A deferral may not extend beyond the end of the fiscal year in which the message reporting it is transmitted to Congress (see chapter 7).

Deficit When annual outlays exceed annual revenues, measured by fiscal years.

Deposit insurance The expenses of the Federal Deposit Insurance Corporation and the funds it incorporates, the Resolution Trust Corporation, the National Credit Union Administration and the funds it incorporates, the Office of Thrift Supervision, the Comptroller of the Currency Assessment Fund, and the Resolution Trust Corporation Office of the Inspector General.

Direct loan A disbursement of federal funds to a nonfederal borrower that is expected to be repaid by the borrower.

Direct loan obligation A legally binding commitment by a federal agency to make a direct loan.

Direct Spending Authority As defined by the Budget Enforcement Act of 1990, entitlement authority, the Food Stamp Program, and budget authority provided by laws other than appropriations acts. Direct spending is generally within the jurisdiction of an authorization committee, not an appropriations committee.

Discretionary spending Outlays controllable through the appropriations process.

Discretionary spending cap A limit placed on certain categories of discretionary spending. Separate caps exist for both budget authority and outlays. For fiscal 1991–1993, caps were provided for three separate categories of discretionary spending—defense, domestic, and international. For fiscal 1994–1998, the three categories were combined into a single category that includes all discretionary spending. Any legislation that is enacted that would cause budget authority or outlays to breach the cap will trigger a sequester.

Earmarking The practice of dedicating appropriations or collections for a specific purpose.

Economic assumptions Estimates of how the national economy will behave. The four main economic assumptions that affect the budget are unemployment, inflation, growth in the gross domestic product (GDP), and interest rates (see chapter 1).

Emergency appropriation Discretionary appropriations that the president designates as "emergency requirements" and which are similarly designated by Congress in legislation subsequently enacted into law. Any spending designated as an emergency will result in the discretionary spending cap being adjusted to accommodate the additional spending. A sequester will not, therefore, be triggered that year because of the emergency appropriation.

Entitlement A program that requires the payment of benefits to all who meet the eligibility requirements established in the law. Examples of entitlement programs are Social Security, Medicare, and veterans' pensions (see chapter 1 and also *backdoor authority* and *controllability*).

Expenditures Actual spending, generally interchangeable with outlays.

Fiscal policy Federal policies on taxes and spending intended to promote the nation's macroeconomic goals, particularly with respect to employment, gross domestic product, inflation, balance of payments, exchange rates, and national savings.

Fiscal year Any yearly account period. The fiscal year for the federal government begins on October 1 and ends on September 30. The federal fiscal year is designated by the calendar year in which it ends; for example, fiscal 1995 begins on October 1, 1994, and ends on September 30, 1995. The federal fiscal year used to begin on July 1 and end on June 30. This was changed by the Congressional Budget Act of 1974 starting in fiscal 1977 to October 1 through September 30, primarily to give Congress additional time to work on spending, tax, and budget matters. A three-month "transition quarter" was added after the end of the old fiscal 1976 on June 30 and before the new fiscal 1977 to make this possible.

Forward funding Budget authority provided in an appropriations act that allows funds to be committed to a specific purpose (obligated) this year for programs that will be implemented next year. Forward funding often is used for education programs so that grants can be made by the federal government before the start of the school year and local school officials can plan their budgets.

Full funding Providing the budget authority to cover the total cost of a program or project at the time it first is approved. This differs from "partial" or "incremental" funding, where budget authority is provided only for those obligations of the program or project that are likely to be incurred in the budget year.

Function or functional classification The system of presenting budget authority, outlays, receipts, and tax expenditures in terms of the principal national need the programs are intended to serve. Each program is placed in the single functional category that best represents its major purpose, regardless of the department that administers it. Both the president's budget and the congressional budget resolutions are supposed to be presented primarily by function (see chapter 1).

Government-sponsored enterprise (GSE) A corporation created by a U.S. statute that has a federal charter; is privately owned, that is, has stock that is owned by private entities or individuals; is under the direction of a board of directors, a majority of which are elected by the private owners; and is a financial institution with the power to make loans and loan guarantees for certain purposes and raise funds by borrowing to guarantee the debt of others. A GSE does not have the power to commit the federal government financially nor does it exercise powers that are reserved to the federal government as sovereign (such as the power to tax or to regulate interstate commerce).The current GSEs are the Farm Credit System, including the Farm Credit Banks, Banks for Cooperatives, and the Federal Agricultural Mortgage Corporation; the Federal Home Loan Bank System; the Federal Home Loan Mortgage Corporation; the Federal National Mortgage Association; and the Student Loan Marketing Association.

As private corporations, GSEs are "off-budget" and so their outlays and revenues are not included in the deficit calculations. However, detailed statements of financial operations are included in the president's budget as supplementary information.

Gramm-Rudman-Hollings See *Balanced Budget and Emergency Deficit Control Act of 1985* and *Balanced Budget and Emergency Deficit Control Reaffirmation Act of 1987.*

Grant A cash award given by the federal government to a state or local government. The two major forms of federal grants are "block" and "categorical." Block grants are awarded primarily to general purpose governments, are distributed to them according to formulas established in the law, and can be used by the recipient for any activities that fall within the purpose of the grant as stated in the law. Categorical grants can be used only for a specific purpose and usually are limited to narrowly defined activities.

Guaranteed loan A nonfederal loan which the federal government agrees to repay if the borrower defaults.

Impoundment An action by an officer or employee of the federal government that prevents the obligation or expenditure of budget authority. Deferrals and rescissions are the two types of impoundments (see chapter 7).

Incremental funding Providing budgetary resources for a program or project based solely on what is expected to be spent in the budget year (see full funding).

Line-item veto A presidential power to veto a particular spending item rather than the whole bill including that item.

Look-back A type of sequester created by the Budget Enforcement Act that reduces the limit set next year for a particular category of discretionary or mandatory spending by the amount that the current year's limit has been exceeded. A look-back discretionary sequester can only be triggered if legislation is enacted that breaches the current year cap after June 30. (See chapter 6.)

Mandatory Outlays for entitlement programs and certain nonentitlements that are controlled by Congress by defining eligibility and payment rules rather than through appropriations.

Maximum deficit amount The maximum deficit allowed for fiscal years through 1995 as established by the Balanced Budget and Emergency Deficit Control Act of 1985, the Balanced Budget and Emergency Deficit Control Reaffirmation Act of 1987, and the Budget Enforcement Act of 1990.

Mid-session review of the budget An updated version of the president's original budget proposal, prepared by the Office of Management and Budget and required to be submitted to Congress by July 15. In addition to an update of the budget submitted by the president earlier in the year, the mid-session review includes the latest information on the previous year's spending and revenue totals.

Obligated balance The amount of obligational authority obligated but not yet actually spent. Unobligated balances are the amount of obligational authority not yet obligated. Unexpended balances are the sum of obligated and unobligated balances.

Obligational authority The sum of budget authority newly provided in a fiscal year, the balance of budget authority from previous years that has not yet been obligated, amounts of offsetting collections credited to a specific fund or account during that year, and transfers between accounts or funds.

Obligations Spending commitments by the federal government that will require outlays either immediately or in the future. This includes orders placed, contracts awarded, services received, and similar transactions.

Off-budget Programs and agencies whose transactions have been excluded by law from the unified federal budget (see chapter 1).

Offsetting receipts Money collected by the federal government that is deducted from the totals for budget authority and outlays rather than being included as a receipt. Offsetting receipts usually come from market-oriented government activities or intragovernmental transactions. Offsetting receipts usually are displayed in the function in which they occur and are deducted from the functional or agency budget authority and outlays, but some are undistributed and are deducted from total budget authority and outlays (see also *Undistributed Offsetting Receipts*).

Outlays The actual amount of dollars spent for a particular activity.

Total outlays in any year result from both new budget authority provided this year and from unexpended balances of budget authority provided in previous years (see chapter 1).

Outyear Any of the five fiscal years that follow the budget year. For example, the 104th Congress will convene in January 1995, and will debate the 1996 budget. This means that the current year is fiscal 1995, the budget year is fiscal 1996, and the outyears are fiscal 1997–2000.

Pay-as-you-go An enforcement mechanism created by the Budget Enforcement Act that requires any enacted legislation that either reduces revenues or increases mandatory spending above the baseline to be completely offset by some combination of revenue increases or mandatory spending reductions. If a full offset is not enacted, then a pay-as-you-go sequester will be triggered.

Pay-as-you-go scorecard An accounting of the deficit impact of mandatory spending and revenue legislation. The official scorecard is compiled by the Office of Management and Budget although the Congressional Budget Office compiles its own estimates for advisory purposes.

PAYGO See pay-as-you-go.

President's budget The proposal sent by the president to Congress each year as required by the Budget and Accounting Act of 1921, as amended (see chapter 3).

Program An organized set of activities directed toward a common purpose or goal, undertaken by a federal department or agency to carry out its responsibilities.

Projection Estimates of budget authority, outlays, receipts, and other budget amounts extending several years into the future.

Real economic growth Increase or decrease in the gross domestic product, adjusted for inflation, consistent with Department of Commerce definitions.

Recession The Budget Enforcement Act of 1990 defines a recession as either of two events: (1) if either the director of OMB or CBO determines that real economic growth is or will be less than zero during any two consecutive quarters over a six-quarter period starting with the quarter before the current quarter and continuing through the four quarters after the current quarter or (2) if the Department of Commerce announces that the rate of real economic growth for the current quarter and the immediately preceding quarter is less than 1 percent. Either of these two events can trigger a suspension of most of the key Budget Enforcement Act provisions.

Reconciliation The process used by Congress to force its committees to comply with the fiscal policy established in a budget resolution (see chapter 4).

Rescission An action of the president and Congress that cancels previously appropriated budget authority. A proposed rescission must be reported to Congress and the comptroller general by the president in a rescission message. If both houses do not approve of the proposed rescission within 45 days, the president must obligate the budget authority as it was originally intended by Congress (see chapter 7) in an appropriation bill.

Revenues Money collected by the federal government from duties, taxes, user fees, or premiums from social insurance programs.

Scorekeeping The process of estimating the budgetary effects of pending and enacted legislation. For purposes of the legislative process, the Congressional Budget Office, the House and Senate Budget Committees, and the Joint Committee on Taxation are responsible for scoring. For purposes of sequestration, the Office of Management and Budget is responsible.

Sequester and Sequestration The cancellation of budgetary resources provided by discretionary appropriations or a direct spending law. The sequestration process was originally created by the Balanced Budget and Emergency Deficit Control Act of 1985 to cut spending if Congress and the president did not enact laws to reduce the projected deficit to the maximum deficit amount set for that year. Under the procedures established by the Budget Enforcement Act of 1990, a sequester will occur if a discretionary spending limit is breached or if revenues are cut below or mandatory spending is increased above the baseline without offsetting changes that will eliminate any impact on the deficit. (See chapter 6.)

Spending committees The standing committees of the House and Senate with jurisdiction over legislation that permits the obligation of funds. The House and Senate appropriations committees are the spending committees for discretionary programs. For other programs, the authorization legislation permits the obligation of funds without an appropriation and so the authorization committees have the spending power. The revenue-raising committees are also spending committees when they deal with spending programs within their jurisdiction.

Supplemental appropriations An act appropriating funds in addition to the 13 regular annual appropriations. Supplemental appropriations are supposed to be enacted when the need for additional funds is too urgent to be postponed until the next regular appropriation is considered, although they are often enacted for other reasons as well.

Surplus The amount by which annual revenues exceed annual outlays, measured in fiscal years.

Tax expenditures Losses of revenues that result from provisions of federal tax law that permit special exclusions, exemptions, deductions, credits, preferential tax rates, or deferred tax liability. Tax expenditures are subsidies provided through the tax code rather than through federal spending, although the impact on the deficit is the same in both cases.

Transition quarter (TQ) The three-month period between the end of fiscal 1976 and the beginning of fiscal 1977 (July 1 to September 30, 1976) that resulted from the change from a July 1 through June 30 fiscal year to an October 1 through September 30 fiscal year. See *Fiscal year.*

Trust funds Federal funds collected and spent to carry out specific purposes and programs under trust agreements or statutes, such as Social Security, highways, airports and airways, and unemployment. Trust funds cannot be spent for purposes other than those for which they are specified by law.

Undistributed offsetting receipts Money collected by the federal government from various activities that are not attributed to the function which best describes their substantive role but are instead listed in a separate function and used as an offset to total spending. These are the collections of employer shares of employee retirement payments, rents and royalties on the outer continental shelf, and sales of major assets.

Unified budget The present form of the budget of the federal government in which receipts and outlays from federal funds and trust funds are consolidated into a single document.

User fee A fee charged by the federal government to users of certain goods and services. User fees generally apply to activities that provide special benefits to identifiable recipients beyond what is available to the general public and are usually related to the costs of the goods or services provided.

INDEX

77706009 2

DATE DUE

N